A Song Inside is a tribu[te to] motherhood, the celebration [and] of loss. I loved this book fo[r] its ability to get up close to [i]shying away but most of all, [the] exploration of a mother's relationship with her son – by turns, infuriating, challenging, joyful, painful but always filled with love."

– Kerry Fisher, author of The Woman I Was Before

"In 'A Song Inside', Gill Mann charts the course of her son Sam's life and death. In it she tells us that 'grief's course ... isn't linear, but a constant moving' and, we learn, so is love's. This is a book no mother would ever want to have to write, nor any parent, friend or sibling read, but in Gill's gentle and loving hands, her son's story sings and blazes a trail for all who have loved and lost, and reminds us that love and grief are composites of all that is and all that ever has been; it is a timeless reminder that we carry the precious burden of both these things with us always."

– Claire Dyer, author of The Moment

"This beautifully written and tender tribute to a beloved son is full of sadness but also of love. I learned a lot from it."
– Cathy Rentzenbrink, writer, journalist and author of the Sunday Times bestselling memoir The Last Act of Love

"Sam's story is that of many young men: different, trouble, beloved and lost. His mother's story, and the family's is all their own but will raise echoes for many of the process of memory, understanding, and resolution."

– Libby Purves, radio presenter, journalist and author

"Schizophrenia remains greatly misunderstood. By telling the profoundly personal and deeply moving story of how it changed the life of her son and her family, Gill illuminates the truth of the disease."

– Orlando von Einsiedel, Oscar-winning film director of *The White Helmets*

"If you get the chance to read this shatteringly beautiful evocation of family relationships, grief, death and most exquisitely – love – grasp it with both hands. In a word it's breathtaking."

– Jan Kaneen, author of upcoming *The Naming of Bones*

"None of us wants to lose a child. It's every parent's worst nightmare. In 2016 Gill Mann's much loved son, Sam died from schizophrenia at 22. In this beautifully written memoir she charts how she came to a fragile acceptance of his death, after he and the whole family struggled for years with such an unpredictable and devastating illness. *A Song Inside* describes the vital part Sam played in the lives of this close-knit family and the impact his illness and consequent death had on them all. It is inevitably far from an easy read and often brought me to tears. This is an unsentimental, sensitive and at times raw dissection of living with illness and coping with grief. *A Song Inside* is both moving and honest; ultimately Gill Mann has written an uplifting love letter to her son, Sam."

– Ali Thurm, author of *One Scheme of Happiness*

A Song Inside

The Boy Seen Dancing

Gill Mann

ISBN paperback: 978-1-8380430-0-1
ISBN eBook: 978-1-8380430-1-8

Retreat West Books
retreatwestbooks.com

To Rosy, Sam and Ellie,
with all my love.

'And those who were seen dancing were thought to be insane by those who could not hear the music.'

Attributed to Friedrich Nietzsche.

Part 1

IT'S DARK OUTSIDE my window and the wind is singing in the trees. Soon the sky will start to glow at the horizon as it softens into dawn. It's a bit like life with you Sam. Even in the pitch of night I knew the light would come.

I've written this for you. I've written it for me. It is my song of love to you.

5 May 2014

I KNOW EXACTLY why she's here. They didn't say on the phone but it'll be about the break-in and the burglar's DNA left smeared on the door-handle.

I watch through the sitting-room window as she parks her car, springs from it despite being heavily pregnant, and walks purposefully across the gravel drive. She isn't in uniform, but in a denim skirt and white blouse. Perhaps their uniforms don't accommodate such an advanced bump.

As I let her into the house, and she follows me to the kitchen, there is small talk:

'What a lovely home,' she says. 'Have you been here long?'

'Yes, over twenty years. I'm not sure where they've gone.'

'I've just made us a cup of tea,' I gesture towards two mugs sitting on the side. 'Would you like one?'

'That would be lovely,' she says. 'Is someone here with you?'

'Yes, my partner, Paddy.'

'Well you might as well get him.'

Through the kitchen window, we see Paddy emerge from the garden shed.

'Let's go outside,' I say. 'It's such a beautiful day.'

At the garden table, mug of tea in hand, I sit and wait for the young policewoman to speak. It is Bank Holiday Monday: a day of bright sunshine and impossible clarity. Colours around me shout and sing. Blood-red geraniums in terracotta pots, fresh-cut grass as green as newly minted peas, wisteria hanging in swathes of smoky mauve.

'You have a son,' she says, placing one hand on the swell of her unborn child. It is such a simple statement of fact, a lovely truth, but a strange one for this young woman to be telling me, sitting in my own garden beneath a sky of cobalt blue. It seems she doesn't expect an answer for she is carrying on, but 'Yes,' I agree in my head, 'I have.' She tells me his name too.

'Samuel Edward Roberts,' she says.

'Yes,' I agree in my head, again, and then I realise. Of course, not the burglary. It's about Sam's passport, stolen ten days ago as he slept on a train from Bangkok to Chiangmai.

More words come, yet still there's no mention of the

passport. I feel a sudden, cool waft of foreboding, as fleeting as the shadow of an aeroplane passing before the sun. Then a strange thing happens. The words cease to belong to the young woman opposite me. They take on an embodiment all of their own. I can see and feel them, floating on the garden air.

'He's travelling in Thailand, in Mae Hong Son province,' her words continue, relentless. Suspending themselves in the space between us, above the table, they hang in the air like an executioner's axe.

There is no faltering, no change of pace or tone when she speaks again. 'Your son has been found dead in his hotel room. We've been contacted by the Thai police.'

There is silence as the words sway in front of me. Such an innocent conglomeration of consonants and vowels; but put together, such devastating words. Words which must not be allowed to turn that simple, lovely truth, 'You have a son,' into a terrible lie.

Everything becomes still and intense: the geraniums, the freshly mown lawn, the bird song all freeze for a moment. And all the while my mind is whirring, unbidden, arming itself with alternative explanations. Hotel room? Sam isn't in a hotel, he's in a bamboo hut on stilts, and he's in Pai, not the place she mentioned.

'No, no,' I say, as suddenly it all becomes clear, 'it won't be Sam. It will be the person who stole his passport.'

'His passport was found with his body,' she says.

I hear my voice, insistent. 'Yes, but it was stolen, his passport was stolen ten days ago. It could be the *stolen* passport they've found with someone else's body.'

She is patient; understanding perhaps why I need to believe this.

'Yes, I see. There's a number at the foreign office. Why don't you call it now?'

She gives me a name. Paddy fetches the phone. I have it in my hand and, sitting at the table in the sunshine on this heavenly spring day, I make the call. But the person I want to talk to isn't there, and I find myself explaining about a body found in a hotel room in Thailand and the police thinking it's my son but my thinking it might be someone else with the passport that was stolen from my son when he was in Bangkok. I need them to check the date on the passport, I say. I wait as they do so. My mind is empty now, save for a strange hum, like static, fizzing and crackling in my ears. A voice cuts through. It tells me that the passport found with the body was issued on 24 April, 2014. It is the replacement passport issued to Sam in Bangkok.

Now there is nowhere to hide from those hideous words. Try as I might to push them away, to dismantle their letters, change their order, undo their meaning, I cannot, for they have set like concrete in the warm spring air.

This woman is telling me my son's life is over. She's sitting there with a hand resting on her future while, in one sentence, she takes mine away from me. I want the sky to dim and the birds to fall silent. I want leaves to wither and fall to the ground. I want the world to acknowledge that everything has changed. Forever.

But nothing happens. The earth proceeds on its slow revolution round the sun. The garden all around me swells with new life; bluebells unfurling in the long grass, wisteria in every shade of purple, the magnolia tree slowly opening its petals, tongues of white velvet shot with pink.

The policewoman is still talking. I wish she'd stop but I don't know how to ask her to. I listen mutely as she tells me there's more information we will need. I can't take anything in. Words slide over me, water over stone. She wants to write things down and needs some paper. I push myself up from my chair. My legs work, though I'm not sure how. They don't seem to belong to me. The gloom of the hallway is a relief after the searing brightness of the garden. I'd like to crawl into a dark corner, curl up small with my arms over my head, and stay there.

I need paper but I can't think where to look. I see a used envelope discarded on the kitchen table. I take it, head back outside and hand it to the policewoman. Paddy sits silently, head bowed. She talks as she writes. Telephone numbers to call, times people will be there, Foreign Office references, the importance of getting on to Sam's travel insurers. These insignificant facts mean nothing to me, when all the while I am holding this new and terrible knowledge, this dreadful thing. There are people I have to tell: Sam's father, Simon; his sisters, Rosy and Ellie; Simon's new partner, Kim and their daughter Imogen; Paddy's daughter, Lily; and grandparents, aunts, uncles, cousins and friends. I've been handed something toxic, that can only do harm, yet I have no choice but to pass it on. Somehow I have to find a way of doing so without doing too much damage. As if that were possible.

Simon doesn't answer his phone or respond to my text messages. Have they even returned from their trip to Slovenia yet? I text Kim. Are they back? Yes, they've just picked up Imogen and are on their way home.

'Could you please pop in?' I write. 'Quite important.'

I think about that second bit carefully. I don't want them to go through what I've just been through; the small talk, the cup of tea, and then the axe descending from nowhere. I want them to be a little prepared, to erect, unconsciously, a small psychic defence, so that when the blow falls there's a protective barrier already in place to absorb at least a tiny part of the trauma. I've worked as a therapist with trauma victims and I think I know my stuff. I've thought about Imogen too and the need to protect her from the moment of telling and the raw grief that will follow.

But then Simon is out of the car and walking towards me, demanding to know what it is, which child, and I say, 'I'm so sorry Simon. It's Sam. He's dead.'

And Simon crumples. He physically crumples. It's terrible to see. But Kim hasn't heard, she's asking me what's happened and I start to move towards her so that Imogen's out of earshot but at the last minute Imogen runs over and Kim scoops her up into her arms, and I say it again and little four-year-old Imogen starts to scream, an ear-piercing shriek and I don't seem to have got it right at all.

Simon is angry. It's what he does – converts difficult feelings into anger. It's the "*Quite important*" he objects to.

'I'd rather have heard it straight out,' he says. 'Just a straight 'Sam's died'. It's been agony wondering which child it is, which one is dead: Sam, in Thailand; Ellie, in South America; or Rosy, in Bristol. Why did you have to say that?'

There's no point trying to explain. Part of me wants to ask why he automatically assumed that one of our children has died. But we all do that: imagine the worst in the hope that the reality will be better. And somewhere I know it isn't really me he's angry with. Just as I know that it isn't the policewoman's fault that Sam is dead. It just feels as though it is.

She's still there. She'd offered to stay in case Simon had questions. I didn't know how to ask her not to.

'Get rid of her,' Simon says.

I walk back through the house and into the garden.

'Thanks for staying,' I say, 'but I think you've told us all you can. You should get on your way now.'

We talk about how to tell the girls. Rosy is twenty-four, studying in Bristol at Circomedia. Ellie's just eighteen and abroad on a gap year. They love Sam. This is news that every fibre of my body resists telling them, but I know I must.

Simon and I are at odds again. He thinks we should phone Rosy, be direct, even brutal, no preamble, just come out with it, 'Sam has died.' It's what he would have preferred for himself, what I failed to do for him. I don't agree. I feel strongly that we should go to tell her in person, even prepare her a little in advance. For me, anxiety, however uncomfortable is also an opportunity to fore-arm. It's better than trauma. Simon disagrees. He knows because he's just been through it. Of course, I have too, but that doesn't occur to me at the time.

We compromise. We will drive to Bristol and tell her in person, but with no forewarning. We will simply arrive.

The light is fading and it's raining as we draw up in her street and park at a distance from her house. We sit in the car and debate how to deliver the news. I want to be the person to tell her, as gently as I can. Simon wants to come straight out with it. And then I hear a front door slam and see a diminutive figure with curly mop-top hair run across the road. We leap from the car.

I'm ahead of Simon, about twenty metres from Rosy.

I call her name. She stops and turns, sees us both, a look of delight on her face, raises both palms to the sky, shouts down the street, 'What the hell?'

I say nothing and keep on walking. She drops her arms to her sides, looks questioningly at my face, sees something there that warns her of what's to come. She starts to back away from me, lifting her hands as if to fend me off.

She's shouting now, 'No, no, no!'

'It's Sam,' I say, 'I'm so sorry, Ro, he's died.'

I take her in my arms, in the rain, on a Bristol street, and she howls as I say over and over again, 'I'm so sorry.'

Her front door opens and her two house-mates run out.

'Rosy, what's wrong? What's happened?'

They look at me accusingly. She composes herself and goes to them. Her voice reaches me across the rain-soaked street. 'My brother's died,' she says softly.

We go into the house, squeezing past bicycles in the hallway to get in through the door and into the sitting room. Her house-mates are still there looking on, helpless observers, as Rosy continues to howl and then starts to stamp her feet shouting, 'No, no, no.' She attacks a large house plant, karate-chopping its leaves and branches.

She stops as suddenly as she began.

The next thirty-six hours are torture. Simon, Kim and Imogen visit often. There's a powerful need to be together. We talk ceaselessly of Sam. We still don't know how he died. There's no obvious cause, no sign of drugs or physical harm. There will be an autopsy. We try to fill in the gaps. Was it drugs? Did he mean to die? Was it an accident? There are no answers. We speculate on his state of mind, on the text messages Simon and I received on the day we think he died: upbeat and positive.

Things in Pai are great. Rented a scooter so I could

drive 8 km to the waterfall which was well worth it! I'm going on a hot spring trip by the end of this week. X love Sam.

A photo of him and a girl, smiling into the lens.

This is the German girl I spent the day with in Bangkok. We spoke about possibly spending the week together on one of the islands. Love Sam x

Yet he appears to have died later that day. Nothing makes any sense.

And when it becomes too much, we move onto Ellie. There's an unspoken relief in all of us when we pass from a subject that holds only pain, to one where there's still something we can do, however difficult. We can't get hold of her, so we can't tell anyone else about Sam. She mustn't hear the news from anyone but us. I'm a prisoner, unable to answer the phone or respond to text messages, unable to leave the house for fear of bumping into someone.

I don't seem to be inside my body. I don't know where I am. I can see myself doing things and hear myself speaking, but I'm not really present. I'm going through the motions of living but inside I'm numb.

Finally, at 10.30 pm the next day Ellie sends a message on WhatsApp:

It's ok Mum. I'm still alive!

She actually says that. I want to weep for her, for the innocence I'm about to shatter.

I've been to the salt flats. I'm having the most amazing time. I'll tell you all about it later. Can we FaceTime in about an hour?

'Yes,' I reply. Just that. I don't have the energy for more. Whatever's been keeping me going until now has simply drained away. I'm shattered and I need to sleep. Rosy is with me and watching me like a hawk. I think she's scared I'm going to break down.

'Please don't sleep, Mum,' she pleads. 'You might not be able to wake up properly. Let me read to you, talk to you, anything.'

'It's okay Ro. Just twenty minutes, right here on the sofa. I'll set an alarm on my phone. I will wake up and I'll be okay, but right now I need to close my eyes.'

When I open them again she's still there. I don't think she's moved. After forty minutes the waiting becomes unbearable. I send Ellie a series of WhatsApp messages.

Finally she responds.

Mum!!! Give me twenty minutes. I'm booking our bus journey for this evening.

We need to speak to her now.

I call her on FaceTime. It takes a while for her face to appear. She looks tired but happy. I start to speak. I think I'm doing well, being quite normal, but suddenly she's sitting upright and saying insistently into the screen,

'What's wrong, Mum? Something's wrong, I know it is. Is it Sam, Mum? Tell me, please. Tell me.' Her voice dips to a whisper, 'Is he dead?'

I hear myself responding, 'Yes, Elle, I'm afraid he is. I'm so sorry.'

She's howling, something primal, raw. Rosy breaks into a howl too. My two lovely daughters, distraught because of what I'm saying. I've failed them both. My role is to protect them, to shield them from pain, but I can't.

I say, 'We're coming, Elles. Rosy and I are flying out to be with you as soon as we can. We will be on a plane. We just need to know where you are.'

Her relief is palpable. She gathers herself, we start to make plans. We will meet in La Paz in Bolivia.

I still haven't told anyone else. It seems so wrong, but there's nothing I can do. We have to book flights. The need to tell someone is overpowering. I make one phone call, to a friend.

I hear a voice whispering into the phone, 'Sam's dead.' It doesn't seem real. It seems to be saying something that has no connection to me. I can hear the sadness in my friend's voice. I don't want to. It might connect me with those dreadful words.

The next few hours are a blur. I'm incapable of coherent thought. I'm simply not functioning. Simon and Paddy take over. They find flights via the USA with a six-hour stopover in Miami. Rosy completes the online forms for our transit visas. It is already the early hours. We need to leave by eight. I go to bed and try to sleep.

For some reason our tickets haven't been confirmed next morning. I call the airline. There's a technical glitch in the system. If I don't mind holding, they will try to sort it out. Ten, twenty, thirty minutes pass. Still no one in my wider family knows that Sam is dead, and I'm about to leave for Bolivia. These are valuable minutes I can't afford to waste. I call my sister on my mobile, keeping the landline still connected in my left hand. It's a terrible way to make the call, to deliver news like this, with my mind only half engaged, the other half focused on the airline, waiting for them to speak.

7-9 May 2014

I FEEL THE thinness of the air as soon as we leave the airport. I haven't been at such high altitude before. We say 'yes' to the first taxi driver who approaches us despite his furtive glances left and right. His dented car with its front bench seat rattles and slides our exhausted bodies up and down the cobbled streets of La Paz. At the hotel we call Ellie, agree to meet next morning, climb into our beds and try to sleep.

Ellie arrives at the hotel escorted by two friends from home. They disappear but at lunchtime she wants to know if they, my nephew, Ed, and two more friends she met in Buenos Aires, can join us. We're eight in total. We eat in the hotel. When awkward silences fall, Ellie fills them with her chatter. Afterwards she goes back to the hostel with everyone else.

Neither Rosy nor I question any of this. I'm not sure we have the energy. We know the time will come when Ellie will have no option but to face the reality she's trying so hard to avoid.

After another night in the hotel, the three of us set off on our long journey home; three flights and two long stop-overs. It's in the airport in Ecuador that Ellie finally breaks; her body racked with sobs that sound as though they might tear her apart. At Madrid airport she drags behind us, refusing to talk, then curls up on a seat in the terminal and covers her head with a hoodie. When our plane boards she has no choice but to emerge. Her eyes are full of pain. She looks at me defiantly as if to say, 'Don't you dare try to talk to me.' Her flip-flops drag along in our wake. Once on the plane she takes the hoodie and places it tent-like over her head and face.

10-12 May 2014

PADDY MEETS US at Heathrow and drives us home. I'm ill from the moment I arrive – a violent stomach bug that has me vomiting and running for the loo. I take to my bed. I refuse all visitors. I send messages to family and friends to tell them about Sam; and to my clients to explain that owing to a bereavement I'm having to take an unexpected break from my work as a psychotherapist.

I've stopped being sick by the time Paddy, Rosy, Ellie

and I set off, less than forty-eight hours later, to catch our plane to Bangkok, but I'm still very unwell. Simon, Kim and Imogen flew there the day after Rosy and I left for Bolivia. They've been dealing with the Embassy, the undertakers and all the miserable administration involved in a death abroad. They phone to say they've been to Pai and have spoken to the police and the family who run the accommodation where Sam was staying. People have been kind but there are no answers. We still don't know how he died.

There's a curious comfort in all this travel. I've headed sixteen hours west, stayed two nights, then twelve hours east, spent two nights at home, then travelled twelve hours further east. But in physical terms I have no idea whether it's night or day. I don't know where I am. This sense of dislocation mirrors what I'm feeling internally. Nothing feels real. I can locate myself only in my grief. I cry in airport lounges and on planes. Cabin crew hover helplessly at my elbow asking if there's anything they can do. I don't explain, I simply shake my head. I have no words, only memories.

I think of Sam's spirit and energy and I wonder how I can ever accustom myself to the idea of a life without him in it. It doesn't seem possible that I will never again hear his voice; nor watch his face break into a smile at the sight of me; never again feel the comforting weight of his arm as he slips it over my shoulder; nor be caught up in his irrepressible, infectious laughter; never again be driven to distraction by his stubbornness, his contrariness, his wackiness. This is the thing I cannot grasp. I can know it on an intellectual level, yet I cannot feel it. There is something inside me that cannot take it in. It's simply inconceivable that all that made up Sam, his physical and emotional being in all its complexity, is no more.

***

The first time I saw you properly Sam, was at my twenty-week scan. You were a bit of a blur at twelve weeks. I can still remember it: the shock of cold gel, the slight pressure of the probe as the sonographer moved it across my bump in long sweeping strokes, her eyes fixed all the while on the screen above. I might not have been there, so intently was she focused on her task. A small sigh escaped her lips as she shifted the angle of the probe and then an, 'Aah' as the grainy black and white of the screen resolved itself into a baby in profile: the curve of a back, an over-sized skull and tiny kicking legs.

'Do you want to know whether it's a boy or a girl?' she asked. 'We should be able to tell at twenty weeks.'

'Yes please,' I said. And as I spoke I saw you move, white against the black. A small arm shifted upwards and flexed at the elbow as a tiny hand headed for the skull. The thumb stretched out as it found its target, the fingers straightened and splayed outwards in a perfect arc with equal gaps between each digit.

'Aah, look at that,' she said, finally turning towards me. There was a small click and the screen froze. 'He's sucking his thumb.'

I have the image still, in grainy monochrome, its corners curled and frayed. I keep it in a box with the plastic bracelet

I cut from your tiny wrist when we came home from hospital. There's a rectangle of pale blue card in the bracelet. Boy of Gillian Mann it says in loopy left-leaning handwriting. Below is a date and time: 22.2.92 @ 14.35.

In the latter months of pregnancy, I grew huge with you. So huge that when I sat down I had to move my legs apart to make space for you. The midwife took one look at me – five foot four and normally around eight and a half stone – and my gigantic bump and reached for a tape-measure, stretching it round my middle.

'I think you might have polyhydramnios,' she said. 'It's nothing to worry about, it's just that you've got too much amniotic fluid.'

I grew more and more. My due date passed but still my waters didn't break. I went for an appointment at the hospital. I could have cried with relief when they said they'd book me in for you to be induced.

Much of the labour passed in a blur, but the final bit is imprinted on my memory like a series of screen shots, as though I'd had a camera in my hand and clicked the shutter every second. I can see the midwife, hear her telling me she can see your head. Then she's telling me to push. You were wedged at the shoulders. She tugged and tugged. You didn't shift. She tugged again. I felt something give. Perhaps you'd decided this was a battle you weren't going to win. It'd be the one and only time if you had, Sam.

'Push,' she said. 'Well done. One more time.'

I pushed again and, arching forwards, looked down towards the foot of the bed. A shiny dark grey torpedo shot into my line of vision and down the plastic mattress, propelled by a huge whoosh of water. A tidal wave. It poured off the sides and end of the bed. I heard the spatter of it hitting the floor, like a bathtub being emptied onto concrete. The torpedo meanwhile was skidding to a halt against the metal bed frame where it transformed itself into a baby.

You.

The midwife seized you and slapped you hard on the back. There was an intake of air and then a wail of outrage. She checked you over quickly then placed you gently on my tummy.

'He's turning a normal colour now,' she said.

Even then I could see you were beautiful.

I can still picture that moment twenty-two years ago when you appeared between my knees, borne aloft on a wave. I'm not sure it can be real. Perhaps our memories are shaped by what comes later. But that's the image I have in my head. You surfing into life: your life, my life, the family's life. It couldn't have been a more appropriately dramatic entry. And now I'm expected to believe that you've left us. I'm behaving as though everything is normal: boarding planes, criss-crossing my way around the globe, checking in baggage, going through passport control, walking up to hotel reception desks.

But nothing is.

***

13 May 2014

AT THE HOTEL in Bangkok we find Simon, Kim and Imogen. They all look tired. We go up to our rooms. I lie on the bed and try to sleep. I've never felt more depleted in my life. The jet lag, stomach bug and emotional exhaustion seem all to have hit me at once. And I feel horribly disconnected; not just from myself but from family and friends. I find myself picking up my phone and composing a message to the people who I know would want to be here if they could.

'Sam will be cremated at noon on Wednesday, 14th May, so if you happen to be awake, join us in thought as his spirit soars ...' I write. For many it would be early in the morning, 6 or 7 am, for others early evening. I don't know what to expect but I feel better for having done something. I need to know that people are thinking of us, holding us in mind and sharing something of our pain.

I need to feel less alone.

We go out for supper to a restaurant called Cabbages and Condoms that raises money for good causes, birth control among them. We're greeted by life size mannequins whose costumes are made entirely from condoms. All round the restaurant are flowers and decorations also fashioned from rubber. The terraces are strung with thousands of fairy lights and lanterns hang from every tree. As we leave we pass a giant bowl, above it a huge sign, 'Sorry, we have no mints. Please take a condom instead.'

After our meal we take two tut-tuks back to the hotel, waving at Imogen as they draw up alongside us at the traffic lights. We're going through the motions of living life but there's a hollowness to everything; no substance to any of it. It's like a muslin veneer, stretched taut and thin. We all feel its fragility.

14 May 2014

AS WE WALK into the dining room next morning, Sunshine welcomes us with a radiant smile. She greets each of us personally, in turn, our names tripping from her tongue like a tinkling stream: 'Good Morning Gill, Good Morning Paddy, Good Morning Rosy, Good Morning Ellie, Good Morning Simon, Good Morning Kim, Good Morning Imogen.' This is her party piece. The smile and the names never falter. She fusses around us, trying to persuade us to eat and drink more. It's the morning of Sam's cremation. Surely someone's told her why we're all there? I force my face into a semblance of civility as I politely decline her repeated offers, and fight the urge to punch her.

A minibus arrives to collect us. Harry, the German undertaker recommended by the Embassy, has arranged everything. We've chosen a Buddhist ceremony because we know Sam would have liked that. We want to take him home but it isn't possible. We can't even see his body. He's too decomposed. I say 'he' and 'his' but I'm not sure why. There seems to be no connection at all between the Sam I knew and loved, and the dreadful idea of that. When Simon said we wouldn't be able to see him, I couldn't accept it at first. But I had to after he told me about the Thai policeman who found Sam. His broken English wasn't up to describing the scene but he acted it out for Simon: how he ran from the hut and was violently sick.

So, we're not going to see Sam. There will be no final words of farewell, no kiss on a pale, cold forehead. No comfort of a face in repose, all cares dissolved. The only thing we will be able to say goodbye to is the coffin.

We drive through busy, crowded streets, then onto more open roads past frangipani and tulip trees, before turning into the compound of Wat Chong Lom temple. It's huge: not just one temple but a whole complex of them large and small with interconnecting walkways. Everything is ornate: walls and ceilings painted in patterned pastel shades of green, pink and blue; carved wooden fretwork finished in gold leaf. In the centre is a large pagoda-like tower and from it are strung thousands of tiny fluttering prayer flags in vibrant shades of every hue, crossing the compound like ribbons from a giant maypole.

Harry is there to greet us with his quiet Teutonic efficiency and discreet but business-like sympathy. He's explained that the monks won't charge for the service but that we should provide them with a gift of several robes. He has it all in hand. He leads us to a row of seats at the edge of a small, open side-temple. We sit beneath an ornate roof with an intricately carved golden frieze. Small birds swoop in and out between the red and gold pillars. Drapes of bougainvillea hang low from the eaves.

I only remember any of this because I made myself take photos after the cremation. It felt all wrong, as if I were a tourist capturing the scene for my holiday album. But I knew that I'd want to know what it all looked like afterwards and that photos would be only the way as most of me would have to be absent. That would be the only way to bear the pain.

The coffin stands ahead of us on a painted dais. It seems to bear no connection to Sam at all. I hate it instantly, with its tacky, light wood and nasty tin handles. There's a sheet of heavy plastic around the base that goes halfway up the sides, attached at the top with brown sticky tape, that has stuck to itself in places. No one mentions the alien addition of the plastic and its reason for being there, but it must be in all of our minds. On top of this horrible coffin is a stilted arrangement of red and yellow chrysan-themums. I hate them too. I would have liked a cascade of soft white petals and young green leaves.

Paddy tells me later that it wasn't plastic at all, but silicon glue. It's strange how the mind remembers things. I can still picture the sticky tape. It's quite possible the coffin wasn't tacky at all. I just needed it to be. I needed something to be angry with.

Three barefoot monks in saffron robes file in and stand in a row to one side with their backs to the wall. Simon steps forward to read a short poem. His voice breaks as he tells us how, as they waited to board the plane to Bangkok, Imogen came to him from the play area with a book of poems in her hand, *Now We Are Six* by AA Milne – a favourite of all the children. As she handed the book to him, it fell open at *Solitude,* a simple eight line poem about retreating to a place to be alone. Simon wept as he thought of the little hut on stilts where Sam had died.

The monks begin to chant: low and rhythmic. We stand, the seven of us, huddled together, waiting for the moment when we will approach the coffin. I feel nothing. My mind resonates with a soundless hum that both fills and empties it. Minutes pass, then abruptly the chanting stops, and the monks file silently away.

We're gestured to move closer to the coffin. Ahead of us four figures slip out of the shadows. Teenagers, dressed in dirty T-shirts, baggy shorts and flip-flops. They seize the coffin and begin to manhandle it. There's no other way to describe it. I want to shout at them, to tell them to be gentle, to take care, but instead I watch mute with horror as they struggle, staggering right and left. Then they're in front of the mouth of the crematorium. They push Sam in.

One of them takes a large white paper flower from a basket, lights it from a flame in a lantern, before inviting me to take a flower too. Harry has explained this part of the ceremony to us: we will each be invited to take a paper flower, light it from the flame and place it on the coffin with our letters and mementoes for Sam. I'm to go first. But as I step forward to light my flower the man extinguishes the flame in the lantern. I'm totally thrown. I don't know what to do. I'm hit by an overwhelming sense of loss, a feeling that I've been deprived of something that matters terribly. I need to light my flower from the flame. I have to do it for Sam. It's something to do with being his mother, a way of granting my blessing to this new journey he's taking. A final act of maternal love.

I stand there not knowing what to do. It feels like minutes but it's probably seconds and then I lean into the mouth of the crematorium. I light my flower from the flower that's already burning on his coffin and I place it there with a letter I've written to him and step away.

I don't know what I say to him. I fear I say nothing.

Rosy follows me, then everyone else in turn. Ellie's sobbing. Kim carries Imogen, clutching the brightly coloured picture she's drawn for Sam. Paddy leans in with his letter containing the pressed wild flowers he's brought from one of our favourite walks; and finally Simon, who stands for longer than any of us before the coffin, saying a long goodbye, desperate to keep Sam with us; expressing for us all our silent wish to delay the moment when the heavy doors slide shut and take him away.

But the doors do slide shut.

There's no velvet curtain to shield us. We watch in silence as the doors grind their way across the opening, eclipsing the coffin from view. Ellie breaks into a howl of grief as Sam disappears. One of the boys in dirty shorts and flip-flops steps forward and casually begins rotating dials and flicking switches. We carry on standing in front of the doors as though waiting for something, not quite sure what to do. Reluctant to leave. Not knowing where to go. There's no formal ending, no comfort from a final prayer, no words, no actions, no organ swelling to fill the silence, no shuffling feet, no quiet hum of people starting to talk in hushed tones.

It's over but there is no ending.

Afterwards I stand in the temple compound and watch a thin plume of smoke rising from the tall industrial chimney in the centre. The chimney is patchy white and grey against the azure blue sky; stark and unadorned. It couldn't look more out of place in the midst of all the splendour. I take a photo of the plume, several photos, because I want to capture Sam's last journey. But when I look at them later there's almost nothing there. I wanted a billow, a statement from him. But all he gave me was the tiniest wisp.

As I write this I feel as though there's still a part of me standing in front of those doors, waiting for someone to explain, someone to tell me how this could be; that I am still here, breathing, living, with a future ahead of me. But my son is not. Perhaps writing is, in part, my attempt to allow it to be real. I didn't consciously plan to write. It simply happened, just as it had fifteen years ago, when Simon left me with no warning. I struggled to accept that too. But night after night, I sat at my computer after I'd put the children to bed and tapped away at it. It helped.

Maybe I'm hoping this will too. I'm trying to be honest as I write, to tell the whole story. It would be easy to focus only on the easy parts: the prayer flags and bougainvillea hanging low; the swooping birds and the swell and fall of the chanting of the monks. But I would be keeping the painful parts at bay. I took comfort from knowing that Sam would have loved its otherness, but I found it deeply dislocating too. I missed the familiarity of a Christian ceremony, the containment of knowing what was coming next, the calm solemnity of the British pallbearer, the presence of family and friends, the hymns and readings. Their absence seemed to prevent me from connecting with the idea that he was truly dead. I knew it rationally, but I couldn't *feel* it. I hadn't seen his body, had a chance to say goodbye to him, talk to him dead, tell him what his death meant to me.

Perhaps that's what I'm trying to do now.

***

I don't know where to begin. Just like I didn't know how to end it as I stood in front of that open crematorium, trying to say goodbye when I couldn't really believe you were gone. So maybe I'll start where I left off just now, with you as a baby.

You were lovely Sam. You did what babies are meant to do; you fed, you slept, you fed, you slept. By the time you were twelve weeks old you were compact and neat with a glow of fine dark-blonde hair. You'd lie on your mat and kick your legs and every few seconds your arms would join in too, in little bursts of frenetic energy. And if anyone appeared in your line of vision your fingers would splay wide, your whole body go into a judder of excitement and you'd grin a toothless grin that stretched from one ear to the other in a perfect arc. The judder was almost a convulsion. Even then, pre-words and pre-crawling, it was as though you couldn't contain your feelings, you had to express them somehow.

At eighteen months you become contrary. It seemed to happen overnight. It was more than the usual 'terrible two's'. You certainly never grew out of it so perhaps it was just you beginning to be you. You started to be stubborn, to dig in your heels at every opportunity, to do the opposite of what anyone asked. You were so impossible it was almost funny. If asked to hurry up, you'd slow virtually to a halt, taking the minutest of steps. Offered apple or orange juice, you'd insist that it was cranberry juice you wanted. On a skiing holiday we asked you children to put your ski kit on after breakfast and to come to the table wearing only your thermal leggings and tops. You arrived next morning in full kit: ski suit, helmet, goggles and gloves. I took a photo: you grinning up at me from underneath your red helmet, goggles on, and a piece of bacon dangling from your mouth. If we'd asked you to come to breakfast fully kitted up, you'd have arrived in your underpants. It was just what you did.

I never understood why you chose so often to swim against the tide. It made your life so much harder than it needed to be. I'd talk to you about it when you were little and you'd nod your head slowly as you thought about it and I'd hope that perhaps some small seed of what I'd said might take root. But then when it came to the next time, I'd see your face set into contrariness and it seemed as though you didn't have a choice. You simply had to opt for the difficult path. For resistance.

It was lucky you had such charm. It kept people loving you and liking you. There was nothing studied or calculated about it. It came every bit as naturally as your contrariness. Just not so often.

Once you skied off a mountain on a holiday we had with the Martins. You were about ten. It was a white-out and we were going down the piste in a nice slow snake: Dad leading us, Pete at the back, Sue and me strategically placed amongst the six children in-between. You were towards the back, ahead of Pete. But instead of taking a left-hand turn, you simply shot off to the right and disappeared over the edge. All Pete could see, thirty feet below, was a huge snow drift and the cartoon-cut-out shape of a spread-eagled body as it entered the snow. Next to it was a ski pole. We all waited at the bottom, wondering where you and Pete had got to. You were full of it when you arrived fifteen minutes later.

'I skied off the side of the mountain and landed in a ginormous snow drift,' you crowed. 'Pete had to climb down

and dig me out.'

Pete simply shook his head. 'I've no idea why he did that,' he said.

At your first ever parents' evening the head of nursery said you were a natural magnet. That when she lost you she simply looked to see where all the action was, and you would always be there at the heart of it. That never changed. I can picture you munching your way through an entire daffodil, much to the appalled delight of the group of boys egging you on. Life was never dull when you were around.

It's going to be so quiet without you.

***

16 May 2014

I'M AWAKE AT five in the morning, sitting up in my hotel bed in Pai. The girls are asleep in the room next door. Everyone else has returned to the UK.

My body has given up the battle of adjusting to time zones, following instead its own haphazard clock, which bears little relation to the rhythms of day and night. I have never felt more tired. Night-times have become a two-pronged torture. Sleep often evades me, leaving me in the dark to magnify my terrors: I've failed as a mother, I should have been able to save Sam, the girls will die too. Waking is as bad as the sleeplessness: undefended – numbness and disbelief not yet in place – I feel the physical blow as I remember. All over again. Pain as I've never known it, so intense that it takes my breath away. I don't understand how I keep going.

It's a relief to see the sky lightening on the horizon and to hear the stirrings of life in the world outside my hotel room window. In no time at all there are cockerels crowing, a choir of frogs in full croak and a bird shouting 'fuck it, fuck it, fuck it' in a repetitive, guttural call. The air swells with wolf-whistles and cracking whips, a dissonant tide of sound and song rising and falling and rising again. Fingers of light creep into my room. One cockerel has gone into overdrive and there's a young man in a sarong down by the pool, taking off covers and sweeping up fallen leaves. I look around, trying to absorb it all. I can see it, hear it and smell it but it's a tableau. I'm not a part of it. I make myself picture the last forty-eight hours: the golden eaves of the temple, four young men taking hold of Sam's coffin. I still feel nothing. Still just numb.

Bizarrely, that word reaches me.

I feel its meaning in the truncated sound of it; I feel the way the 'm' is deadened by the 'b'. That final, soundless 'b' resonates within me. I feel the numbness of the word numb, in a way I cannot yet allow myself to feel the dreadfulness of those two words I wrote moments before, 'Sam's coffin.' Perhaps I'm not yet ready. Perhaps I can allow myself not to be ready.

I look again at all the text messages, emails and photos I received from around the world on the day of the cremation. I see and hear of families gathered together at home, of candles lit in botanical gardens soon after dawn, of walks taken on beaches, beside rivers; of candles lit in churches, in synagogues, in temples. In England, New Zealand, Portugal, Jerusalem, the USA, Australia. I feel the collective sorrow and love of all these people who loved Sam or us. It gives me strength.

I wait for the girls to wake up. They are, of course, the reason I keep going. I'm glad I have one. I'm not sure what would happen otherwise.

17 May 2014

TODAY WILL BE all about Sam: where he was staying, the places he went to, where he died. It will be a day of Saminiscing. The word comes to me as I lie in bed. I like the sound and shape of it and the way it makes me feel connected to him. I'm surprised to have the capacity to like anything. Perhaps the numbness is receding.

We start by looking for Art in Chai. It's a tea shop Sam mentioned in passing as his favourite. I wrote the name down. It made me feel better to know there was somewhere I could go to look for him if ever we lost track of him on his travels. We find it on a narrow lane behind the main street. It's easy to see why Sam loved it, with its low tables scattered amongst the bookshelves, prayer flags and fabric draped from the ceiling, the walls dotted with artwork and the wooden floor with brightly coloured rugs. Normally its quirkiness would appeal to me too but all I can feel is an unbearable weight of sadness that we can never tell him we came. A song is playing in the background. The girls want to know what it is. There is a need in each of us to grasp at anything which connects us with Sam, painful though it is. As we get ready to leave, a torrential downpour strikes from nowhere. Great stair rods of warm, hard rain. Thunder rumbles overhead. Rosy and Ellie go and stand in the rain, arms outstretched, faces turned skywards. They stand still and silent as the rain courses over them. I remember the text message Sam sent when he got here.

> *Just arrived in Pai. Lightening striking! Already met tons of cool people. It's lovely here x*

We walk through the narrow streets to the place where Sam was staying when he died. It's exactly as he described it: on the bank of a wide river, spanned by a swaying, rickety, bamboo bridge – narrow but long, its handrails missing in places. We cross it in a line; me, then Rosy then Ellie. Ahead of us is row upon row of simple cane and bamboo huts. We follow the directions Simon has given us, wordlessly reducing our pace, walking ever more slowly as we approach the place. I can feel the resistance within me. Part of me doesn't want to see it or imagine Sam living here. To do so also means accepting that he died here.

Then we are standing in front of it, a tilting hut on stilts. Rough rectangles of corrugated iron, off-cuts of wood and hardboard lie beneath it. Baked earth. Dust. Uneven, open steps lead up to the entrance; the door shut tight. There is a thin-stringed hammock on the terrace and a half-filled plastic water bottle next to the doorframe.

Music drifts from another hut, a voice calls out and a peal of laughter follows.

I cannot feel a connection with him here. My mind rejects the very idea of it.

I hate the meagre hut. I feel angry with Sam for dying here, amongst strangers, with no one to notice his absence, no one to look out for him, no one to find him soon enough to save him. I'm angry at the lives still being lived around this hut, the towels slung carelessly over balconies, the sandals waiting outside doors for feet to be slipped inside them. How dare these other lives carry on, so casually, when Sam's is over and ours has changed forever. It's spartan, this place he chose to stay. He lived simply. I feel a sudden surge of guilt that our hotel is so luxurious in contrast to this flimsy structure, tilting beneath its film of dust.

I stand silently and make myself look properly. I want to connect with Sam, to imagine his life here, to picture him opening the door, coming down the steps, see him sitting on the terrace as he peels a mango. But I can't. My mind won't let me. Instead I just feel anger and guilt; hard, ungiving emotions. Then, worst of all, my mind is battling with unbidden, fleeting thoughts, leaping from one to the next. I can't prevent them. Without warning they take over.

Does the person who's staying here now know that someone died here only two weeks ago?

Perhaps I can wear the black dress with the external zip to his UK remembrance service.

Was there a commotion when the police arrived? Did people leave their huts; take off their head-sets; put down their phones; stand and stare?

And if I wear that dress, then I can wear those new suede boots.

How did they get his body down those rickety steps?

But what if it's too hot for those boots? What to wear on my feet if it is?

And then. Most dreadfully of all.

Was it the smell of Sam's decomposing body that alerted other people? Is that why he was found?

This final, disturbing thought is the last. My mind empties. Becomes a mindless blank.

We leave Sam's little hut. Rosy and Ellie are silent as we cross back over the rickety bridge. A water-wheel rotates lazily in the river as dusk creeps in over the tree-clad mountains. It's quieter on the other side. Sound reaches us across the water but it's soft and muted, like the fading light. Heat falls away, and there's a hint of evening dampness in the air as it settles on the sun-baked soil. We start to walk towards the village. But something makes me stop. I realise I'm not yet ready to leave this place which meant so much to Sam. I ask the girls how they feel. They don't want to leave either. We find a table at a restaurant on the riverbank opposite the huts. We can't see Sam's hut, but we know it's there. I hold the knowledge of it deep inside me. We talk of Sam, of nothing but Sam. And while we talk the sky and the river suffuse with pink, deep and intense, as the sun slips down behind the mountains. Daylight dies around us.

I start to feel again; small pricks of feeling, cutting through the numbness. Lanterns are lit on the opposite bank. They pierce the darkness; shimmer towards us across the water.

I feel guilt and anger slip away as swiftly as the equatorial sun.

And in their place comes sorrow.

Back at the hotel I start to pack my bag. As I stretch up into the wardrobe to reach for my clothes, take each garment from the hanger, lie it on the bed to smooth and fold, my mind seems to go through a similar process. I think about our visit to Sam's hut and my struggle to connect with him there. I stretch into my mind and pull out the feelings of anger and guilt. I lie them out before me and look at them. I look at them as a psychotherapist. I ask myself what function they fulfilled, in that moment; what they protected me from. I see it immediately. They shielded me from sadness, from the unbearable pain. Next I pull out those strange, off-kilter thoughts. Of course, they do the same. They are a form of psychic flak, launched to protect me from being overwhelmed by the pain. They deflect my mind from confronting the real issue. Numbness too prevents anything from reaching me. It's caused not by an absence of feeling but a surfeit. It's simply that I'm overwhelmed.

It helps me to remind myself of this. It's a relief to see it this way, rather than as something for which I need to berate myself. I know that there's nothing to be gained in accumulating sticks with which to beat myself.

Tomorrow we leave for England. I feel curiously ambivalent about going home. I've almost become used to this strange life of being on the move. It's been dislocating to be away, but the constant change and sense of otherness has protected me too. It's provided a barrier between me and the reality of Sam's death. Going home means facing it head-on. I'm not sure I'm ready to return to the place where I learned of his death. Perhaps as well as losing him I will have lost the sense of home as a safe and happy place. And I'm returning to a life that has changed. I'm worried I won't know how to be around people whose lives are still the same.

18 May 2014

WE ARE UP at 5.30 am to take a taxi to Chiangmai. From there we catch a plane to Bangkok and then a connecting flight to London. We arrive home in the evening. Paddy comes to pick us up at Heathrow. Simon and Imogen come to meet us too. Everyone looks tired.

'I need to tell you about Sam's ashes,' Simon says. 'I've put them on his bed. I thought you'd want them there with you all at home.'

'Thanks, Simon,' I say, and I really mean it.

'I brought them through customs without declaring

them. I knew he'd approve. I'm calling it Sam's last scam.'

***

I went to see your ashes as soon as I was home. They were in a box, wrapped up neatly in brown paper, inside a smart carrier bag, with a picture of sky and sea and the name of the undertakers, 'Alison Monkhouse,' emblazoned across it.

It was impossible to believe this neat box was all that remained of you. Your room spoke so loudly of you still. All those packets, bottles and jars — spirulina, organic green barley grass, Ambaya Gold zeolite, tinctures of Siberian ginseng root, organic poppy and astragalus. The shoes kicked off under your bed and books piled up on the pine blanket box next to it. It looked as though you might walk back in at any moment. I hated the silence of it. I wanted you to be sitting on your bed, calling for me through the doorway, 'Mu'um,' with the extra syllable you always added when you shouted for me. I wanted to hear you doing what you always did: repeating your call of 'Mu'um,' the pause and then the question: 'Paddy, do you know where Mum is?' I wanted that instead of silence.

How could this inert, insensate box possibly represent you: irrepressible, complex, impossible you? I think of the energy you brought to things. 'Hackavis,' you'd shout as you bounded up with something for me to see, or 'Hackavat,' as you pointed something out, running your words together in your excitement. And in more pensive moments asking, 'Do cows wee milk?' and, 'If there were no clouds would it always be summer?'

I think of the shows Rosy used to organise for me, Dad,

Sue and Pete. You were always out of control and beside yourself with excitement. You'd end up revealing punch lines moments before they were due to be delivered, or miss a carefully timed cue and burst in mid-action. One Halloween, Rosy was bringing the show to an end with a magic trick involving a match box, a disappearing coin and a thick middle-European accent. As the trick reached its climax, your piping voice broke through. From your vantage point behind her, you'd sussed it out. 'I saw what she did with it,' you shrieked. 'It's up her sleeve. It is, it is!' You were triumphant. Rosy was devastated.

There was often something manic about your energy, as though you couldn't quite contain your feelings. Sometimes they spilled out and into others. When they were positive feelings, you brought an energy that enlivened everyone around you. You were quirky and funny and people couldn't help but respond. But when they were negative feelings, you were a nightmare. Even as a child you knew exactly which buttons to press. You could sabotage any gathering, excursion or plan. You'd push and push and push until someone snapped (an adult) or protested or broke down (a child) and then you'd be all right again, the change palpable, simply because you'd managed to discharge your uncomfortable feelings into someone else. I can see all this now and, after my training as a therapist, can give it a name: projective identification.

You were never short of friends, which is surprising given how difficult you were. I'm not sure you were always kind either. You simply loved getting something going and would happily lob a couple of grenades into a conversation or activity. Just to watch the fall-out. That seemed to matter more than other people's feelings.

Perhaps your ability to laugh at yourself kept people on board. You were always happy being the butt of others' jokes. You set yourself up for it. You'd say the most outrageous things and if someone pulled you up on it you'd laugh: that rolling throaty chuckle that grew and grew until you were doubled up with laughter at your own ridiculousness. It was impossible not to join in. And even though part of you knew you were being ridiculous, there was another part that half-believed what you'd said; or wanted to.

'I can hot-wire a car,' you said at six. And, 'I can split the atom,' at twelve.

'Aah, Sam's on the ludicrous slide,' Dad would say because one preposterous claim would slide into another, and another.

'I am definitely the most skilful driver in the family,' you claimed at eighteen.

'But Sam,' I said. 'You haven't even taken your driving test. The first instructor arrived back from your initial lesson looking shell-shocked. She said she couldn't take you out again because you didn't listen and thought you knew best. The next instructor loved you because you had such interesting discussions about philosophy and religion. You brought home a copy of the Koran, but never a driving licence.'

You grinned and put your arm round my shoulder. 'Oh come on Mum, you know I'm best. What does a piece of paper matter?'

You were always unusual Sam. You experienced life differently from other people. Even as a small boy you had your own reality. I remember filming you, the camera lens focused exclusively on you.

*'Why won't you photograph **me**?' you whined, into the lens, although you knew I was.*

A moment later Rosy shouted, 'Come and play with us Sam.'

'No,' you retorted, and turned to me, 'It isn't fair, they're not including me.'

You weren't simply being perverse. I could see you believed what you were saying. Your reality was simply different from ours.

*You had a habit of starting a conversation as if halfway through it, 'So Mum, like I said, I thought I would ask Ryan if he wanted to come over.' Or to Dad as he came through the front door to pick you up for the weekend, 'Well, Dad, Mrs Smith said she **does** think I could move into the top Maths set.' You seemed to assume that something in your mind must also be in the mind of the other. You did it with your friends too. I remember seeing Simon T, even when you were both in nursery, looking at you quizzically as he tried to work out exactly what it was you had assumed he already knew.*

You were impossibly competitive too. If you were winning you were full of it, but if someone else out-performed you at something, you simply feigned a loss of interest and began to rubbish whatever you'd just been beaten at. I can understand your childhood competitiveness, sandwiched as you were between an older sister who excelled at everything, and a younger sister with blonde curls and a ready smile. It must have been terribly hard. I'm not sure I helped you enough with it. I tried to but you were so hard to help.

When you were at Sixth Form College, one of the philosophy tutors confessed to being both admiring and despairing – in equal measure – of your free-thinking mind and your capacity to think outside the box.

'He just wasn't made for an A-level syllabus and a system that requires a tick list,' he said, shaking his head. 'I think he was born into the wrong era. He'd have fared better as a gentleman traveller a couple of centuries ago, free to pursue his own eclectic ways of thinking.' He smiled, 'But I have to say, my class is never dull with Sam in it.'

It was always a relief for us, as parents, when people 'got' you. We'd become so used to teachers shaking their heads as if lost for words, before embarking on a tentative, 'Well, yes, (long pause) Sam ...' So we were always especially grateful when teachers saw beyond your disinclination to apply yourself and conform. You appeared not to care about what people thought of you, but I know you did. You cared deeply. I think of the message I still have on my answer-phone, delivered in breathy excitement and pride, 'Well, Mum,' as though we're mid-conversation, 'I got an A/A star for my English coursework, and Mr Golding said it was the best in the class, and he's printed off my opening paragraph to give to the whole year.'

You were diagnosed with dyslexia at thirteen and ADHD at seventeen. You found it very hard to listen to anything – instructions or advice. It didn't matter how much I tried to prepare you for something in advance, explaining what was expected of you and the potential consequences of doing it otherwise, you had to do it your own way. It turned life into a series of battles. It was as though you were programmed to do or want what others didn't. Your outrageousness was often funny and made people laugh. I'm not sure you always understood why. There was even something endearing about your contrariness at times. I think we all knew you used it to hide your vulnerability. And when you lowered your defences and stopped fighting us all, allowed yourself to engage and enjoy something it felt so incredibly rewarding. It made everything feel worthwhile. And every now and then, just as we'd all got ready for you to be contrary, you would turn the tables and do exactly as you'd been asked without a word. You constantly confounded.

Above all else, Sam, you were a joy. I loved being your mum and you couldn't have been more loved. I don't think any of us can imagine life without you at the heart of it.

***

21 May 2014

SIMON AND I are going to meet the undertaker in Henley. I need to take Sam's ashes with me. Paddy suggests I go on the train, making the journey Sam made for two years when he went to Henley College. I sit in a carriage full of students; lively, chatty, talking about UCAS and offers of university places, of grades and exams. Sam sits on the seat next to me, in the small box wrapped in brown paper inside the carrier bag which brought him home from Thailand. I feel a powerful urge to tell these students that

I have one of their number with me; that he took this train which they take now, that he shared their hopes for the future, that he was one of them – young and full of life.

I don't.

I walk with Sam through Henley. I'm early for our appointment so I stop and sit on a park bench in the sunshine. I put him next to me. Parents with toddlers in push-chairs pass by, a mother coaxing a recalcitrant four-year-old, a father with a curly-haired little boy in his arms, head resting on his shoulder. I watch and listen and think of all the hours and days and weeks and months and years of loving, of effort, of investment in Sam … and I am overcome with a terrible sense of waste, that it has all been for nothing. I have another sudden raw urge to speak out; to tell these young parents at the start of their journey, that this is my son, in a box, in a carrier bag. I want them to know. I want the world to acknowledge my loss.

The undertaker is a nice man, a kind man. He expresses his sympathy for our loss and talks us through the options: caskets for the ashes in various woods or willow, temporary plaques in wood, brass or plastic. We go next door to view the real things. We make our selections. We produce the ashes, undo the brown paper packaging, tear open the box containing all that remains of our son. It seems surreal, this normality, when all is turned upside down.

Inside the box is a brass urn, a pretty, tasteful urn. The undertaker murmurs his approval. He takes it out and turns it round in his hands.

'It's so much nicer,' he says, 'than the plastic containers you get in the UK.'

'It's so small though,' Simon comments. 'I wonder whether it actually contains the whole of Sam.'

The undertaker starts to answer and, warming to the theme, begins to describe cremation in detail. 'It's a very complex process,' he says. 'Much more complex than people realise. They use magnets you know, to extract hip and knee replacements. You wouldn't believe the unexpected things that turn up. All sorts of things. Coins, screws, paper clips.' He raises his hands in disbelief.

'And ashes,' he continues, both shaking and nodding his head in one movement. 'They're not what most people are expecting at all. It's the bone. It doesn't reduce to ashes at all. People call them ashes, but they aren't really ashes. They're much harder than that. It's a fascinating process,' his face lights up, 'truly fascinating.'

He glances up, catches himself and falls silent. Perhaps he feels some shift in temperature in the room or sees something on my face to remind him that Simon and I are parents grieving for their twenty-two-year-old son. I feel sorry for him. He's a kind man who simply got carried away. Perhaps Simon and I need to be reminded too that if we hide the emotions that lie beneath the surface and appear to be okay, then people will take their cue from that. They can't be expected to know what we're really feeling. We're both too good at doing the right thing, at giving the appearance of coping.

We go for a coffee afterwards and talk about our past, sadness at choices made, happiness found since. We talk of Sam and the girls and how we are all going to get through this. Afterwards we stand in the street and carry on talking.

It's hard to part when we've just left our son's ashes with a stranger.

***

The family feels thin and unfinished without you. The shape's all wrong. I hate this new reality of having only two children instead of three. It feels too few. It's not 'you lot' any more or 'you three' or 'all of you'; it's 'you two' or 'the girls.' It doesn't feel right not to include you. The dinner table seems empty with four rather than five, incomplete, as though we're waiting for you to arrive. Which of course we are.

Your presence never went unfelt at mealtimes. Or anywhere. You loved nothing better than to pick up a strand of spaghetti and twirl it around, oblivious to the spattering sauce and people diving for cover when it did its final flick as you sucked it noisily into your mouth. You'd add gravy to your roast chicken until it threatened to pour over the edge of the plate. Once the chicken was gone, you'd slurp it up noisily. It was almost impossible not to be on your case all the time. You weren't wilfully naughty or disobedient. You just didn't see the problem. As well as being the messiest eater I've ever known, you were also the fussiest; your vegetables weren't allowed to touch your meat, and if they did, or someone coughed near you, you'd put down your knife and fork and refuse to eat.

You were always on the move. If it wasn't a shoulder twitching or an arm shooting out sideways, or a constant shifting in your seat, you would leap up without warning and start walking round the table. Round and round and round as you talked. You did it when you were particularly engaged in a conversation with us all. It was almost as though you didn't know you were doing it. It was hard to know what to do as your parent Sam. Should we have insisted that you sit back down, which would have killed the conversation dead – you would have done that to punish us – or should we have let you carry on so that you remained engaged? I think about these things often now, wondering where I went wrong, what I might have done differently to make things end another way. You never grew out of your steady circling of the table. Later on, once things started to go wrong, I let you circle. I was so relieved to have you engaging with us at all. You so rarely came out of your room.

Teachers recognised the energy and passion you could bring to things and the way you transmitted your delight to others. You didn't generally get the main parts in school plays when you were a child. You were too much of a liability for that. But you did get some of the best laughs. I can picture you aged ten bursting onto the stage and pedalling like mad on a toddler's trike as you played a Chinese take-away delivery man. Your grin stretched from ear to ear. You knew how to make an entrance.

And now we're trying to plan an exit. We're having a Service of Thanksgiving for you. We want it to be a *celebration of you in all your glorious quirkiness. We shan't shy away from the difficulties of your life, but we want that only to be a small part of what people go away with. We want them to understand the whole of you and all the joy you brought to us.*

You did face difficulties Sam, despite your insistence that you were okay. It's hard to pinpoint exactly when they began but by the summer of 2010 things seemed to be starting to unravel. That June when you were about halfway through your A2 exams you simply walked out of one, telling the exams officer that your 'head was all over the place.' You never went back. You were incredibly casual about it, offered no explanation, refused to speak to your tutor or see a doctor. You said there was nothing wrong with you. You'd simply made a choice to sit your exams the following January instead. You were immovable.

You were extreme about what you would eat by then. It started with insisting on organic food but soon you'd become vegetarian, then vegan, then raw vegan. You spent endless hours on the computer, reading about all the things we ingested which were bad for us. You refused to eat anything bottled or packaged in plastic, because it leached into food and drinks. You wouldn't drink tap water because it was full of fluoride, part of a government conspiracy to "dumb down" society. When we all went to Devon for Dad's 50th birthday you refused to eat any food the hotel provided as you couldn't be sure it was organic. Nor would you drink the water because it came in plastic bottles. All you ate all weekend was two bags of organic rocket, which we managed to find in a local supermarket. You insisted on walking barefoot for two days when we walked the coastal path, saying you wanted to connect with nature. You wouldn't wear sun cream because it was full of chemicals. It was ferociously hot and you burned terribly but you wouldn't budge. When we got home you took to your bed and broke down and cried. You'd convinced yourself that you'd contracted Lyme's disease from walking barefoot. You were inconsolable. It was heart-breaking.

Something strange happened to your body clock too. It seemed to be out of sync with the world outside. You took to sleeping during the day and getting up at night. I'd hear your soft footfall as you padded round the darkened house, the clunk of doors and kitchen cupboards opening and closing as you went on the rounds of your nocturnal life.

One morning I asked you, 'Are you sleeping okay Sam? I often hear you up at night. Is everything alright?'

You looked at me with pained irritation.

'Of course it is. I've never felt better. I'm simply moon-gazing. You should try it.'

'Well, yes, maybe one day, Sam, but don't you need your sleep? I know I do.'

'But you make such terrible choices,' you said, shaking your head. 'Moon gazing is amazing. It's good for you. Yogis do it. The ancient Indians did it. It's healing, it brings clarity of mind, it increases your psychic abilities. You just have to open your mind, Mum. You're so closed off. About every-thing. Each day you poison yourself with the food you eat. Why won't you listen to me? It would make you live longer. I'm going to outlive everyone else my age because of the way I live.'

You might have been right on lots of the things you said

Sam, but you weren't on that last one.

Do you remember your watermelon fad? It began that summer on holiday in Sicily. We were staying on the coast next to Syracuse. I went to the supermarket after we arrived and bought food for the next few days. On my return you looked in the fridge and the cupboards and declared with exasperation that there wasn't a thing you could eat.

'Oh come on Sam,' I said, 'Surely there's something there you can eat.'

'No,' you said with absolute finality, 'there's nothing. I need to go to buy my own food.'

'You could've told me earlier, Muelo. You could've come with me.'

'Well you didn't ask me if I wanted to.'

'Well I didn't know you were going to refuse to eat everything I bought.'

'Well I didn't know you were only going to buy food that I can't eat.'

'Oh, come on Sam, I'll take you,' Paddy cut in.

You left in the battered Fiat 500 that had been waiting for us at the airport. Paddy stayed in the car while you shopped. After ten minutes or so he glanced in his rear-view mirror. You were approaching the car, grinning broadly, pushing a giant trolley loaded high with watermelons. Only watermelons. You unloaded them into the boot and, when you ran out of space, onto the back seat. Back at the apartment you ferried them in batches from the car.

'Look what I've bought, Mum,' you shouted excitedly as

49

you wedged them into cupboards and piled them high in the kitchen until every surface was covered.

'Blimey Sam,' I said. 'That was an unusual shop.'

You ate only watermelons all week. Instead of coming down to the beach with us or joining us on that day trip to Notte, you stayed in the apartment. You slept all day and went to the beach as the sun dipped low. You waited there until the moon rose and you stayed all night. You expounded the virtues of sun and moon-gazing in a tone that suggested you were talking about things we couldn't possibly understand. You were right, Sam. I didn't understand. There was so much about your behaviour then that kept me awake at night. But you had a way of sensing when I was reaching the point of irredeemable concern and then you'd start behaving more normally again. You did it on that holiday.

After four days of daytime sleep and night-time vigils on the beach you surprised me by agreeing to come too when the apartment owner offered to take us all out on his boat. You were your old self again. You exclaimed at the clarity of the turquoise water in the caves, admired the bleached limestone of their walls and leapt noisily into the sea. That evening you even agreed to come out for a meal with the rest of us. You were in high spirits as we set off to walk into the old town. In the restaurant our waiter wore starched white and had the air of a man who'd seen everything. He produced his order pad with a flourish and went round the table noting our starters. You requested a rocket salad. The waiter moved on to the main course and went round the table a second time. You ordered another rocket salad. The waiter raised an eyebrow but no more. We ate. He reappeared with his order pad.

'Puddings,' he said.

When he got to you, you looked up and smiled. 'Rocket salad please.'

He clapped his hands in delight and disappeared through a door into the kitchen. After a while it swung open and into the restaurant walked five or six kitchen staff. Behind them came the waiter. He approached the table bearing your plate aloft on one hand. He presented it with a small bow. You grinned and returned the bow. The staff all clapped and cheered.

When we got back from that holiday you moved up to London to look for work. You were eighteen and said you wanted to live independently. You walked everywhere until the soles of your shoes – those purple suede loafers – wore through. I still have them in your cupboard. They're stiff and flattened at the heel where you walked on the back of them. I can't bring myself to throw them away. Not yet.

You came home intermittently and when you left again you filled my largest wheelie-case with dozens of glass bottles of water. You dragged it behind you clanking as it sank into the gravel on the drive. You were going to catch the train and walk from Paddington. You refused my offer of a lift. When I asked you whether it wouldn't be easier to buy the water in London or even order it online and have it delivered, you shook your head as if I were missing some painfully obvious point.

You bought yourself an electric earthing mat and a piece of polished zeolite that you wore round your neck on a leather lace. Both were incredibly health-giving you said. You sat and slept with your feet resting on the mat. Its blue electric lead trailed incongruously from under your duvet at the foot of the bed. It spoke to me of otherness. To you it was the only way to live.

When I came to visit you, we'd always walk to Planet Organic. It had become the only place you'd buy your food and supplements. You consumed spirulina – that strange powdered seaweed – by the tablespoon. You were entirely unself-conscious about the dark green-black residue it left on your teeth and around your mouth.

One day as we walked, you stepped off the pavement to cross the road without looking either left or right. I grabbed your arm as a black cab sped by.

'For God's sake Sam,' I said, 'you've got to look before you cross.'

You gently detached yourself, looked at me kindly and said, 'But Mum, if it's my time, then it's my time.'

'But Sam, you're only eighteen. You've got a whole life ahead of you. Of course, your time will come but don't go bringing it forward. You have to take care of yourself. You can't be so fatalistic.'

You smiled and raised your eyebrows in a way that told me you were an adult now and making your own choices in life.

***

26 May 2014

THE MEMORIAL SERVICE occupies us all. Paddy and I are in the study trying to connect a new printer so we can print off photos for a montage. I move a pile of papers and rest them on my keyboard. Both girls are out but suddenly I hear sounds of someone moving around, of doors opening and closing. I think it must be an intruder and I motion to Paddy to make no noise. We both stop and listen. Then, right next to us, we hear a voice. We hear Sam talking. It's coming from the computer.

Without saying a word to one another we draw up chairs. We sit and listen. It's a recording I made of Sam and me when we were out at Pizza Express for lunch. There's a second recording too, made at home a few days later. It plays automatically when the first one ends. I knew they were on my phone but I'd no idea they were on my computer. By placing the pile of papers on the keyboard I have unknowingly pressed a combination of keys which has set them playing. Sam would have called it synchronicity. He liked seeing connections between things. He'd attribute them to some greater power.

Paddy and I barely speak about it afterwards. It's too strange and everything is simply too raw.

28 May 2014

A HUSH FALLS as we walk through the door.

I see a full church: row upon row of extra chairs set out at the back, all occupied. At the front the choir stalls are filling up. There must be three hundred people there. I want to cry with gratitude.

Paddy, Rosy, Ellie and I make our way forward to join Simon, Kim and Imogen. The casket containing Sam's ashes sits on a table with a large photo of him in a silver frame next to it. He is wearing a long-sleeved T-shirt with navy and putty-coloured stripes. Round his neck is the carved, polished stone on a leather lace which he brought back from Hawaii. He has sun-lightened curly hair and a wispy goatee beard. Looking slightly to his left he is smiling in a dreamy sort of way. For a moment I am back there with him on a perfect summer's evening with the palest of blue skies tingeing orange in the evening light.

We take our seats and wait for the service to begin. I can feel the tension in the girls. They are sitting to the left of me. Simon, Kim and Imogen are on the other side of them and Paddy is to my right. All the while latecomers are streaming in, filing up to the choir stalls, squeezing in at the ends of pews. It is a relief when the service begins.

Simon is the first to speak. 'Sam was born on 22nd February, 1992,' he says. And pauses. 'Even Sam couldn't argue with that. He would probably take issue with just about everything else that now follows.'

I laugh. Everyone laughs.

It's going to be alright.

29 May 2014

I WAKE UP early, just after 5 am. I pull on some clothes, pick up the Order of Service, copies of the tributes and poem, some photos, and creep out of the house. I'm going to visit Sam. I park at the churchyard, walk through the lychgate and past the church. There's no one about.

It's only when I'm sitting by his grave that I realise. That despite the service, none of it feels real yet. I still can't believe that he is dead. I only know him alive.

The sun is already up. I look through the photos and read. I start to cry, to properly cry and in the quiet and comfort of the churchyard, I am finally able to speak to him. I tell him how much I miss him, what his death means to me and I berate him for leaving me.

I cry until I'm spent.

No one is there to require anything of me. I sit with my thoughts of him and, in my stillness, I become invisible to the squirrels. They run behind me on the flint and brick wall and in front of me across the grass. I feel at peace, as though something has shifted for me: the beginnings perhaps of an understanding that Sam will never be coming home again.

***

I've been used to your coming and going with all the travelling you did after sixth-form college. Hawaii was your first destination. It was September 2010 and you were back from London. We were terribly nervous about your going but you assured us you'd be okay, would stay in touch and that you'd return to sit your A levels the following summer, not January as you'd previously said. The night before you left you damaged your eye 'gazing' at a strobe light. Somehow that lack of judgement and recklessness seemed to epitomise everything I was scared of.

You set off with a small backpack, walking shoes, a tent, a sleeping bag and a vague plan to work on an organic farm. You said you wanted to go where the wind took you. After the plane landed you headed off on foot and walked to the nearest beach to pitch your tent for the night.

You did stay in touch, sporadically. We heard nothing from you for the first ten days, but finally you emailed to say you were loving Hawaii and meeting fantastically interesting people who 'shared your views.' That didn't exactly fill us with joy but of course that was part of your reason for choosing Hawaii: knowing you'd meet like-minded people there. You travelled round the islands for three months and said you'd never been happier. Your emails were full of your usual exuberance, but they did little to allay my anxiety.

I was terrified you might just drift away into your new life and stop getting in touch. I wanted to hear from you so that I would know where to come to find you if you did. In my emails I tried to pin you down on details of where you were staying and what you were doing, but you remained resolutely vague. You didn't want to phone. We understood your need to establish a bit of distance. You were almost nineteen and looking for independence.

Your emails became stranger. You took to signing off as 'ONE' and sending 'blessings.' You asked for money to be transferred to you in multiples of 111. A week before you were due home you requested £333 to tide you over. Dad asked if there was some significance in the number 333. You explained in an email:

> 'The brain operates between 0-40 hz, in a similar way to broadband the connection can either be slow or fast. Most people use little more than 1-2% of their brain and operate using 0.2/0.3 hz. 3.33 although a seemingly small number on the bandwidth is actually when the left and right hemispheres of the brain align

and more meaning is experienced. Interfacing with classical music, meditation and the like can elevate our frequency to this level.'

Alarmingly, the same email ended:

'Love! I got bitten by a brown recluse spider, the venom of which is actually more poisonous than a rattle snake so the story ever proceeds onwards. The bite was a massive gift but has obviously come with its price, an irregular heartbeat. I am now going to focus on recovery!'

A few days later the phone rang at three am. It was a terrible line and we struggled to hear one another. It didn't sound like you at all. Your voice was different, the intonation had changed, and your laugh too. I might have been talking to a stranger. I think you sensed my discomfiture because you ended the call quite abruptly. I wanted to blame my sleepy state, the poor connection and background noise for the strangeness of the call and the overwhelming feeling I had of not being able to connect with you. It seemed as though we were each having a conversation that the other couldn't hear.

When Dad and I drove to the airport to collect you on Christmas morning, I was nervous. Your plane arrived early, so you were already through customs and standing just outside the entrance to the terminal. You didn't move as we approached. You just stood there, feet apart, arms aloft, your face fixed in a beatific, trance-like smile. You waited for us to reach you, then stepped forward to enfold us both in your arms. It didn't feel like a hug. It felt like some strange religious ritual in which you were trying to confer something on us. There was a look of ecstasy on your face, yet it felt as though you weren't really there. You weren't the young man we'd waved off three months earlier.

On the journey home I couldn't speak. What I was seeing and hearing was too terrifying: the non-sequiturs in your speech, the incongruent laugh, the wildness of your eyes, the constant hand movements. Your clothes were in rags, and dark with grime. Dad was fantastic. He kept on talking to you and asking you questions despite your inability to answer them. I was mute with terror. The smell was terrible. We had all four windows open wide because of the stench. Later I discovered that you had suppurating wounds on your feet from walking bare-foot on volcanic terrain, and two terrible spider's bites oozing pus and seemingly eating away the flesh on the inside of both your knees.

When we arrived home, Ellie was first to the door. She was so excited about seeing you again. She stepped forward to greet you. You took her in your arms and held her in a too-long embrace. I watched her face from behind you as the look on it changed from pleasure and happy anticipation to confusion and then fear.

'What has happened to Sam?' she mouthed at me over your shoulder. You hadn't even spoken. It was that palpable, the change in you.

It was a desperately difficult day for us all, but especially for you. You walked back into a family Christmas: sixteen of us. You did your best. We all did. You came and said hello to *everyone. You spoke in sentences that didn't make sense, laughed when there was nothing to laugh at, didn't seem to hear when people asked you questions. You tried to connect with us. We tried to connect with you. But we were on different wavelengths. You sensed our discomfort, and I saw the pain and confusion of that in your eyes. You excused yourself and withdrew to rest.*

After a while I came upstairs carrying Imogen, who was only eleven months old.

'Come here, Mum,' you called.

We came into your bedroom and you leant towards Imogen and gave her one of your new, too-long smiles, your eyes full of rapturous joy. You wanted to communicate your love to her. It was too much. She shifted uneasily in my arms and tried to avoid your gaze. Even she sensed something different, something other. You wanted to take her in your arms. I made an excuse and withdrew.

*'She's **my** sister,' you called after me angrily. 'You're not anything to her.'*

I understood your anger and it broke my heart.

You reappeared after your sleep. Nothing had changed. It seemed that we had lost the young man we knew.

After you'd gone to bed, Rosy, Ellie and I sat down together and wept for you. We still had one another, but we knew that you were alone in a world that now felt alien to you. We could only hope that we were seeing something caused by drugs, or disorientation from tiredness, dehydration and jet lag rather than something more sinister. We knew your journey had included a twelve hour stop-over and that you probably hadn't eaten or drunk all trip. We were clutching at straws but didn't know what else to do.

We talked endlessly about that: what we should do. Family and friends advised waiting for a few days, to give you time to re-orient yourself. You wouldn't hear of seeing a doctor. I look back now and wonder why we didn't go against your wishes and call in medical help there and then. Would it have changed anything? Might you still be here if we had? I don't know. It's one of the many unknowns I have to learn to live with.

Simon T came to see you. You and he went back so many years: best friends since you met on your first day at nursery just before you both turned three, your birthdays only four days apart. When Aidi and I became friends too, we worked out that we must have been in hospital together. We organised joint birthday parties for you both. I have a photo taken at your fourth. You're standing one on either side of a magician's box, both wearing lumberjack shirts, tucked into trousers. Yours are ruby red corduroy, Simon's are olive moleskin. Your outfit is topped off with a matching moleskin waistcoat with satin back, Simon's with red wellington boots. You both look incredibly solemn and a little terrified. The magician was elderly and rather strict. He must have realised over the years that crowd control was rather more important than his act. You were about to blow out the candles on the cake and he was making you wait. You said afterwards that you hated him.

It was three years before I saw you both look so solemn again. That was at Aidi's funeral at the end of her long battle with cancer. After the service you ran about together in the way that children do as if, in that moment, neither of you had a care in the world. You were dealing with a dreadful blow then too, though not as bad as Simon's. Two months earlier Dad had suddenly moved out. You were devastated. You and Simon remained firm friends despite going to different schools when you were eleven. Perhaps even at that age sharing such painful experiences created a closeness that isn't easily broken.

On that visit, you and Simon spent the whole day together in the green room, your chosen venue because it had the computer in it. You emerged only to prepare lunch. When I drove him home at the end of the day, he said his mouth and throat were still on fire from the rice you'd cooked. You'd tipped two entire packets of ground chilli into it. You'd looked surprised when he said it was hot. You hadn't reacted to its spiciness at all. Simon thought drugs might be to blame for your mental state. You'd told us both about helping a man to build a hut and being paid with a large bag of cannabis and magic mushrooms but that you hadn't done other drugs. Simon advised against a medical intervention. He thought it might do irreparable damage to our relationship with you and that you'd probably leave to live on the streets if we did.

You told me that you'd lived with the homeless during your last month in Hawaii and had loved it. You'd slept in a bin bag, having left your tent, sleeping bag, walking shoes and most of your clothes behind you when you travelled to your second island. You liked the thought of someone finding them and making them their own. You always returned from your travels with very few of the things you'd taken with you and whenever you saw a homeless person, you'd dart into a *shop to buy them some fruit.*

When you first arrived home I washed your feet – the water in the bowl turned black – and bathed your wounds. You wouldn't let me put anything on them and refused to see a doctor because you didn't believe in Western medicine anymore. You said you'd treat them yourself with Ayurvedic methods. You sprinkled some sort of powdered silver onto them. It worked. And within a few weeks they'd healed, leaving only scars. It provided you with ammunition for your arguments, as well as healthy legs.

Dad and I went to see our GP. He listened carefully and said, 'It's hard to say. It depends really whether he's just wacky or more wacko.' He referred us to a psychiatrist who when we described your behaviour also said that it was hard to say, but it sounded as though it could be schizophrenia. You refused to visit him.

We found a psychiatrist who came to the house. I explained that someone would be coming to see you. You were furious and said you'd refuse to talk to her if she came, but when she knocked on the green room door and introduced herself to you, your good manners got the better of you. You sat and chatted to her for an hour or more.

She spoke to me afterwards and said you were showing signs of psychosis and had almost certainly been having a psychotic episode but she couldn't say whether it was a one-off, was drug-induced or the first signs of schizophrenia. You were adamant that you wouldn't take any medication so there was nothing to do but wait.

You gradually found some sort of equilibrium and we started to be able to connect with you again. I think that was as much a relief to you as it was to us, Sam, though you never acknowledged there had been any problem. Initially it was just the odd moment of connection. Sometimes just a smile, a glance, something in the way you looked at me and I'd know that you were back.

Then there would be whole conversations when you were you again and, in time, whole days. You weren't the same you, but we could at least make contact with one another. It was your psychosis – the losing touch with reality – that made you seem so different. I hate it that so many people think schizophrenia is the same as a split personality. They're totally different, but people are scared of schizophrenia because they think it's a Dr Jekyll and Mr Hyde-type illness. I would see the fear in people's eyes when we were out together and it would break my heart.

I think there was something about coming home that grounded you. It always had. Even when you were little, I would sense a palpable change in you as you walked in through the door and breathed in the air of home.

You stopped using your bedroom. The green room became your home. You'd lie on the floor at night to sleep, gazing at the stars and moon through open-shuttered windows, wearing the same clothes you'd worn day and night for weeks. You didn't wash or change your clothes or cut your nails except under extreme duress from me or Dad. You withdrew more and more from family life. We all tried so hard to engage with you. You hardly ever came to family meals. You preferred to prepare and consume your raw fruit and vegetables on the Georgian knee-hole desk on which the computer sat. Peelings and cores and half-eaten food and discarded packaging built up around you. You stopped seeing or contacting friends.

The way you lived your life became gradually more and more extreme. You wouldn't wash in tap water because it contained potentially lethal fluoride. You kept a bottle of vodka in the bathroom and poured it onto cotton wool pads to wash yourself. Very infrequently. We installed a filter on the shower hoping that might encourage you to wash. It didn't. Personal hygiene became a major battleground between us. You foreswore most soaps, toothpastes and deodorants as full of chemicals. We made frequent trips to Planet Organic on Westbourne Grove where we spent a fortune on products you promised to try, but rarely did. Most of them are still in your bedroom, unopened. You stocked up on supplements and tinctures too. You didn't believe in washing your hair; it was long and sun-bleached and starting to form dreadlocks. You said it would clean itself.

You spent all your waking hours meditating or on the computer listening to music. You weren't depressed or low in this withdrawn state. You were happy, ecstatically so. You said you'd never been more fulfilled, that your life had never been richer, never more complete. You were on a spiritual journey to higher levels of consciousness than we had ever attained, and you argued passionately and cogently for this life of spiritual fulfilment that you'd chosen. You became so engrossed in the rich world inside your head that you didn't want to leave the green room even to relieve yourself. Instead you peed into empty bottles. They built up around you on tables, on the floor, next to your bedroll; in different sizes and subtly varying shades of yellow and orangey brown, alongside half-eaten food and fruit and vegetable peelings, like some monstrous modern art installation. You looked at me as though I were mad when I made you empty them and suggested you use the loo instead.

Whatever was happening in your head affected your senses too. It seemed that a switch had been flicked to reset your thermostat. On a bitter winter's day, you'd sit scantily clad in the green room with the sash window fully open in a blast of icy air. And on hot days you'd wear two coats on top of jumpers as you lay huddled beneath the duvet.

You simply did not understand where we were coming from when we expressed concern about your well-being. We might as well have been speaking in a foreign language. You refused to see a doctor. You denied the validity of most things we said, talked of making your own choices, finding your own path. You responded with outrage and disbelief if we persisted, ultimately refusing to listen, saying that we were imagining things. Then you'd turn the tables altogether, saying the problems we saw lay within us, not you, and perhaps we should talk to someone about our own mental health. You often accused me of being mad. It broke my heart, but sometimes, when I was feeling vulnerable, it felt as though you might be right. It was hard to hold onto my own reality when you presented yours with such conviction.

We called the local Community Mental Health Team (CMHT). They sent someone from their Early Intervention in Psychosis team to see you. Again, you were outraged and swore total resistance, but again good manners prevailed. You would explain politely to everyone who would listen that

GILL MANN

*there was nothing wrong with you, that it was your mother
who had the problem and needed to see the psychiatrist. They
came repeatedly, but each time we were told the same thing:
that although there was evidence of psychosis, they did not feel
that you were ill enough to be sectioned under the Mental
Health Act. Each time you threatened to leave, to go to live
on the streets, where at least you'd be free from our meddling.
I lived in terror of you simply disappearing one day.*

*The CMHT talked of 'watchful waiting'. The gentle
onomatopoeic lilt of that term does not begin to describe the
dreadful reality of it. It was torture. It went on for more than
eighteen months.*

***

30 May 2014

WE ALL GO to Heathrow to see Ellie off to South
America. I understand why she's going back. She's missed
a whole month of travelling with her friends, but perhaps
more than that, she needs to get away. It's too painful to
be at home without Sam. By cruel coincidence she's flying
from the same airport, the same terminal, where only six
weeks ago we waved farewell to him. It's hard to let her
go. Rosy cries inconsolably. I take a photo before she
heads off through security. I didn't take one of Sam. I
knew it would irritate him.

In my mind's eye, I'm back again with him at
Heathrow in April, as he sets off on his final trip. He and
I are standing near the entrance to the security checks. We
have arrived in good time and withdrawn money for
emergencies. A large group approaches, pushing several

trollies side by side. I see Simon behind them, dodging and weaving in an attempt to pass. He fails, shrugs his shoulders, raises his hands in defeat and pulls an exasperated face. Sam laughs. They hug. We go through all the normal parental requests: *stay in touch, call if there's any problem, stay safe, remember you can come home at any time.*

He agrees to text at least once a fortnight, weekly if he can. We hug and kiss in turn. He doesn't want to linger. I can sense his impatience to get on his way, back to Pai, a place he feels most able to be himself. He looks us each in the eye, smiles his slow broad smile, and is off, striding in that way he does: purposefully, confidently, without a backward glance. Slim-hipped in his black jeans, white T-shirt and light merino sweater.

The detail matters so much now. I want to imprint Sam into my mind's eye, fix him there forever so that I can close my eyes and conjure him up at will. I want to be able to see him, to fill in every detail. I don't want him to fade with time. I think of all the photos I've developed in my dark room. The white, blank sheet of paper lying at the bottom of the developing tray beneath a film of liquid. Then something starts to emerge. At first no more than shadow: tones, different shades of grey with no real form. But gradually the image takes shape, contours turn into outlines, areas of light and dark become distinct, details form. And then it is there, the inverted image I saw on the negative, coming to life under the eerie red light. I see Sam's freckled nose, the sun-bleached hair around his temples, the crinkled, smiling eyes.

I'm scared that now this process can only happen in

reverse: the details erode, the outlines fade, the shades of light and dark merge into something shapeless and unformed. I'm scared I will lose the picture of the last time I saw him.

Rosy leaves for Bristol to rejoin her year group at Circomedia. She has missed a month of her course and needs to pick up her studies again.

The house feels horribly empty. I go onto Facebook and am confronted with the evidence of others' lives going on: a friend counting her blessings in her children and new grandchild, another proudly celebrating her son's first-class degree, yet another posing happily with her child at graduation. It increases the sense of distance I feel between me and other people at the moment. I see their sorrow and their love for me, but I feel strangely un-moved. Perhaps I can't bear to be moved by their grief in case it puts me in touch with my own.

When it does come, my grief hits me in quiet, unsus-pecting moments: when Paddy's grandson Charlie announces excitedly that he's finally 1.4 metres tall and can go on all the rides at Thorpe Park. Sam promised to take him there as soon as he was tall enough. Writing a birthday card and finding my pen moving automatically to write 'Rosy, Sam and Ellie.' It's almost unbearable not to include him.

31 May 2014

OUR HOLIDAY TO Ibiza has been booked for months. Everyone says it will do me good to get away. I'm happy to trust others' judgment at the moment. It's hard to know what I want or what will be good for me. I still feel hollow and strangely insubstantial, bobbing on the surface of life like balsa wood or pumice. I think perhaps it doesn't matter where I am, that even home doesn't feel entirely real at the moment. But as soon as I leave it, I'm hit by a sense of loss. It's dislocating to be on the move again.

At the villa we're greeted by the owner's agent. I go through the motions of being a normal holiday-maker, but nothing is normal. I feel lost.

***

I'm used to feeling lost. It's how I felt during those eighteen months of 'watchful waiting.' I quite literally didn't know how to make sense of what was happening to you.

At times things felt almost normal, as though we had the old you back with us – funny, quirky, warm, rational, happy to engage and join us for meals or walks or days out. But then just as I was daring to believe that it was all okay, everything would change. You might become overly exuberant, disinhibited and expansive, making outlandish and grandiose claims that you were an author, a music producer, a poet, an athlete. At other times you would be remote, unreachable, silent, withdrawn. You could spend days on end doing nothing, lying still and quiet, seemingly content but unable to find the motivation to move. At others you would be filled with restless energy which made you pace the room and move your arms through the air as if warding off some invisible – to us – threat.

When Dad and I talked to you about where your life was going you argued forcefully and articulately for the choices you were making. I struggled to know where the truth lay. Perhaps we were making more of your eccentricities than necessary. You had always been extreme. You liked to be different. You loved to shock. You revelled in and played on your eccentricities – though you wouldn't have called them that. They'd become a part of your identity. Much of your odd behaviour might be just another 'Samism:' making a dramatic entry for a meal with the Martin children dressed only in cotton pyjama bottoms – your torso glistening with olive oil; insisting you were going to spend the night in a sleeping bag on a heavily frosted lawn because the sky was clear and starry; sitting down on the lawn to chat with Ellie and Rae, your cousin, completely naked. Perhaps these were simply extensions of the sorts of things you had always done. And your claims to be a philosopher, a yogi, a guru, a sage, were just a small step up from your boyhood claims that you could split the atom and hot-wire a car. It was all very you. Were you ill or were you simply being a more extreme version of yourself?

You had always been passionate, obsessive and dispropor-tionate when you found something that you loved. After your ninth birthday you spent all your money on two Tama-gotchis, those digital 'pets' that needed to be cared for. But once you'd had the thrill of buying them, you lost interest in them and didn't care when they both 'died' within 24 hours. As a boy and young teenager, you'd moved through endless fads: magic cards, World of Warcraft, mini motorbikes, strawberry laces, Pokémon, blueberries (four packs at a time), BB guns. You embraced each fad with single-minded zeal, casting aside the last to gaze on your latest obsession.

When you became a vegetarian and then a vegan and then a raw vegan, you embraced your beliefs with the same disproportionate fervour. You became a mine of information on nutrition and health. But as always you were extreme and made your own rules, ignoring recommended dosages along with my advice to pay heed to them. You consumed tinctures as though they were water. Large bottles of life-giving potions which should have lasted for months, were consumed within days. It was the same with your interest in spirituality and meditating. It became your life. But it was so hard for us to know what to make of all this. As you pointed out regularly, you weren't alone in your devotion to meditation, to your 'earthing mat' and the energy charm you wore round your neck. A whole community of people worldwide shared your practices and beliefs; and fuelled your interest in conspiracy theories. These people weren't ill, they just had a set of extreme beliefs. It was very hard to know with you where those beliefs ended and the illness began.

You didn't sink into gloom or depression. It might have made you want to seek help if you'd struggled in some way. Instead you rose to dizzying heights of bliss and euphoria. You were entranced by the beauty and richness of what you saw and heard and felt. You had no need to engage with people or life. You had a world of wonder and awe inside your head and you didn't want to leave it. I would pop in to see you when I finished work and ask you how your day had been, knowing you'd done nothing all day but meditate and *listen to music on your computer, your eyes half-closed, eyeballs flicking upwards in ecstasy. Your answer was always the same: 'AMAZING!'*

At other times you were more irritable and withdrawn. You resented intrusions into your world because they took you away from where you wanted to be. If I came in to try to engage with you, you'd either ignore me or ask, 'Yes?' irascibly, like an over-worked boss being interrupted by an incompetent secretary. It became very hard to have a normal conversation with you. All attempts to talk about money – the need to earn a living, responsibilities to others, volunteering instead of doing nothing – got us nowhere. You made it clear that you had no interest in the stuff of normal life: people, relationships, work, events. You were engaged in higher pursuits, in attaining higher levels of consciousness. You looked on our world with disdain and made us feel stupid, boring, dull and pedestrian.

Life fell into a rhythm of sorts. You continued to live in the green room. The CMHT visited regularly and advised that it was too early for a formal Mental Health Act Assessment; we should continue with our 'watchful waiting'. We all worked very hard at including you in our lives, trying to coax you out into the real world; to join us for a meal, to come away for a weekend or a holiday, to head out with us for a walk or a trip to the cinema. Persuading you to do anything was a cause for celebration. You didn't want to leave your room or tear yourself away from what was happening inside your head. The real world was humdrum and tedious by comparison. Sometimes what you saw would make you laugh out loud, a huge guffaw of mirth.

We went on a guided tour of the Chelsea Physic Garden.

You were behaving strangely, repeatedly opening and closing doors to the greenhouse as if engaged in some private ritual, trailing after the group and looking suspiciously behind you. I saw people clocking you. We were gathered together with the guide who was talking when a huge guffaw broke from you.

'Have I said something to amuse you?' she asked caustically.

'I'm sorry,' you said, in that way you had of rising to the occasion when required and pulling yourself back into reality. 'What you said reminded me of something funny'.

Your apology hung in the air, unacknowledged. She remained affronted. Others looked at you nervously. My heart bled for you.

Your behaviour was hard for people to decipher, and I would see the seeds of discomfort you scattered unknowingly in your wake. You made frequent hand movements, as though shifting some invisible object from one place to another. You stared piercingly at strangers, holding their gaze for longer than was socially acceptable or comfortable for them. Sometimes there was a hostile edge to your gaze, at other times something emotional and overly intense. You'd walk along the street, jump up and swivel 360 degrees in the air before nonchalantly continuing on your way. I asked you once,

'What's the jump and swivel about, Muelo?'

*'I dance if I feel like dancing,' you replied tetchily. 'You're just so **locked up**. You really need to let go a bit.'*

In the early weeks of 2011 and only a short while after your return from Hawaii we went on one of our trips to Planet Organic. You were not in a good place that day although you didn't know it. I could see you felt threatened.

73

You walked repeatedly up and down an aisle where two shop assistants were chatting as they filled the shelves, slowing almost to a stop each time you passed them. You crouched down to look under shelving units.

'Can I help you, sir?' one said.

You narrowed your eyes and gave him a long, searching look, as if you knew some dark secret about him. Without replying you spun on your heel and marched back down the aisle, stopping only to turn and repeat the stare.

We sat down to eat and an elderly lady bumped into your chair as she tried to pass. You swivelled round angrily, fiercely protective of your personal space. Before you could speak the old lady said loudly,

'There was no need for that, young man. What bad manners and loutish behaviour.'

You immediately stood up, held your arms aloft and started declaiming at the top of your voice, 'I am not a lout. I did nothing wrong.' You looked around the room at the fellow diners. 'Citizens of Planet Organic, I appeal to you all. Did I do anything wrong? Tell me, did I?'

People shifted uncomfortably in their seats around us, but you didn't notice. By then you were away.

'Of course I didn't,' you said indignantly. 'I have travelled the world. I've been to many places far, far away. I'm a philosopher, writer, musician, yogi. And I have many, many friends. Yes, many, many friends.' You turned to the old lady. 'I have more friends than you. I'm greater than you. Yes, much much greater.'

By now silence had fallen and all eyes were on you. The old lady shuffled off. You sat down, satisfied.

In the hush that followed I saw pitying glances directed at

*me. You were oblivious. Later she approached me. 'I'm sorry,'
she said, 'I hadn't realised ... '.*

*'No, don't worry,' I said. But I wanted to weep. Inside I
was struggling with a bewildering mix of feelings: anger with
her for being so disagreeable, so quick to go on the offensive,
for 'not realising'; but most of all I felt defensive of you; my
poor, lost boy. I wanted to protect you and yet I didn't know
how. I felt such sadness for you. And sadness for me too. Both
of us adrift.*

*We left Planet Organic. I couldn't bear to stay. In the car
you immediately clamped your headphones over your ears and
lost yourself in music. I'd never felt more despairing and
lonely.*

*Life carried on but then, terrifyingly, within two months of
being home you told us you were going off travelling again
and had already booked your flights.*

*During those eighteen months you went on three more
trips: another to Hawaii in June 2011 and two to Pai, one
in March 2011 and one in April 2012. You'd discovered
how much further your money went in Thailand. That
mattered as you were funding it all yourself with money you'd
inherited. We tried to talk you out of it each time. But you
were immoveable, adamant that it was what you wanted to
do.*

*I can't begin to describe the anxiety we felt each time you
went away. We thought about hiding your passport or
destroying it, but we knew we'd only be delaying the
inevitable and even more importantly would be risking losing
your trust. We didn't want to do that. You always stayed in*

touch, if erratically, and made it home each time. You were always in a parlous state when you did, though never as bad as that first time.

When you left for your second trip, in March 2011, you'd booked a return flight to Hawaii. I took you to the airport and waited as you checked in your luggage.

'You should go now,' you said. 'I'll go through security after I've bought a couple of things.'

We heard nothing for two days and then a text message arrived.

LOL. I'm on a train from Bangkok to Chiangmai. I decided to go to Thailand instead.

As though you'd simply changed your mind about where to buy your groceries. You saw nothing unusual in having to retrieve your baggage or pay for more flights.

Another time you arrived back more than a day late. You didn't think to let us know, even though you knew we'd be waiting for you at the airport. We discovered, from the airline, that you'd been detained for 24-hours on your stop-over in Canada. You didn't know why.

In-between your travels you continued to live in the green room and we continued with the awful, unspeakably painful process of 'watchful waiting'. It was a time of such confusion for us all. When you were in a good phase you argued cogently for the life you were leading. Your arguments were passionate and powerful. I found myself engaged in a constant mental tussle as I weighed up the evidence of what I was seeing and what it might mean. Like most mothers I'd always been finely attuned to you all. With you, especially so. I'd had to be. You'd always been such a challenge. My feeling, from early on, was that you were ill. But others disagreed. They thought you were just being obstinate and contrary, just a more extreme version of who you'd always been. People would listen to my concerns, then tell me that when they'd last seen you, you'd seemed to be okay. They'd perhaps hint quietly that I should try being firmer with you, giving you more boundaries. Often the mental health professionals would report that you'd seemed quite lucid and grounded. It was very hard not to doubt myself. I wondered often whether I was being neurotic and imagining things. I wanted to believe you when you said you were fine. And sometimes I did. But at other times I simply couldn't. I knew you so well.

Initially, it was a relief when you seemed to recover from the terrible state you'd been in. But as the weeks and months passed it became harder and harder to manage the fact that there was no predictable, linear progression to what was happening to you. You just continued with your bewildering array of different behaviours.

Every morning, every time I came home from work or being out, I simply didn't know what I was going to find; the Sam I knew or this stranger. There was no logical reason for the constant changes in you. They swept in and out, like uncharted tides, causing the ground to shift beneath my feet, carrying with them anxiety or hope, relief or dread. In time it seemed that my feelings responded only to the tug and pull of these tides which were beyond my control. I found it harder and harder to separate my own happiness from what was happening to you. I would feel upbeat and optimistic when the old you appeared. Just a smile, a feeling of connection, could lift my spirits and give me hope; but then in an instant *it could move to anxiety and a sense of dread when I lost you again. I found myself in a state of heightened awareness to even the smallest shifts in your mood or behaviour. It was impossible not to be on full alert. I didn't know what to do for the best, how to help you, how to help the girls, how to help myself. And above all else I didn't know how to parent a son who at times behaved normally and at others seemed to exist in a world I could not enter.*

If it was agony for us it must have been even worse for you. You believed fervently that you weren't ill. In your mind you were simply making legitimate choices about how you wanted to live, and we were to blame for everything, with our outdated, unenlightened views. You felt wounded and betrayed by a mother who had, 'called people in'; by a family who simply didn't understand you. You told me often that with a different mother, one who loved and accepted you for who you were, your life would be better. Dad popped in often to see you. You told him the same thing. It was heartbreaking to see your confusion and bewilderment.

I felt failed by a system that left a family to bear witness to the disintegration of a beautiful, bright young man; a system that seemed powerless to intervene until things got even worse. And I felt that I was failing you too. Somehow as a mother I should know what to do, but I didn't.

***

2 June 2014

I BUMP INTO an old university friend by chance. He's staying in Ibiza and he's heard about Sam.

'I know what you're going through,' he says as he

clasps my hand meaningfully, but soon the conversation moves on.

I don't want it to. I want it to move back to Sam, to my loss. Does it not warrant more than a few words and a quick clasp of the hand? I feel anger growing inside me. How can he possibly think that I'm interested in these meaningless, petty things? Does he want me to laugh, to smile as he and his friends are, when all I can think of is my dead son?

It's lonely being so out of step with others. I don't know how to bridge the gap.

Sam's picture is on my phone, smiling at me every time I turn it on. Often I stop to look at it, take in his gaze. His smile was for me. At other times I move quickly past it. It's a rejection, a conscious decision on my part not to engage with him. In those moments I feel a small electrical charge within me, something more like anger than pain. I can't look at his smiling face because he's left me; broken his promise to Ellie to keep himself safe when she was away on her gap year; jeopardised Rosy's end of year show at Circomedia; caused Simon to crumple. I am angry with him. We still don't know for sure how he died. But I have an idea. He wasn't depressed or desperate. That was never part of his experience of the illness, whose existence he denied. He felt deeply that he had been wronged, misunderstood – but I don't believe he ever felt he *couldn't* go on living; just that he might not *choose* to.

The Thai police reported that they'd found no evidence of drugs, but Simon came across some empty diazepam packets in the bin of his hut on stilts. Sam liked how they made him feel. He wouldn't have thought about risk: the ferocious thirty-nine-degree heat and the airless, non-air-conditioned room, the need to remain hydrated, the potential side-effects of his medication – to compromise the body's capacity to regulate its temperature. I don't think he actually *chose* to die. But he was almost certainly reckless with his life.

All these things are in my mind when I refuse to engage with him. I feel angry with him, even though I don't want to. The guilt always comes later.

3 June 2014

I'M LYING ON a sun bed under the dazzling blue of an Ibizan sky. The guilt has arrived. What sort of mother am I to be angry with my dead son? Perhaps Sam was right, that with another mother all would have been different.

A series of small cotton wool clouds drifts across the dome of the sky, high above me. There is a solid nucleus to each cloud, but as they pass in front of the sun, small sections detach themselves one after the other and swirl in ever-shifting patterns around the perimeter. They form limbs that stretch and bend, an arched back here, a cartwheel there, a tumbling exuberance as they break free of the whole. It seems they are engaged in a never-ending, glorious dance. I want them to keep going for ever.

I feel Sam in these clouds. There is something so

unfettered and irrepressible in them. Guilt makes way for a sense of celebration and awe. I feel him so powerfully and perhaps he's saying, 'I'm okay Mum. I'm free. And it's alright for you to be angry.'

***

There were happy times too in that period of watchful waiting when your exuberance was so infectious, so intense, that I couldn't help but be drawn into your positive energy.

*For Mothering Sunday in 2012 Rosy came home from Bristol and we all went out for supper. Your dietary stipulations were strict – organic, raw, vegan – so it was hard to find somewhere to go. Often you'd agree to come but decline to eat; your empty plate sitting on the table like a silent reproach, a symbol of your otherness and increasing distance. But that day you agreed to come **and** to eat. I knew it was your gift to me.*

Paddy took photos of us all before we set out. There's one in particular I treasure still: of you and me, both laughing as we turn towards the other. You were full of a manic, explosive energy, which escaped in bursts of speech and laughter, inappropriately loud. Your eyes burned bright with unexplained zeal. You were wild and unkempt with your straggly dreadlocks and wispy goatee. You looked possessed. Rosy and Ellie both look strained in the photos, even stricken.

We sat at a table in a little booth and it turned out that our waiter had been at Henley College with you and you'd been friends. You were on cracking form, making quips and asides to your friend, darting your head out of our booth like a lizard capturing flies as you waited for him to return. Ellie sat ever smaller on the red banquette, slipping lower and lower on the seat in a silent plea for an escape from the disapproving stares of fellow diners; Rosy sat quietly with a look of anxious concern.

I recognised the place they were both in. It was often so hard to see beyond the evidence of your illness and see you. Fear and anxiety drew our focus away from you and onto your behaviours. But I was in a different place that evening, one in which I could enjoy your manic love for the world and the quirkiness of your thinking. I could laugh with you freely, wonder at the originality of your mind, join you in your ebullience and joy of life. For once I was inured to what others saw or thought. Without consciously knowing it, I was already storing up my times of happiness with you, determinedly enjoying them, despite the terrifying subtext of their meaning.

There was another evening too, a football match in the 2010 World Cup. We watched it after supper, the five of us together with Charlie – just six – and Katherine. You were like an excitable child. You couldn't sit still for more than a second. You'd crouch on the arm of the sofa, springing onto the floor, then up again, back onto the sofa and round the room. If you could have, you would have been walking up the walls and across the ceiling. Your commentary was witty, wacky, wild. It should have been infuriating because we were trying to watch a game of football, but it wasn't. It was hilarious, infectious, and impossible not to be drawn into your excitement and passion.

Adam, your sports teacher at Dolphin school, wrote after

you died, describing you "zigzagging across the sports field like a manic imp". It made me smile. I could picture you running in that determined way you had: head down, limbs pumping and flailing like an unbalanced train whose wheels were about to part company with the carriages. Another Dolphin parent wrote too and described a Year Eight inter-school rugby match where you fronted up to the opposing team with a haka shouting, 'Come on big boys! Come and get us!' — particularly reckless given that you were tiny by comparison with your peers and still waiting for the hormonal kick that seemed to turn some boys into men overnight.

I've done that thing I always do, that need in me to counter the difficult stuff with something good and happy. It's as though I can't bear to let myself really know how hard those years with you were.

They were hard. I can allow them to be hard.

And this is hard too, the writing of this. I'm trying to get it right, to get the balance between the pain and the joy of life with you. I'm not sure I am. I'm not sure I even know where the balance lies. Those years are such a muddle in my mind in every way. Perhaps how it was for you. It was a roller-coaster for all of us. I can't imagine how it felt to be inside your head. I can barely remember how it felt to be inside mine, but I do know that you never stopped surprising us. You seemed to have a sense of when you were losing us and just as we would all be at the point of despair, you would confound us all by emerging from the green room and asking if anyone fancied doing anything: a visit to the cinema, a walk, a trip to Planet Organic? You would be cogent and engaged, show extraordinary insight into something subtly nuanced, present a logical and coherent argument about something that had caught your attention. And we would dare to hope again that everything was going to be alright.

When you arrived home from your fourth set of travels in June 2012, you seemed more dislocated from reality than ever. You brushed away our concerns and set up camp in the green room again. It became your sanctuary and the more you isolated yourself from the outside world, the more difficult you found it to operate within it. You often seemed ill at ease away from the green room. Your behaviour would become erratic; staring at people, calling out to strangers, gazing into the distance. You became more and more bothered by the movements of people around you.

*You and I went out for supper one evening. We placed our order, but when the food was delivered, you insisted that the waiter had come out of the 'wrong' door. There **was** only one door in and out of the kitchen, but you wouldn't budge. You refused to touch either your food or drink. The waiter was perplexed. At the end of the meal you stood up dramatically and slid the pizza from the plate onto your hand. You rotated it at the wrist, raised it to shoulder height and marched out holding the pizza aloft, like a silver service waiter delivering some great delicacy. You rested it on your knees in the car and said you were looking forward to eating it once we were home. You ate it cold and declared it* *delicious.*

Another evening you arrived back with Dad and Ellie after a meal out. First out of the car, you were ecstatic. It had been the most beautiful, the most wonderful evening you had ever spent together. A moment later Ellie ran past us in floods of tears. She was traumatised by the oddness of your behaviour, the discomfort of the way you had gazed adoringly at the waitress, your inappropriately loud comments and incongruent laugh. You shook your head in confusion. You didn't know what she was crying about. Dad shook his head in sorrow.

We all went for a family therapy session. The idea was to address the gap between how you saw things and how we did. You refused to come. We went without you. I wanted the CMHT to understand that it wasn't just me who was seeing these things. The response was unprecedented. When I finished work the next day, I found four missed calls and messages saying they wanted to arrange a home visit urgently. It was hard not to conclude that they had seen me as an over-anxious, over-involved mother and needed to hear it from others before they took it entirely seriously.

Still you weren't ill enough to be sectioned.

As a family we continued in the dreadful role of being informers against you, providing evidence to the CMHT of your increasingly bizarre behaviour. It felt treacherous and yet we knew we would be failing you if we didn't. I lived in terror of your realising that information brought up by health workers must have come from us. That you would leave and go to live on the streets. But perhaps the reality was that you were no longer capable of making that link between them and us. Certainly you were losing the ability to look after yourself and to keep yourself safe.

One morning in July I came downstairs to find you standing in the hallway, wearing your favourite pale lilac striped pyjama bottoms. You seemed unusually distracted.

'Would you like some breakfast, Sam?' I asked.

You shook your head. I went into the kitchen, put on the kettle and the porridge, came back into the hall. You were standing where I'd left you.

'I'm going to go and have a shower, Muelo,' I said. 'Do you need anything before I go back upstairs?'

You shook your head again.

When I came back down the front door was wide open. There was no sign of you. Your phone was in the green room.

All day a light rain fell. We couldn't find you anywhere. I was frantic with worry. Seven hours later the front door opened and you walked back in, still wearing your pyjama bottoms. You'd added a T-shirt, but no shoes.

'Sam,' I called, 'Thank God you're back. Where have you been all day?'

You looked at me with irritation.

'Out,' you said.

'But where? Where did you go?'

You looked at me coldly.

'I walked into Reading. If you have to know. Is there anything wrong with that?'

Then you walked into the green room and closed the door behind you.

The next day my phone rang. It was a woman I knew from Dolphin.

'I hope you don't mind,' she said. 'I thought I should let you know I saw Sam yesterday. He was walking down the central reservation of the A4, where it's a dual carriageway. I've never seen anyone walking there before so I suppose that's why I noticed. And because it was raining and he wasn't wearing many clothes. He had one hand stretched out ahead of him as though he was trying to catch the rain. There was a small pause. 'He seemed to be talking to himself,' she added apologetically. 'I just wondered if everything's all right.'

'Not really,' I sighed, 'but it's a long story. Thanks for letting me know.'

I called the CMHT. I hated doing it. I hated being a mother who informed on her son but I couldn't see an alternative. You were showing signs of slight paranoia too. You'd turned all the family photographs towards the wall, because you didn't like the feeling of being watched; and were suspicious of Paddy, insisting he was ahead of you and within your line of vision when we went out.

Much later you told me about the things you used to see: energy and auras around people; radiant, glowing shapes in the sky, dragons leaping from star to star, rainbows exploding into glorious colours. I understood then why, when we'd been walking on a grey day, the sky as flat and dull as a hammered nail, you would gaze at it and wonder out loud at its extraordinary beauty. You described two spirits who were your constant companions – little balls of energy, one green, one blue. You were matter of fact about it as though everyone lived with spirits. You found them entertaining and would smile broadly as you looked cross-eyed into the distance in an unfocused way. You didn't see it as a problem but rather as evidence of how sensitively attuned you were to the spiritual world. You were on a path towards enlightenment and this was part of your journey.

Others didn't see it that way and after my call you were formally assessed and – on 5 July 2012 – sectioned under the Mental Health Act and hospitalised for the first time. It was devastating to both you and us.

***

4 June 2014

PADDY AND I go out for supper to La Paloma. It's a pretty restaurant in an old farmhouse, with duck-egg blue shutters and painted wrought-ironwork. We sit outside on the terrace beneath a vine hung with small green glass lanterns. Paddy orders us each a vodka and tonic. He leans back in his chair and smiles at me. He's already caught the sun. He tans so easily. It's a gentle smile and within it is a quizzical look that's asking me if I'm alright. The truth is that I don't know how I am.

I feel the kick of the vodka as I take my first gulp. I'm grateful for it. I have little appetite, so I order something light. There are strawberries in the risotto and sprigs of lavender on the plate. Later, I stand waiting for the loo to come free. There's a mirror straight ahead of me. In it I see a silver-haired woman. She's made an effort with her appearance, there's a touch of make-up – lipstick, a smudge of eye-liner – a pretty top and I say to this woman in the mirror, 'Your son died a month ago. You are a woman who has lost a child. Should you look so normal? Are you meant to look like that?'

She doesn't seem to know the answer.

5 June 2014

EVERY DAY I visit the little white-washed church in the village of San Carles to light a candle for Sam. It's not a real candle, just a box into which I slip my one Euro coin, watching anxiously to catch the moment when a new electric bulb flickers into life among the red replica candles in the glass case.

It seems to matter that I know which candle is for him.

I am grateful to have this peaceful place to come to; a place to feel close to him. It is a pretty church with pale lilac paint on the ceiling and woodwork, and gypsophila bowers draped like ribbons across the altar rails. I sit in the quiet gloom and take out Sam's order of service. I look into the smiling eyes in the photos. 'Hello Mr Mueloman,' I say in my head as I run my thumb across the smooth, lightly glossy paper. For a moment it feels as though I am stroking his cheek again.

Sam had lots of nicknames. Sammy, Muelo, Mue, Mueloman, Mr Muelo. After he was hospitalised that first time, he wanted to be called Samuel. He enunciated and lengthened each of the last two vowels. 'My name is Sam-u-el,' he'd say to me crossly when I forgot. Perhaps it was his way of communicating to the world that the Sam who came out of hospital was not the one who had gone in.

Sadness seems to come in waves. Big rolling waves. I have no choice but to ride them. Sometimes they rise up from nothing, like a tsunami, gathering depth and pace until something causes both them and me to break: a song, an act of kindness, a sudden memory. Sometimes they roll on and on before they slowly subside, leaving a dull ache in their place. I compare notes with Simon, Rosy and Ellie. We've all been aware of them. Simon names them, 'Sad Sam Waves'. Something jars in me. I don't like the way the word 'sad' seems to attach to Sam rather than the waves, so I rename them 'Sammy Sadness Waves'. You'd never describe Sam as 'sad'. Even at his most depleted by medication, or his most unreachable and chaotic through schizophrenia, he was never a sad case. He was too stoical, brave and passionate for him ever to be called that. He'd always been the same, even when he was little.

***

Do you remember going into hospital Sam when you were four, to have your tonsils and adenoids removed? I can picture walking with you from the ward to the operating theatre. You were wearing your own slippers and a little hospital gown. When we got there you simply let go of my hand, bent down to take off your slippers and handed them to me. There was no drama. And when you came round and were horribly sick, you made no fuss. You never once complained about the pain.

I had my tonsils and adenoids out in the same hospital as you, even the same operating theatre. Like you I was four. In those days no one was allowed to stay or visit and for four days I wondered why Granny had left me there. I'd never felt so confused and so alone. I can remember the feeling, even now.

I can't bear to imagine how you felt at times. It's hard for me to think about, even now. You never understood that you were ill: in your mind you were being incarcerated against your will and forced to take toxic medication. But despite all this and all the indignities you had to suffer, you never lost your capacity to be philosophical and to put yourself into the hands of fate. Even when you were fighting the system and had no option but to surrender to its greater power, you were brave and dignified. You voiced your hatred of your medication with its crushing side effects and loudly deplored the removal of your liberty and the humiliation of a life under lock and key. But you never surrendered to self-pity, and you never gave up. You were a stoic through and through. Even at your lowest ebb you managed to hold onto something of your spirit. Despite everything.

I know it was torture to have to submit to a regime and a system you didn't believe in and one that, in your eyes, had so grievously misunderstood you. Yet, still, you acted with dignity.

I tried to tell you I was proud of you, but at that time you didn't want to hear anything I said.

You never accepted your diagnosis, scoffing at the idea that you had schizophrenia. I'd often warned you of the dangers of drugs, especially for teenagers with developing brains and someone like you; sensitive, a thinker, a bit wacky. I told you about my cousin Francis; the schizophrenia he suffered from for almost twenty years after he started experimenting with drugs, the tragedy of his suicide. You didn't listen. You always knew best. I know you experimented a lot in your sixth form years. Was it a coincidence that your strange behaviours started then? That you developed full-blown psychosis after your first trip to Hawaii and all the dope you smoked there? We will never know but it's hard to imagine it was.

***

6 June 2014

OUR WEEK IN Ibiza ends tomorrow and we will be flying home. The thought makes me nervous. I've been away so much since I heard the news of Sam's death. I've been protected from facing the reality of life at home without him.

In some ways I've been doing the easy part so far. I've been in a bubble: spending time with immediate family and closest friends who knew and loved him. It's been intense but shared. It will be harder once I'm home. I will be faced with the incontrovertible evidence of others' lives moving forward. As they must. I don't want to have to face that yet. I don't feel ready.

And I know that, however much I want to share my family and friends' pleasure in their children's lives and successes, it will be more complex than that. There will be sadness for me too in every success, in every milestone achieved that Sam did not. And there will be uglier feelings: envy, resentment, anger, potentially destructive feelings that could jeopardise relationships and, if allowed to, turn into bitterness. They already creep in from time to time. They make uncomfortable companions. I mustn't try to suppress them altogether or they will pop out unexpectedly and do harm. I must acknowledge them, process them, try to move beyond them.

7 June 2014

IT IS HARD coming home. The house lies empty and Samless. I turn the key in the lock and walk into the hall. There is no shout of, 'Mu-um' from upstairs, no question or statement requiring an immediate response before he checks himself and asks, 'So did you have a good holiday then?' No clatter of feet on the stairs, no face appearing around the corner with its broad grin. The house remains silent. He is not there.

8 June 2014

THERE'S A WOOD pigeon sitting in the wisteria outside our bedroom window. Its asymmetrical, circular song reminds me of the ditty my mother would chant when she heard them, 'Two cows Taffy, take two cows Taffy, take two cows Taffy, take.' In my half sleep I find myself searching for alternatives: 'Do get going, oh do get going, oh do get going, oh,' and then, 'Morning Sammy, good morning Sammy, good morning Sammy, good.' My mind drifts on to how he might have responded as a little boy; initially with shy pleasure and then with wild exuberance at the thought that the pigeons were singing for him, with their slow, sleepy song.

I see him running up and down the landing, shouting to the girls that the wood pigeons have chosen to sing for him, not them; see his face scrunch up in concentration as I tell him that the final 'good' was a special message for him about behaving well that day; and then a scowl as I remind him later what the wood pigeons told him. I feel a sharp stab of regret as I remember that I can't share anything with him anymore.

Regret is a regular visitor at the moment. I am constantly assailed by thoughts of opportunities not taken and chances missed. I cannot escape the feeling that I could or should have done more, that I failed Sam in some way. It's tempting to push these thoughts away, but I know it's better to stay with them and let them run their course.

In Pai I found myself questioning why we hadn't arranged a holiday there with him; hadn't allowed him to introduce us to the things he loved. But when I started to work through the idea, I realised that he'd discovered Pai for himself, not us. Part of its appeal for him was that it was a place we didn't know – it was his alone, his escape. Thinking it through allowed me to keep these thoughts and feelings in the territory of regret, rather than catapulting them into that of its much more corrosive cousin, guilt.

Recently I've had similarly uncomfortable feelings about passing up the opportunity to spend the afternoon with Sam in London the week before he set off on that last trip.

We'd been to the Thai embassy in South Kensington to hand in his visa application form. It had been a two hour wait in the dark, crowded and chaotic basement. Emerging into the bright sunshine of a cloudless spring day, he tried to persuade me to spend the afternoon in London. I resisted. There were things I needed to do at home. I had a friend coming later.

We returned home. It haunts me now. All I can think of are the happy memories I might have had from those extra shared hours. It feels somehow monstrous that I allowed other things to be more important than spending time with him.

I want to push it all away into a closed-off part of my mind where it can no longer trouble me. But I resist the impulse. Instead, I acknowledge the pain of having made that choice. I make myself think about it, and as I allow myself to reflect on that day, I start to remember other things too, and a slightly different picture emerges. The whole week comes back to me. That wasn't the only day we went to the embassy. We went there the previous day too.

***

We parked near the Natural History Museum and set off for the embassy on foot. It was warm and sunny and you were in high spirits.

'I hope all my paperwork's okay,' you said, clutching a dog-eared sheaf of papers in one hand.

'Well, we'll soon find out,' I replied. But we didn't. The front door was locked, with a small white sheet of paper pinned to it explaining that it was closed for a Thai holiday.

I raised my eyebrows at you, 'Did you check on the website, Muelo?'

'Mu'um,' you said reproachfully, 'of course I did. That's where I printed off the application form. It didn't say anything.'

I checked later. It did of course, but it was easy to miss.

We'd paid for four hours' parking, and it was a lovely day, so I suggested a visit to the Natural History Museum and then an early lunch at The Kensington Crêperie.

'Sounds good,' you said as you pushed your hands into your jeans pockets and headed off in the wrong direction.

'Sam,' I called, 'it's the other way.'

You spun round on the ball of one foot and grinned sheepishly. Your poor sense of direction was legendary.

We walked towards the museum beneath a kaleidoscope of blue sky and silver London plane trees. Arriving, we found the queue snaking in front of the building, out of the gates and onto the pavement. We looked at one another, shook our heads in unison and set off instead towards the nearby coffee shops. You chose a table outside on the pavement and ordered a double espresso with four extra shots. When the waitress questioned your order, as you knew she would, you grinned at me conspiratorially. You never did things by halves and you still loved to shock, despite the anti-psychotic medication you were now taking – aripiprazole – the only ones that didn't give you terrible side-effects.

We headed around the corner and went into a little bookshop piled high with paperbacks stacked on their sides. I bought a stash while you waited outside and when I emerged you offered to carry the bag for me. I thought how lovely it was to have you back – your third and last stay in hospital seemed to have returned you to us – and how lovely it would be to have you living independently in the barn in the garden once it had been renovated. I could see it really working.

At the crêperie, the owner greeted us and showed us to a table in the window. We looked out from under the striped awnings watching people come and go, recalling the many lunches we'd had there over the last twenty years. I reminded you how I'd fallen in love with the hole-in-the-wall restaurant on Flask Walk in Hampstead when I was just a year older than you and doing my first job in London; and how excited I'd been to discover its sister restaurant in South Kensington on the door-step of all the museums we used to go to when you and the girls were small. No trip to London was complete without lunch there. It was one of those rituals that became part of our family life.

You ordered your favourite: savoury crepe with cream cheese and spinach, and we shared a bottle of Breton cider. We laughed about how much more you'd enjoyed the lunches than the trips to the museum.

'Do you fancy a sweet one?' I asked.

'I don't think I do,' you replied. But then sensing my disappointment, you added, 'but you have one if you want to. Go on. Do.'

I did.

***

Am I doing that thing again, of trying to cancel out the painful stuff with some happier memories? Maybe I am, but I'm not sure it really matters. They were as much a part of my life with Sam as the more difficult times were. And because they didn't happen very often when they *did* they counted so much. Perhaps what matters more is that I still have these memories to comfort me. They might all have been lost if I'd allowed regret to turn into guilt and reached the point where the only way to bear the pain was to avoid it by shutting it all away.

Thinking it through helps me to see other things too, factors that affected my decision at the time. With Sam I had to be active in my parenting still. He needed to understand that I had a life too and couldn't simply drop everything on a whim and let other people down. And we *had* spent the previous day together.

So although I still wish I'd made a different choice and spent that second day in London with him, the feelings of regret are easier to bear.

10 June 2014

I LIKE TO keep Sam's bedroom door open. I want him still to be a part of my life. If I find it pulled to, I open it tetchily as I pass, as though it's part of a conspiracy to take him away from me, to make me face some unwelcome truth.

I still find it difficult to take in that I shall never see him again. It is the hardest part.

I have gone through the motions of acknowledging

his death – the cremation, the service of remembrance, the condolences – knowing that he is dead; yet without really knowing it, without really understanding and accepting what it means. That part evades me still. I don't know how to make it real. He feels so alive to me. I can picture him lying on his bed, his duvet wrapped around him, the soles of his feet protruding. I can hear him coming downstairs, keys jangling as he shouts that he's going to Tesco, the click of the front door as he closes it behind him. I can see him standing on the pavement when I pick him up from somewhere, raising a hand in acknowledgement of my arrival. He watches me pull up in the car, opens the door and climbs in, pulls Sigmund, our black Miniature Schnauzer onto his lap, then turns to me and smiles. I ask him how he is, a small pause as he thinks about it, and then 'Good' – always 'Good,' in spite of everything.

As I go to pass his room this morning something draws me in. It is early, only 5.45 am and the sun streams in through the wisps of wisteria, unfurling against the windowpane. On his desk I find a battered leather wallet, brittle and stiff with use. Inside are a few hundred Thai baht and a small pink post-it note, folded over, dog-eared and stained. He has written on it in his spidery hand:

KRSNA
To develop sense of wholeness and Resolution
To meet a most beautiful female partner

To develop all relationships, especially those with the gods
To become as beautiful as I truly am

I come downstairs, this small remnant in my hand, and place it carefully beside me on the sofa. Then I write this diary entry, to try to make sense of everything. I don't know that I can. But as I glance again at this small gift of words from him, I find myself hoping with all my heart that he has found wholeness and resolution, that he has become as beautiful as he truly was.

11 June 2014

WHEN SAM CAME out of Prospect Park hospital in August 2013 – his third stay after his third sectioning – he moved into supported accommodation a few miles away from home, in Wokingham. He wanted to live independently.

It was a nice house, a small Edwardian red brick villa with a painted, green front door, owned by a Housing Association and funded by the local authority. He shared the rest of the house with three other people. He often came home to stay for a few days or sometimes just for the day if I could tempt him with a favourite meal or someone else being there. But he liked the idea of having his own place to go to.

Sue Martin had asked him to go along to the opening night of the Living Advent Calendar to take photos for the charity she worked for. He agreed begrudgingly.

'Do I *have* to?' he asked me.

'Well no, of course you don't *have to* Sam, but you

would be helping Sue and it's a good cause.'

'Are you sure you didn't *ask* her to ask me?' he added suspiciously. 'It's just the sort of thing you'd do, to try to *get me out more.'* This last bit said as if imitating me.

'Sam, it's completely up to you,' I said, dodging the question, because I *had* cooked it up with Sue, so worried was I by his inertia. He so rarely left his room. 'The Mayor of Wokingham is going to be there. That's why Sue particularly needs someone to get some photos. And you never know, you might even enjoy it.'

'Okay,' he said, 'I'll do it, but only because it's Sue. So don't go getting ideas about me and any *volunteering.'* Again in my voice. 'And actually I'd quite like to see the Mayor,' he added mysteriously.

He showed me the photos a couple of days later. They weren't bad. There were lots of the Mayor in his ceremonial robes, with his chain of office across his chest.

'I went and spoke to him afterwards,' Sam said.

'Really? What did you say?'

'I thanked him for paying for my room in my house. I said it was very nice of him and I really appreciated it.'

'Oh,' I said, 'and what did he say?'

'Well he didn't say anything really. He looked a bit shocked.'

I laughed. I couldn't help it. Sam laughed too.

He had his own bedroom in the house paid for by the

Mayor and shared the kitchen and bathroom with other 'service users'. What a terrible term that is, though I can't think of a better one. There were staff there during the day and he had his own care-worker who came to see him once a week and took him out for coffee. He lived there until he left for Thailand on 22nd April 2014. He often booked things for the 22nd if he could. His flight home was booked for 22nd June. Twenty-two was his lucky number. It's one of the things that makes me think he didn't mean to die when he did. He would have made sure it was the 22nd if it were planned. He liked the idea of synchronicity and he wasn't above a bit of tampering with fate in order to create meaningful coincidence.

And now we need to clear out his room in Wokingham.

Simon and I go together.

Sam is everywhere. In the cigarette burn in the duvet, the kicked-off shoes, the sticky pan handles (ostensibly clean, but not quite), the giant glass I bought with him in the supermarket, the half-consumed bottle of Tanquerey gin, the Pro Plus caffeine tablets scattered everywhere, and the can of Red Bull energy drink. He is there in the pile of discarded coins ('I'm only really interested in paper money'), the boxed DVD sets and the fallen cigarette ash still nestling in his sheets. He is there in the Waitrose receipt (carrot and coriander soup, Fentimans old fashioned lemonade, Paysan Breton luxury cream cheese – none of them cheap), in the bag full of laundered socks ('Mum I have no socks!' 'Muelo, you have so many socks, they must all be in a bag somewhere.'). So that's where they were. I feel a flash of self-righteous victory followed instantly by the hollow realisation that there is no Sam to tell and tease.

He is everywhere in the room and yet he is nowhere. After he became ill, his life became so simple, so reduced. His material needs were so few that he would live in a place without trying to impose anything of himself on it. He wanted to be independent, to feel that his life was moving on, and he wanted to do it *his* way. He declined offers of armchairs, sofas, lamps, artwork, photos, cushions, anything that might have made it more comfortable. He wanted it as it was.

When Simon goes out of the room for a moment, I find myself moving the bedside chest of drawers to look behind it, beneath it. I think I am looking for something more, some sign of Sam, something elemental. A little later I see Simon do the same thing, as though we might have missed something. Perhaps we are both searching for the things we can't actually have; something of Sam himself, or some explanation.

Simon flattens out crumpled receipts, studying them intently, as if some answer might lie within them, something to explain how this could be, how it could be possible that his son no longer exists. I find myself burying my face in his duvet, breathing in his smell, stroking the bed on which he has sat, as though it might give me something in return.

We have been told not to clean the room, that it will be cleaned professionally later in the week. But as I sit on the bed for one last time, I feel a powerful urge to clean. I cannot bear the thought of someone else, some stranger to Sam who doesn't care, sweeping up the remnants of his life: the scattered cigarette ash, the small sticky pools of Ambaya Gold and Siberian Ginseng tincture, the discarded bottle tops and scraps of paper and packaging. I resist the urge. I don't know why; some ridiculous need to follow the rules.

I'm left again with a sense of having failed him. Clearing up after him, picking up the pieces is what I do, is what I've always done; sometimes with exasperation but always with love. I'm allowing a stranger to do it in my stead. Even worse perhaps someone who will judge him for how he lived. Judge him without understanding.

It's almost unbearable to leave.

The sense of desolation is complete when we close the door behind us, clutching Sam's belongings, but no Sam. It is a painful, empty replica of all the trips to halls of residence and student flats we've made with Rosy over the last five years.

It's all I can do not to go back into the room to retrieve the bag of rubbish we have left there, to go through it one final time, as though I might find something that makes this absence bearable, that somehow explains the inexplicable, that makes sense of the overwhelming nonsense of outliving one's child. It defies understanding.

Once I'm home I unzip the bag of clothes and bedding. I pull them out one by one, breathing in the familiar smell of stale cigarette smoke, body odour and after-shave. I go through the pockets of his two winter coats. I find two pound coins and a twenty pence piece. These are coins he has touched. I hold them in the palm of one hand, then find myself stroking them. I want something from them, but I'm not sure what.

There's a temporary myWaitrose card, and a Costa receipt – for a Massimo latte, with two extra shots – a Costa gift card and the 100% certified organic cotton T-shirt I bought for him in New Zealand. I can remember the delight I felt when I found it, when I found anything that I thought Sam would like. I want to feel that pleasure again.

I bury my face in the T-shirt.

12 June 2014

I FEEL ANGRY from the moment I awake. It's an impotent sort of anger where I want to rail against the world. I go for a walk – one of Sam's favourites – but even the shaded calm of an old drovers' trail, the swaying ears of ripening wheat and the aeroplane trails drifting lazily across a clear blue sky, can do nothing to assuage my terrible anger with the world for simply carrying on.

I return in my car via the churchyard and his grave, and there I vent my anger on the flowers already wilting in the vase, on the ants who have dared to take up residence beneath it, and on Sam for not being alive.

I say over and over to him, through angry tears, 'I don't want you to be *here*, Sam. I want you to be at home, where you belong. I don't want to be tending flowers on your grave. I want you to be at home in bed, just stirring from your sleep. I don't want you to be *here, Sam.*' It is my song of grief. Like some dreadful parody of the wood pigeons with their soft, circular call.

Driving home I pass a single magpie, hopping along the grass verge. Yes, that's just about right. There's nothing but sorrow for me now.

Back at home Paddy brings me an envelope: two letters, from a husband and wife who live nearby. We had supper with them a few weeks before Sam died. They are lovely letters; thoughtful, kind, caring. I am touched that they have both taken the trouble to write. The anger ebbs, just a little.

***

I'm in your bedroom absent-mindedly working my way through a pile of papers on the side when I come across a worksheet from the drama course you enrolled on at Reading College in September 2011. Students were asked to describe what would happen if they failed to follow rules and respect staff and other students. You had written in your lopsided, spidery scrawl, 'a bit of mayhem.' It makes me smile. It's so you to qualify an extreme concept such as mayhem with a diminutive like 'a bit of.'

You only lasted three days on the course. You didn't mention that you were withdrawing. You simply stopped going in. A few days later I stuck my head round the door of the green room.

'What's going on with the course, Muelo?' I asked. 'You don't seem to have been in for a couple of days.'

'Oh that,' you said casually, 'I've quit.'

'Oh blimey, that's a bit sudden. Any reason?'

'Do I need a reason?' you asked irritably, wanting to get back to your computer.

'Well, I'm interested,' I said. 'I thought you were quite enjoying it.'

'I have my thoughts and you have yours,' you said mysteriously, and put on your head-phones.

I let the college know and waited for a refund of the fees. After about six weeks, when no cheque had arrived, I called the course tutor.

'I sent it weeks ago,' she said. 'In the post. You should have had it by now.'

'That's strange,' I replied. 'I wonder what's happened to it. I certainly haven't received it.'

'I sent it to Sam,' she said. 'The cheque was payable to him.'

'Oh, okay, I'll check with him. I expect he's forgotten to let me know.'

'We were sorry to lose him,' she said. 'He's an interesting young man.' She hesitated a moment. 'I did wonder though whether everything was ...' She let the sentence hang in the air. I didn't help her out. I didn't want to get into a conversation about whether you were okay or not. I didn't

know.

I went to find you.

'*You know that cheque I've been waiting for Sam? Well I've just spoken to the drama tutor at Reading College and apparently they've sent the cheque and it was payable to you. Does that ring any bells?*

'*Oh yeah,*' *you said.* '*I paid it in.*'

'*Paid it in where?*'

'*To my account. It said Samuel Roberts on it, so that's what I did with it.*'

'*But Sam, I paid the fees in the first place, so obviously any refund should have come to me. It was just a mistake.*'

'*I don't think so,*' *you said.* '*It was paid to me for a reason and that clearly means it's mine now.*'

'*No Sam, that's not how it works. It's my money. It's a refund. So were you not planning on letting me know?*'

'*I didn't need to,*' *you said bemused.* '*The cheque was made out to me, so it belongs to me now.*'

'*Well, it's not actually Sam. It's come to you by mistake. I need you to pay it back.*'

'*Well that won't be happening,*' *you said.* '*That's outrageous.*'

Earlier that same September you'd transferred £500 of my money via PayPal to buy a ticket for Bestival. I'd expressly told you I wasn't going to pay for you to go. When I realised what had happened and asked you about it you were equally bemused by my reaction and entirely unrepentant.

'*But I wanted to go,*' *you said, as though that was the end of it.*

It was a long time before you paid any of it back. In the end I confiscated your passport and told you. You called the police and reported it as theft. They took a statement but didn't pursue it further. By then you were in Prospect Park. You seemed to see things differently once the medication started to work and paid me back without protest.

***

13 June 2014

I WAKE UP early again, as I do most mornings now – somewhere between 4.30 and 5.45am – and go downstairs. This week I've been greeted by sunshine every day and the extraordinary early morning June light: clear, razor-sharp, like a high definition screen with impossibly high resolution, and warm. I look out of my study window where the morning light falls on a bright red geranium in an old terracotta pot, against a backdrop of the almost too-green lawn. The effect is electric, not quite real.

Simon and I used to have a phrase to describe such mornings. 'Too bright, too early,' one of us would say as we drew back the curtains, because past experience had taught us that it always seemed to have clouded over by the time we were up. It became a shorthand for acknowledging the potential for things, however lovely, not lasting forever; a sort of inverse nostalgia, where the wistful ache is there in the moment of being touched. I feel a similar sort of ache nowadays when something moves me; the ache of knowing that Sam isn't here to see it.

Yet, despite this, things do still touch me. It surprises me, this capacity within me still to see and feel the beauty in life. I would have expected it to be snuffed out by sorrow.

I feel it again when we go to Rosy's end-of-year show. My nephew, Ed comes with us. The Martins too. It's a solo performance, the last on the bill. I know how much it's cost Rosy emotionally to re-engage with her course and devise this piece.

She draws the audience into her fantasy of a longed-for relationship, using a Lonsdale punch bag to represent the object of her passion. Much of it is pure comedy as they dance and smooch together and later, as the relationship begins to fail, when she berates it for failing to talk to her, for being so passive.

But there are moments too of overwhelming pathos and when the mood shifts seamlessly between hilarity and pain, I find it almost unendurable.

In the final minutes a hoop spins in slow rotation above her as she tells the audience in a low, soft voice that despite the emptiness inside her, she isn't drowning. She grasps the hoop with both hands and pulls herself up into it as it rises. There is total silence as she moves through it, round it and over it in slow, balletic movements. She spins round, suspended by the small of her back as the light fades to total darkness. The audience is silent too. I hold my breath.

Then the clapping and whooping begins.

As we speed back home along the motorway in the darkness Ed says,

'I'm so glad to have been with you all this evening. It's meant so much to me to feel so close to you all since Sam died. I know it doesn't make it any better, Gilly, but it's Sam who has drawn us all together.'

'It does make it better Ed,' I say.

And I mean it.

In the stillness of the night I think how extraordinary life is. How it throws together such extremes, the highs and lows; a bizarre juxtaposition of powerful emotions, of loss, of gain, of things being given and things taken away; a glorious, terrible melée of joy and pain.

14 June 2014

IT RAINS DURING the night, heavy downpours that bounce off the York paving beneath our bedroom window like nails falling on concrete. The windows rattle as thunder grumbles overhead.

The air is warm and soupy in the morning as I walk with Sigmund. Steam rises from hedgerows bursting with cow parsley and foxgloves, clumps of wild Michaelmas daisies, and garlands of pink and white dog roses. Towards the end of my walk I see a damsel fly trapped in a spider's web, frozen in a final pose that enables me to see it in all its glory.

Two weeks ago the air was shot through with the startling iridescent blue of scores of damsel flies in flight, darting about like shoals of tropical fish, moving in seemingly synchronised motion. I watched, entranced but frustrated that they rarely settled for long enough really to be seen. I look at it now with its spiky blue body, intermittent black stripes and gossamer wings. I think of Sam and how hard it was to see him in the difficult years of his illness. His psychosis and the overwhelming anxiety it provoked in me, stopped me seeing him. They got in the way. Perhaps it is only in death that I've been able truly to see him and to know what I've lost.

We all go out for supper to celebrate Simon's birthday. Katherine – Simon's goddaughter – comes too. She's suffered a terrible blow since Sam died, falling ill with meningococcal encephalitis and waking up from a coma to discover she'd missed her final year Prom and her A2 exams. She's frail and shaken. Our little group feels insubstantial. I think we all feel the thinness.

We give Simon his presents. He's appropriately grateful. Rosy plays with Imogen and makes her laugh. We say how delicious the food is. We do our best. Simon makes a toast: to all of us, his family; to Ellie in South America; to Katherine, for her bravery in fighting and surviving her illness against the odds; and to Sam, still loved.

Silence falls for a moment. And then the evening continues, as it must.

15 June 2014

TODAY IS FATHER'S Day. I've bought a card to give to Simon from Sam. I think about what I might write. Sam never did cards and sometimes didn't manage presents. Once he and Simon T went shopping together for my birthday and bought me nail varnish in Boots, but by the time they got home the Boots bag was empty. Sam was apologetic in an angry sort of way, as though I was to blame and it was my problem now. But he often came home from school trips or holidays with friends, having used all his spending money on a present for me: once a wooden hippopotamus with its jaws open wide in toothy grin; another time a silver spoon for the sugar bowl; another time still a small brass bell. If things didn't go entirely to his liking after the presentation of a gift, he would demand it back. It was as though he needed to recover some ground, having made himself vulnerable by showing he cared.

The Father's Day card sits on the kitchen table all day. I can't bring myself to write in it. I don't know why. I'm angry with everyone, with everything. Perhaps it was the thinness of the family last night. It's an ugly, bitter sort of anger; with life for failing me, with people for falling short of expectation, with the world for carrying on. I don't want to talk to anyone or do anything.

I feel resentful, put upon and unappreciated. I think

of all the years of love and care and worry that I bestowed on Sam. It feels as though it was all a monumental waste: of time, of effort, of investment, in a life which went nowhere. I move on to Simon. He caused me and the children enormous pain by ending our marriage. Yet here I am, about to write a card to tell him what a great Dad he's been.

The card remains on the table all day, unwritten. I go out, buy food for supper and flowers. I take them to Sam's grave. I crouch down to remove the old flowers and wash out the vase. I re-fill it with fresh water, take the flowers, cut, arrange and trim, re-trim and re-arrange and, by the time I come home, something has shifted. Perhaps by doing these simple tasks, by engaging with a wish to keep on looking after Sam, even if only now in death, I've chosen to carry on being his mother and I feel better for it.

I pick up the card, and in it I write, 'Simon, this is the card that Sam never sent you; but should have, because it's what he knew and felt in his heart. "Thank you for being an amazing Dad; for loving me unreservedly, for never giving up on me, for making me laugh even when it seemed that there wasn't much to laugh about." I'm so sorry that Sam isn't here to share Father's Day with you.'

I mean every word of it.

16 June 2014

IT'S SIMON'S ACTUAL birthday today. He comes for coffee as he generally does on a Monday. I give him the Father's

Day card. He cries.

The holdalls containing Sam's possessions from his room are still sitting in the hallway, where we put them five days ago. At the time I removed his clothes and bed linen and immediately started on the dirty washing. Sheets and duvet covers went in the washing machine for repeated cycles. Then I moved on to his clothes. There were T-shirts and socks and a pair of jeans, stiff with repeated wear and bearing the stains of meals and drinks. They went into the machine too. But I couldn't bring myself to press the button to activate the wash. My finger hovered, withdrew, hovered and withdrew. I left it overnight.

Next morning, I returned to the washing machine but again I felt resistance to putting on the wash. I left it and went to have my breakfast. When I returned I reached inside, removed the jeans and other clothes and put the wash on without them. I didn't know why.

And even now, days later, his unlaundered clothes still lie waiting on the floor of the utility room. I feel that I should do something with them, but I don't know what. I can't fold them up and put them away with his clean clothes, yet every time I load them into the washing machine I find myself unable to take it further and, paralysed by indecision, I pull them back out again and there they lie, in silent reproach, until I try again.

I mention this painful dance to my cousin, Nic, also a psychotherapist. We talk it through. It isn't merely a battle between practicality and sentiment that has been at play. In this loading and unloading of Sam's clothes, I have been acting out – in the external world – the tensions in my internal world: the conflict between opposing urges – to hold onto the past, but also to move forward; to accept the reality of Sam's death but also to avoid the *pain* of this reality. Each time I closed the washing machine door I willed myself simply to press the button without thinking and feeling, simply to walk away. But something wouldn't let me.

I can see it now as a healthy part of me. I needed to feel the pain of what I was doing: washing my son's bedding, his clothes, for the last time, knowing that he would never again ease his body into his jeans or pull on a T-shirt over his head. I needed to give myself space to acknowledge that this task, another small gift to Sam, would have an empty ending.

I'm glad I still have his unwashed clothes. I can give myself a real choice now that I understand the moves in my silent dance and can name the feelings lying behind them. I need to think about the part of me that isn't yet ready to give up the lingering traces of him, as well as the part that needs to move forward.

I reach a compromise with myself. I select a few items to save as they are. I wrap them tightly and push them into carrier bags, which I seal and place on the trunk at the foot of his bed. The rest I load into the machine. This time I am able to close the door and add detergent, select a wash and press the button to start the cycle. I know I will lose some traces of Sam. But I know too I will have others to sustain me.

There are similar battle lines all around the house: shoes which will never be worn gathering dust on the rack inside the back door; scraps of paper bearing his illegible scrawl; his anti-psychotic medication sitting on the window sill in a crumpled Boots bag; his wellington boots nestling with others in the porch; corners of now redundant paperwork sticking out of desk drawers; coats and scarves hanging from pegs in the utility room. His possessions in the holdalls.

For now I will leave it all. I know I'm not yet thinking straight. For these decisions I have the gift of time.

When my mother died, after forty-eight years of a largely happy marriage, my father took it upon himself one day to clear out the bureau that held all the family films: slides, cine film, super 8 footage of their wedding in 1949, subsequent christenings, silver wedding celebrations and all the family holidays. And all my mother's diaries of their holidays. He didn't consult a single one of his four children before he decided to throw it all away. In one fell swoop, all that family history was gone, never to be retrieved.

I have struggled to understand how he could ever have thought that it was a good idea, or the right thing. But now I begin to understand something of what perhaps happened: it wasn't that he thought it was a good idea. It was that he simply wasn't able to think. Faced with things that generate psychic pain, we sometimes lose the capacity to mentalise, to *think* about thinking. At the very time when it would be helpful to slow down our mental processes, to ask ourselves questions about *what* we are thinking and why, our unconscious defences kick in and speed things up instead. It simply feels too much to allow those thoughts in, to face that pain. Faced with a record of his happy life with my mother and the pain of all he had lost, my father acted rather than thought. We often live to regret the decisions made in those moments of avoidance and denial. I'm glad I haven't made the same mistake. I'll make others I'm sure but at least I haven't made this one.

17 June 2014

SIMON AND I meet with James, Sam's consultant psychiatrist, and Paul, his key worker in the CMHT. I'm nervous beforehand, but not sure why. Perhaps it's simply the pain of going back to the Old Forge, where the CMHT is based, and being reminded of the desperately difficult meetings we had there with and without Sam over the past four years.

We walk past the exposed brickwork, the blacksmith's tools and oak beams displayed behind a glass window and wait for the doors to be buzzed open. We climb the staircase up to the CMHT reception area. James comes to fetch us and leads us through to a meeting room where Paul is waiting. They want to know how we all are.

There was no need to feel nervous. It's a good meeting for me: helpful, informative, confirming and affirming things I knew or thought I knew. There are no surprises, and it gives a sense of closure to one aspect of Sam's life and death. It would have been strange never to have any contact again with these people who were so involved in his care.

It helps to hear what they have to say about him and most of all to know all over again that they did understand him, they 'got' him and liked him. It helps me to feel that he was receiving the best care he could from people who, like we did, wanted only the best for him.

James talks about diagnosis and says that Sam, like many others, was not a clear-cut, text-book case. He reiterates what he's said before about not finding labels very helpful in the context of mental health.

He turns to look at Simon, 'I'm not sure there's anything I can usefully add to the picture you and Rosy painted of Sam in your tributes at his service. They described him and what happened to him more accurately than a label ever could. But if I had to plump for something, I'd say schizo-affective disorder because of the mood element. It's a type of schizophrenia.'

He leans forward in his chair, places his mug on the round light-wood coffee table between us and asks what else we'd like to know.

'I'm wondering about the prognosis,' I say, 'what life might have been like for Sam in the longer term had he lived.'

James leans back in his chair. 'Well, there were lots of

positive elements: high intellectual functioning, a supportive family. And he was personable, immensely likeable.' He smiles, then adds, 'But of course you need to be likeable if you're going to be as difficult as Sam was, and still keep people on side.'

Paul smiles too.

'He was popular,' he says. 'People liked him. They enjoyed his company.'

James moves on to the negatives.

'Of course, his lack of insight really didn't help. And there was the co-morbidity – a bit of ADHD, some Asperger's traits like rigidity – and then certain personality traits. The need to have things his own way, the endless negotiation required.'

He raises his eyebrows and smiles.

'There's always the possibility of course that, had Sam lived, there would have been a reduction in his day-to-day functioning with each psychotic episode. He would probably have had repeated episodes and hospitalisation, which might, in time, have brought insight. But that might have been especially hard for Sam. He would have resisted the idea of a reduced or even an ordinary life. It wouldn't have sat well with his high expectations of how his life should be. His tendency towards grandiosity would have made it a particularly unpalatable truth for him.'

Paul nods his head in agreement.

'And then there was always the question of risk. It was so difficult to manage with Sam. Insight can be helpful in lots of ways, it normally is, but with Sam it might very easily have made him more of a risk to himself. It was such a difficult path we had to tread, a constant balancing act between *not* treating him – with the attendant risks of self-neglect and his coming to harm through misadventure – and *treating* him against his will, and provoking the feeling in him that his life wasn't worth living.'

'I know,' I say. 'It was a nightmare. And then you add in his philosophical and spiritual beliefs about death not being the end, but a way of moving on to a new and probably better life, and you have a perfect storm.'

Silence falls for a minute.

'He probably could have held down a job, in time,' James muses, 'although he might have struggled with anything that didn't fulfil his high expectations of what a worthy job for him would be. And of course, the notion of working in a voluntary capacity was anathema to him.'

Simon and I sigh in unison and shake our heads. We talk of his recklessness and risk-taking. From his pocket Simon produces the empty diazepam blister-packs and explains how he found them in the bin of Sam's little hut. He asks what they think.

James is silent for a while before he replies.

'I just don't know,' he says. 'It's possible that drugs were a factor in his death, but even if they were, there's still no way of knowing what Sam's intentions were. And committing suicide by taking an overdose never featured in any of his suicidal ideation. He talked about much more dramatic things than an overdose.'

I wonder out loud if anyone could have done more or whether doing things differently might have made a difference. I don't really mean it as a question but James replies.

'I think probably not,' he says simply.

There is comfort in that.

Above all else Simon and I are reminded that James and Paul really understood Sam and put endless thought into his treatment and care. Later I write to them.

The meeting helped confirm for us something we already knew but needed to know again, that you both 'got' Sam. You found things to like in him despite his awkwardness and you understood him in all his glorious, and sometimes impossible, complexity. You didn't just understand the illness, you understood Sam, which was enormously important to us as a family. And because of that you were able to make decisions relating to his care that we, as a family, could trust. I suspect that that is a rare gift within the world of psychiatric services and we are eternally grateful for that.

***

I know you didn't share these feelings, Sam but the meeting reminds me of how much better you were after your third admission to hospital in February 2013. Although you could never see it. You were given a lot of home leave after the first five months, to prepare you for being discharged in August. It had taken you a long time to forgive us, and though you never did, entirely, you'd softened and came home for a weekend in July so you could go out with Rosy and Ellie in Henley for the evening, to meet up with various cousins and friends. *We offered to take you all in the boat and drop you at Marsh Lock to walk along the towpath into town. You were a bit tipsy. You'd had a bottle of cider during supper and then another on the river. But you were on cracking form, engaged with us all and excited about the evening ahead.*

As we made our way down the Thames you called out loudly and enthusiastically to everyone we saw, standing up to take an extravagant bow as we passed by. Ellie wasn't amused. She stomped off down the towpath when we arrived. It wasn't a sense of humour failure, it was fear. She was worried about you, how you would behave and whether she and Rosy would be able to keep you safe.

The next day you were all full of it. It had been a huge success. It was lovely to see you re-engaging with the girls. I know you hated the anti-psychotic medication you were forced to take but it returned you to us and made you part of the family again, able to take part in the small rituals that formed the glue of our family life. You were such an important part of those.

Do you remember those Easter egg hunts I used to set up for you three and the Martins? I'd do those cryptic clues adjusted for age: Rosy and Harry, you and Tom, Ellie and Katherine. You always began with boastful bravado about how you and Tom would win and find your eggs way before everyone else. It wasn't actually a competition, but you turned everything into one. Of course, it was never long before you reappeared, eyes wide in outraged disbelief,

'Our clues are IMPOSSIBLE, Mum. The others' must be so much easier.'

You'd plead with me to reveal the answers, then leave,

affronted, when I refused. You and Tom were always last to arrive back with your eggs.

*And the games of frisbee on the lawn, in which you loudly celebrated all your good moves and conveniently ignored all your mis-throws and drops; your endless capacity to laugh at yourself when you were caught out saying or doing something ridiculous; your knack for saying something that everyone around you was thinking but didn't dare say out loud; your vocal enthusiasm for Paddy's Christmas ham, and then the side-swipe at me that he was **definitely** the best cook in the family. Even though it was his sole contribution to cooking in the entire year.*

I can see you one Christmas morning before Dad left. You were in your Pokemon phase – just one of your many fads over the years. You were all opening your stocking presents on our bed, each of you in his or her allotted space, an allotment reached by unspoken agreement over the years: Ellie is sitting on my side of the bed; Rosy is on Dad's side and you're at the foot, in the centre. You're leaning back against the metal bed frame, red and green tartan pyjamas rucked up from the effort of hoisting your haul up with you. There's a momentary hiatus as you all look at one another, and then, without a word, you are off.

The girls take their time, remove each present from their stockings one by one; squeeze it, gauge the weight, trace its contours, turn it over in their hands. Only then do they start to take off the paper. Small exclamations of excitement greet each unwrapping. They stop and observe one another's gifts, exchange comments, admire.

At the foot of the bed it seems that a small volcano is erupting. You have up-ended your stocking – actually the size of a generous pillow-case – and the contents are tumbling out and forming a small mountain between your feet. You work from the top down. You grab a present, tear the paper from it, then having seen enough, discard it – sometimes only half unwrapped – as you reach for the next. A second mountain soon forms: a muddle of gifts and crumpled paper. You neither look up nor utter a word. You're in a frenzy of anticipation, entirely focused. Within a minute or two you've worked through the heap of gifts. You could be Tom, in a Tom and Jerry cartoon, boring through the skirting-board in search of Jerry. And like Tom you haven't found what you were looking for. You turn to me.

'Is that it?' you ask with undisguised disappointment.

'I think there might be something stuck in the toe, Mr Mueloman. Have a …'

But before I've finished speaking you've grabbed the giant stocking, shoved your hand inside, and pulled it out again. You hold aloft the final parcel. Triumphantly. In a second the wrapping is stripped off. Pokémon cards. Your whole being is glowing with pleasure.

'Thanks Mum,' you shout, then with an apologetic glance at me, 'Father Christmas, I mean,' and you quickly check to see if Ellie's heard. She hasn't.

'Pokémon cards,' you exclaim. 'Look what Father Christmas has brought me, Elles. Look Rosy.'

Oh. My. God,' you continue, each word enunciated with slow drama as you look at us in turn, 'just wait 'til Simon and Laurence see these.' And you start to laugh at the thought of it. Your slow, deep, infectious chortle.

We all join in.

It isn't just the occasions I will miss, but the undefinable *element that you brought to them: the strength of feeling you evoked; the hilarity you prompted effortlessly and often unintentionally, the exasperation you provoked, also effortlessly but frequently intentionally. You were so often completely impossible. But you made everyone feel alive. We couldn't help but respond to you: posing questions no one else would ask; expressing opinions almost always contrary to those already put forward; making people see things from a different perspective. You burned fiercely during your too-short life, sometimes with an intensity uncomfortable for you and those around you. But your presence was always felt.*

In 2012 you once returned home from a night out with a black eye and a small cut on your cheekbone. You were philosophical about it when I asked you what had happened. You smiled at me as you said,

'I think my light was shining too brightly, Mum.'

***

18 June 2014

AS I LIE in bed early this morning, more than half awake but not entirely so, I hear a noise like a door latch opening or closing. That will be Sam, I think, going outside for his first cigarette. It's one of those half-formed semi-thoughts that seep into consciousness, more of a reflex than anything, a reflex based on habit and familiarity and the human instinct to trust that what has been will continue to be. And then I remember. And with the jolt of realisation, I am wide awake. I wonder how to deal with the pain of this new reality – a life without him.

I pick up a book a friend has given to me, *Lament for*

a Son by Nicholas Wolterstorff. It is beautifully written, poetic, insightful, honest, brave. The author writes of seeing his son in his coffin. 'I pity those who never get to see and feel the deadness of the one they love, who must *think* death but cannot *feel* it,' he says. 'To fully persuade us of death's reality, and of its grim finality, our eyes and hands must rub against death's cold hard body, body against body, painfully. Knowing death with mind alone is less than fully knowing it.'

This is my struggle. I don't know how to fully know that Sam is dead.

I continue reading. 'Seeing and touching was also a way of taking leave. Not a full leave-taking – not one in which two *persons* said good-bye to each other. But still, a leave-taking. For though we aren't our bodies, yet of nothing on earth do we have more intimate possession than these. Only through these do we dwell here. I knew Eric through his body. In touching the place of his dwelling, I took leave of him – just as in touching him in his crib, I welcomed him to life. Greeting and leave-taking go best, I think, when we do them with our hands.'

I don't know how to take leave of Sam.

In my mind's eye he's as I last saw him, walking with light but determined step towards the security checks at the airport, no backward glance or wave. He was doing what he wanted to do, happy, hopeful, positive. I can picture how he might have looked, returning from Thailand this Sunday evening, as he should have done, smiling his slow, reluctant smile – reluctant to give away something he would rather not reveal, his love and happiness at seeing his family again. In the start of that slow smile I see it all: the love, the pain, the hurt, but mostly the love. I can picture his smile spreading into a full-blown grin, despite himself. How can I learn to understand that I will never see his smile again? I only know Sam alive. I don't know him dead. Unless I can know him dead, then how can I ever take my leave of him?

19 June 2014

I'M AVOIDING PEOPLE: ignoring calls, rejecting offers of shared walks, coffees, glasses of wine, shoulders to cry on. I appreciate the kindness and love that lie behind them, but I don't really want to talk. Except to people who really knew and loved Sam. Sometimes not even them. Perhaps it's because I am doing so much talking inside my own head, trying to process all that has happened, to come to terms with the idea of a life without him. Anything else feels superfluous and unimportant. I resent interruptions. It's almost a compulsion, this need to process, to make real what has happened, to find a way of *feeling* that he is dead.

21 June 2014

LYNNE, OUR GARDENER, comes every Friday afternoon. She works incredibly hard, rolls her eyes to heaven and ignores me when I say she should leave heavy things for Paddy to do.

Today we are talking about Sam. She reminds me of the lovely summer we had last year, of all the Friday afternoons when he was here and people came and went, spilling out of the back door into the garden.

'It was lovely,' she says, 'such a happy house.'

A computer man came too, perhaps ten years ago. He was called Fred and walked with a limp. He had a passion for ballroom dancing. He spent a whole weekend with us, re-wiring inside and out. It was summer and the children flew in and out through the open back door into the garden. He stood on his ladder and smiled as they pedalled past him, bounced on the trampoline and swung from the climbing frame. We lit a barbecue and Fred laughed when Sam dropped a sausage by mistake but caught it between his knees. 'Well held, Sam,' Paddy and I chorused in unison.

Fred didn't seem to want to leave when Sunday evening came. I thanked him for what he'd done. 'I've so enjoyed it,' he said. 'I've loved being here, in such a happy home.'

It's a quiet home now, a sad home. I wonder if it will ever be happy again.

Sam should have been returning from Thailand in three days' time. The details are there in my diary still. Sunday, 22 June, '*Sam returns 18.30, terminal 3, JAI 0122 from Delhi.*' He gave them to me before he left. He'd become good at doing that sort of thing. Before he left, he even gave me the dates for the massage course he'd enrolled on to start in September. It was lovely to see him engaging with life and with his future.

I don't know how to get through Sunday. I feel a need to go to Heathrow to meet his plane. I know it's irrational and makes no logical sense. I've been told Sam's dead, that the body identified by the police *was* that of the person in the passport found in the room. I have that passport here with me now, propped up against my computer, and I know that, even if this were all some hideous mistake, he would not be able to travel without it. And yet I feel a need to be there when his plane lands. It feels as though I would be failing him, failing as a mother, if I were not there waiting. It's my job to carry the hope, to keep on believing in him. It's what I've always done. I don't want to fail him, for him to think I'm not still there for him.

Or perhaps I actually need to do it for me. Perhaps I need to sit, to watch, to wait, to see people come and go and for there to be no Sam. Perhaps this will be how I *fully* know that he is dead, how I *feel* death as well as *think* it.

We're planning to go to Wales for the weekend. It's my way of escaping, but I know I still might want to go to Heathrow on Sunday. I tell Paddy. He says that's fine, that we can do whatever I need to, drive back early from Wales to get to Heathrow if need be.

We go for a walk. It's one we did with Sam shortly before he left for Thailand. It was a cold, grey day then and we had thrown in skinny chips and a Bombay Sapphire and tonic at The Bell, a favourite local pub, as an incentive for him to come. He complained a lot about the length of the walk, but he kept going.

Today it's balmy and still and the fields are full of ripening wheat with borders of poppies, cornflowers, feverfew and gypsy wort. Sigmund has to spring with small, deer-like leaps to clear the vegetation. I want to tell Sam about the wildflowers. I want him to be there too.

I receive an email from a friend. 'I can well imagine your urge to withdraw, to be quiet and undisturbed. It's like having been wounded, isn't it? Your heart needs peace, to begin to heal.' It helps me to read this. It helps me to combat the inner voice I have that sometimes tells me, unhelpfully, in impatient tone: 'You aren't *ill*. You're not an *invalid*.'

22 June 2014

'I LOVE YOU in your big pearl earrings,' Sam said to me once. I wear them often. It's a way of staying connected to him. I put them on today: the day I should have been welcoming him home. We've come to Wales, but I don't know how to get through the day. We decide to do a walk. It's one he loved: Black Hill in the Black Mountains.

It's a rewarding walk, just a short, steep climb and then you're on a high narrow ridge, with land dropping away on either side of you. Olchon Valley on the left, wild, untamed and raw, and on the right, Herefordshire, with its neatly parcelled fields and milder, gentler hues. There are huge, flat boulders on the ridge, perfect for picnics or drink stops, and flat stones protruding over the drop like diving boards. I picture Sam scampering up the hill to be first to the top, waving his arms in triumph at the rest of us, his piping voice drifting down, 'I won. I beat you all.'

The light is crystal clear, the sun blazing down, the valleys a vibrant green, and as we walk, waves of sound rise up to the ridge from the fields below, a constant soundscape of bleating lambs in search of their mothers, baaing sheep trying to locate their young, and skylarks on the wing, hovering overhead, their song drifting earth-wards. My head is filled with memories of him.

Alongside the memories an internal battle is raging. I want to go this evening to meet his plane at the airport. It's a powerful urge driven by a part of me that wants to hope beyond hope, to believe in the fantasy that it might all be a dreadful mistake, that Sam might arrive or call, that I should be there just in case. As mother to him I've held onto belief and optimism against the odds. It's been one of my roles. I make myself slow down and think. Of course it's hard to accept that he is dead. But do I really need to put myself through the agony of experiencing his non-arrival as some painful step on my journey towards acceptance?

I don't go to Heathrow. I spare myself that.

As I write this, I can see that the decision itself mattered less than the process – the process of battling out internally this wish to go. It would have been easier and less painful in the short-term to ignore it, either suppressing it altogether or dismissing it as the mad idea it was. Alternatively, I might have decided simply to go to Heathrow rather than go through the discomfort of *thinking* about it. I did neither. Instead, I batted it to and fro in my head. It was painful but it gave me the opportunity to work out what was going on, to identify the unconscious impulse and the need that lay behind it. Only then was I able to make a truly conscious decision, one that has the potential to sit comfortably within me.

I know it's going to take a long time for me to feel that Sam is dead, to feel it viscerally. Going to Heathrow would have been part of that, a way of making his absence real. But it would have been a cruel ordeal to put myself through: making myself a witness to happy reunions, to lives being lived; making myself sit through arrival after arrival, having to decide when to call it a day, when to tear myself away and admit defeat. I'm glad I didn't have to do that.

But I'm also glad that I was able to allow it to be a possibility. If I simply hadn't gone because I'd banished the thought as mad or suppressed it because it was too painful to think about, I would have been left with something unprocessed psychically. Like undigested food it might have repeated on me, in the form of doubt, guilt and anxiety. Thinking about it – and the meaning lying behind it – helped me both to recognise something important about my grieving process and to make a conscious and better choice for myself.

Later, back at home, I lean into my bedside cupboard and pull out the small stash of photos tucked in there. I leaf through them until I find the one I'm looking for. I hold it up above me as I lie in bed. He is on the boat, on the Thames. He's in profile, leaning forward slightly, hands cupped around a lighter flame, cigarette clamped between his lips. It shouldn't speak to me as a photo because I didn't like his smoking – a habit he acquired during his final stay in Prospect Park – but it does. It captures something of the essence of him. Although it started as a way of passing time, of relieving the crushing boredom of seven months spent on a locked ward, it became a part of him, a part of the post-Prospect Park Sam, the Sam he was when he left for Thailand.

There is movement in the photo. You can see the tendons in his right hand, taut with the action required to activate the lighter. I half expect him to turn and face me once the cigarette is lit, to acknowledge me there with the camera, capturing a fleeting moment of his life.

He didn't know I was there. I don't think he ever saw the photo, but I think he would have liked it if he had. I gaze at it through my tears. I will him to turn towards me for one final meeting of our eyes.

He doesn't. He remains still, eyes lowered towards the task of lighting his cigarette. He is gone. This is all I have of him now.

Part 2

23 June 2014

I HAVEN'T OPENED any official-looking post for six weeks but I can't keep on ignoring it. There is a huge pile to go through. I carry it through to the kitchen and stand at the counter opening envelope after envelope. It seems to be an inventory of life with Sam: a credit card bill with hotel and restaurant expenses from our trip to Berlin; a letter from Kensington Borough Council, confirming that they will allow my appeal against a parking ticket incurred when he and I went to the Thai Embassy; the annual family membership cards for the RSPB; bank statements addressed to him; his new National Trust card. My mood sinks. There are just three envelopes left: a Notice of Intended Prosecution for speeding over the May bank holiday weekend, requiring completion and return within twenty-eight days; a subsequent reminder requiring a response within seven days. And then finally a letter from a payday loan company threatening to send round the bailiffs for a loan that has nothing to do with me.

These last three letters fill me with a disproportionate sense of dread and anxiety. I know what I need to do, but I'm not sure that I can. I'm overwhelmed, weighed down and paralysed. Sometimes, even the thought of going food shopping fills me with dread; not just for fear of who I might bump into – people who 'know' or 'don't know' are equally challenging in different ways – but also because of the mental energy it requires to think about what to cook, what to buy, what we need. I don't seem to have any.

24 June 2014

LILY SENDS A message to me and Paddy, a group text, to tell us that she's signed up for a TEFL course. She sounds excited. Sam's death has drawn us closer. She was only eighteen when her mum died of cancer. It just left her and Paddy. When he met me two years later, recently separated, with three young children, it must have been immensely hard for her. How not to resent and even hate the woman who threatened to take her mother's place? How not to resent and hate the children who made demands on *her* father? How not to feel abandoned when he moved in with me and my children?

We've been careful, considerate, kind to one another. She's been warm to my children, generous towards their growing relationships with her father; and I have loved her son, Charlie (now ten) and done my best to be a quasi-grandmother to him. My children have loved him too. 'I wish Sam could be my brother,' he said to me once, in a tone which implied that I really ought to be able to arrange it, since he wanted it so much.

But it's taken time. In the early days, when I was

needy and insecure, I sometimes wanted more of Paddy than he could give. It would have been easy to resent the fact that he came with a ready-made life and family, easier to have him to myself. I had to fight those feelings, recognise them for what they were, try never to put Paddy in the position of having to choose between us. But I don't suppose it's felt like that to Lily.

I realise now I should have done more to make her feel a part of our life. Paddy should too. I wish we had. She seemed so grown-up to me then, compared to my own children. I thought of her as an adult, wanting to lead her own life. Now I've seen my own children at that age I can see how wrong I was. Yet despite this, over these last two months I've felt her support and understanding of what Sam's death has meant to me.

It's drawn Kim and me closer too. She wrote to me after Sam died, telling me I couldn't have been a better mother and couldn't have tried any harder with him than I did. It arrived at a particularly bleak moment of self-reproach. I was touched. After all, we have reason to be resentful of one another. I am the woman whose children continue to make demands of, and lay claim to, her partner, their father. She is the woman with whom Simon has had another child, toppling me from the position of being the only mother to Simon's children. These are difficult and painful realities, apt to drive wedges between people, make one behave unreasonably and look for fault in others. We have both resisted that. Instead we have found a way to love one another's children. I love Imogen. I have witnessed Kim's sorrow at the loss of Sam. I can see that she feels it on her own account as well as sharing my pain as a mother.

Blended families are hard work for everyone. Trying to manage difficult feelings, to see them for what they are: acknowledging their ugliness and yet their validity, processing, working through and trying to make better conscious choices. And, when feeling hurt or angry, trying to understand, rather than retaliate. Thank goodness we have all done our best to make it work. It would have been terrible to face Sam's death as a divided family.

I suppose I'm writing here of good things that have come out of Sam's death. They are no compensation for the loss of him, but they are a salve.

28 June 2014

THE HOUSE HAS felt emptier than ever this week, just me and Paddy and Sig.

I haven't written anything for several days. I think I've been in some sort of emotional lock-down, avoiding feeling anything. Perhaps my mind decided it needed a few days' respite from grieving. But I'm not sure it works. I feel extraordinarily tired, a sort of bone-weariness that drags me down. I fear it's the price I have to pay for *not* allowing myself to feel – all the psychic energy required to keep my feelings at bay. Grief is exhausting too but at least it has the potential to lead somewhere positive in the end, perhaps to acceptance. With this I'm just treading water.

In the evening Paddy and I watch Glastonbury on TV. Elbow are playing. The music unlocks something in me. I'm moved by it. I see the billowing flags, the swaying arms held aloft in the golden glow of evening and feelings creep in. As the camera pans out and takes in the thinning crowds at the back, the dying sun casts impossibly long shadows that turn the scene into a Lowry canvas. Tears rise up along with a need to be close to Paddy, who has been such a rock to me over the last two months, to express that feeling of closeness through physical intimacy. But no sooner have I recognised the feeling, than I realise how utterly impossible it seems in the aftermath of Sam's death.

And then I am crying. Deep, painful sobs for all the beauty of this world, that Sam will not see, for all the relationships he won't have, for a life barely lived. It feels so wrong, so profoundly wrong that I should still be part of this world when he is not. Each pair of swaying arms should be his. He will never know happiness, wonder and beauty again; and yet I will. It is wrong.

As my tears subside into something calmer and quieter, I find myself processing all these powerful feelings. It is guilt that I'm feeling, guilt at the idea of deriving any pleasure and joy in a life he has been deprived of. And disloyalty to him if I continue to invest in things he can no longer have. Yet, what else can I do but live the life that I still have?

I let the battle rage inside me.

Finally it stills as I come to a realisation of sorts: that allowing these feelings to prevail would, in a sense, mean opting for a form of death in life. I would be joining Sam in no longer living. I would be allowing what Freud called the 'death instinct' to prevail over the pull towards life. It would keep me stuck in a dark place, where joy and hope are extinguished.

When we go to bed Paddy and I make love for the first time since Sam died. I cry again afterwards: for Sam and all he'll never experience; and for me, trying to find a way to navigate this new life in which I find myself, a life that has changed forever and yet must continue forward.

29 June 2014

MORE THAN A month has passed since Paddy and I sat and listened to the recordings of Sam. I feel ready to listen to them again, to transcribe them. I look for them in my iTunes folder. I'm not sure of the dates but there are only a handful of Voice Memos. There's one recorded on 29th June 2012, just a few days before he was first sectioned. I press play. It's the recording I made at Pizza Express. I must have been there with him exactly two years ago today.

Synchronicity.

***

I've just been listening to your voice Sam. But it isn't the voice I loved. It's your voice when you were psychotic. It was different: the pitch, the tone, the intonation. It's hard to describe but it was strangely mellifluous, almost other-worldly, as though you were addressing us ordinary mortals from a great height. You used flowery vocabulary and spoke in long rambling sentences that often didn't make sense. You'd leave enormously long silences – you couldn't bear it if I interrupted them – and speak with great emphasis, as if talking to a particularly dim child. It wasn't just your voice that changed. Everything was different when you were psychotic: the way you held yourself, the way you looked at people, the way you walked, even the way you laughed. It changed from that wonderful rolling chuckle to a humourless, jarring, Santa Claus-like 'ho ho ho'. It didn't sound like you. But of course it was. You were still there, it was just that you'd lost touch with reality. It's easy to see why the myth of schizophrenia involving a split personality endures even now. It isn't that at all. Although schizophrenia means 'split mind', it's describing the split from reality that occurs during a psychotic episode and the change in thoughts, feelings and behaviours, not a split between different personalities.

You never knew about these recordings. I concealed my phone under the table when I was making them. I hated myself for doing it, but I was desperate, we all were. We'd been watching and waiting for eighteen months by then, but your psychosis came and went and whenever the CMHT visited you seemed just to have emerged from a psychotic phase and would be back to your coherent, articulate self. I needed them to understand about the other times. And I was beginning to be worried for your safety: you seemed so out of touch with reality. That's why I recorded us talking. I didn't know what else to do.

I've hated listening to them again. It isn't how I want to remember you, with your thinking so disorganised and your anger so palpable when I can't discern the meaning behind your words. It reminds me of how painful it was for both of us. I was trying to do what I'd been told: not to challenge your statements, but not actively to collude with you either, to be as calm and steady and grounding as I could be. But not to patronise or be inauthentic because you'd sense it and react badly. It was so much harder in practice than that simple advice sounded.

The irony is that I don't sound like me either. You could have accused me of sounding different too: wooden and stilted. The truth is I don't sound natural because I'm paralysed by fear. Every non sequitur in your speech is a blow to me, every oddness is more evidence that terrifies me. But above all else the recordings remind me of how lonely we both were and I feel overwhelmingly sad for us. Each of us trying so hard to connect but we were inhabiting different worlds, different realities. And although there were moments of connection, most of the time we were like two trains on parallel tracks, moving alongside one another but unable to find a point of contact. You sensed, just as acutely as I did, the huge gulf that had opened up between us and every time I failed to understand you, you felt bewilderment and pain. And because it was painful you were angry with me. I wish it could have been otherwise.

I started the first recording towards the end of our meal. We were sitting outside. You'd re-discovered a love of pizzas by then and sometimes relaxed your strict eating regime. We were having lunch before we went to the cinema. This is how it went:

Me: How was that Sam?

You: It was such a wonderful pizza. It was like receiving a golden land, golden land …

Me: It was like receiving what?

You: Many golden artefacts.

Me: Really? That sounds good.

Silence

You: Many golden and sublime artefacts, motifs, fine, fine tapestries, yes, yes.

Me: What – all in the pizza?

You: To confirm wealth in such a way, possibly.

Me: So have you enjoyed your lunch out, Sammy?

You: I did very much enjoy it. Really something that I would say is, **to** me and **for** me, not only is the world so fantastic and there are so many wonderful things to do within the world, whether that is engaging in activities, whether that is interests and hobbies you have and discuss with other people, whether one is enjoying the technologies and toys, even jet skis and boats and all manners of things, but really what I would say is, all of that stuff can be enjoyed to the greatest emotional reaction that can take place when you share those experiences with another person. In all of the worlds that this earth can offer there is such a tremendous reservoir of pleasure that can open itself up to those who …

Long silence.

Me: Yes? To those who …?

You: No I mean (*quite crossly*) what I said was, there were many points in, and what I said.

Me: I know, darling, but I thought you were going on to say, to those who … what? Are open to them?

You: To those who open themselves to the delights of life. It's like I'm here and when I'm with my friends and when I'm with girlfriends, who are very ultimate people to me, it's like I have the most remarkable, incredible, emotionally enriching, humanly gratifying exchanges and it's, it's limitless when you're with the right people …

Me: Yes, that's true.

You: (very crossly): If I was with finer company, people who actually understand. You see it, the way you did there? If I was actually with a finer, accommodating …

Me: What did I do, Sam?

You: You made a weird noise.

Me: What sort of noise?

You: As if you were expelling hydrogen.

Me: Did I?

You: Yes you did.

Me: Oh, okay. Well apologies for that. Sammy, I know I'm not the finest company for you, I know you'd much rather be here with friends or with a girlfriend or someone really special.

You: No, I enjoyed your company but the reason I would probably be having a funner and more enriching and beautiful time with them is because they would be far more open and receiving to my words and all of the things I like to experience … I have spoken about friends. I've had a long conversation speaking about friends, I've spoken about relationships, I've really actually said a lot. I gave you an audio-visual simulation of a boat trip.

Me: Of a what?

You: Of a boat trip, of a boat journey.

Me: Oh, okay. (*Hesitantly*) Yes. I'm sorry I was just trying to work out what you were talking about.

You: (extremely crossly): I really, really should keep far better company.

Long silence.

Me: Well, Sammy, the limitations of the present company accepted, are we now going to go and watch this film? Because if we are it starts in three minutes.

You: They will definitely have about half an hour of adverts.

Me: Do you reckon?

You: If I reckon something, I reckon something, I'm a reckoner.

The following evening you were in the kitchen when I came and joined you. You were cooking yourself something to eat, and had pots boiling on the hob. You kept lapsing into long, long silences while we were talking, staring into space or closing your eyes and swaying violently forwards and backwards on the balls of your feet. I kept thinking you were going to lose your balance and fall onto the hob. You'd been for a run with Kim in the morning: one of those organised park runs. She said you'd set off at a great pace with your arms held aloft and then dropped out altogether, but you'd returned in high spirits. Those were dampened somewhat when someone from the CMHT popped in to see you. You weren't at all happy about that.

Second recording

Me: Hi, Sammy. How are you darling?

You: Very, very well indeed. Enriched by the connections and conversations that I've had today. Feeling very positive. Feeling outraged that you called up people and, to be completely honest with you, even to have to share space with a mother who thinks that there's something wrong with me. If you think that, it takes a certain degree or manner of emotion to address such a topic, but it makes me slightly sad for you, not only that you could think such a thing but that you have to live with it, that you have to live with that.

Me: I'm sorry about that.

You: You see, the apology isn't enough. You telling me you're sorry, that instigates or implies that you're going to have to live with that problem for the rest of your life. If you can't just see me as me being your son, as me being a person who has many friends, who has better relationships, who's happier than you. I'm happier than you. I'm more joyful than you. I have a finer spirit. I have a poetic spirit. I have the kind of nature and inclinations that make me enthused and want to share stories with other people that make me want to share the finer things with other people. That you can't see that, that you can't see that spirit within me...

Me: I can see that Sam. I can see that.

You: But you say it in that way. If you could truly see it. You only see it through your **jarred** perspective. If you were a **proper** person, the kind of mother that I should truly have, who would both be delighted with everything I said, but who would want to experience my delight that I have, with me.

Me: Sam I'm very pleased that you take a lot of delight in life. It gives me great pleasure that you do.

You: Well, I'm happier than you.

Me: Well you may well be. It's difficult to say.

You: No, I clearly am, because you see a problem in me, therefore you have a problem. Because I'm perfect. Existence is perfect, life is perfect and God is perfect. I have better friends than you. I have better relationships. I can say that because I do believe in a god and that is a part of my life.

Me: Well, I'm very pleased for anyone who has God as part of their life. I think that's an enviable thing to have.

You: You see, you envy. That's why I'm better than you because where I see gratitude you choose a different emotion, which obviously means that I'm more noble than you as well. I have principles on my side as well. I mean, I'm … (*You were really shouting by now*) I'm **eloquenting**. I'm clearly deciphering and showing – not only through my art of language and my perfection and vision of being – how much greater I truly am than you!

Me: Why do you compare yourself all the time, darling? I mean you're you and I'm me.

You: Because I'm having to, because for you it isn't enough just to love your son as he is.

Me: I do love my son as he is. I absolutely love my son as he is. I love **you**, Sam, just as you are.

You: Anyway, I'm savouring finer thoughts, thoughts to be shared with my friends definitely – people who are going to truly experience all of the delights and pleasures that I want to experience with them, all of the most beautiful things that I can share with them. Those are the things I look forward to and obviously have already shared.

Me: Well, I'm pleased. So who have you spoken to today, Sammy? You said you'd had lots of interesting conversations and things.

You: Oh, I've just spoken to the people I've encountered.

Anyway, I'm trying to uphold a far more positive note, a far more positive note. I would much rather be with people who have a different perspective. I have a far more emotional reservoir than you. I understand the beauty of my ancestors' lives. I have far more confidence than you. I am greater than you. Life is always an ongoing process of learning. That's why I'm so wise, that's why I'm respected so dearly by my friends because I see that element, I see that aspect of it and why I'm a master of it, and yes I **am** a master of it because anyone who is an author, anyone who writes, anyone who is an actor, the precise, well I should only talk to someone who actually understood these things and who embellished them within me because that's how an actor goes about his work.

Me: That's true. Do you not think that **I** can understand any of that then?

You: No, I, I hope you can. I hope you can. But you need to get to a certain level or perspective where you can understand that your son has matured into a man.

Me: I **do** know that Sam, I **do** know that.

Long silence in which you closed your eyes and simply stood and swayed.

You: Well, that makes me very happy.

Me: Good, good.

Another long silence in which you again stood with your eyes closed, your head tilted back, rocking to and fro on the balls of your feet, right next to the stove where you had a saucepan of water coming to the boil.

Me: Careful, Mr Muelo, you're going to fall over. *(Silence)* What are you cooking Sam? *(Silence.)* Talk me through your supper. *(Silence.)*

You: You see, as an artist I always savour the pleasures, and as I've said many times before when someone is having a moment of delight and joy, you let them have that moment.

Me: I'm sorry Sam, was I interrupting?

You: Speaking from excellence, yes, you were.

(Silence.)

Me: Sorry about that. *(Silence.)* So, tell me about your moment of joy. Was that thinking about what you were preparing?

You: Ohhh, it was what I was preparing – it was many things that I was preparing. Those aspirations and those joys are obviously things that we always look forward to and things that motivate us and captivate us to go forward and do many things, but one thing that I've really truly been savouring is the accomplishments that I made during my race today.

Me: Oh, oh, good. How did your race go? I didn't hear. (*Silence.*) Sammy, tell me about your run this morning. (*Silence.*) Sam?

Long silence.

You: What did I tell you about just letting someone enjoy a moment? You've got to understand, people imbue feelings and thoughts into every single conversational exchange. If I was with a girlfriend right now, I would have been savouring that moment. That is part of the beauty of life, in letting people express their feelings and their thoughts.

Me: I know, I was just asking. I just wondered because you said you were thinking about your accomplishments.

You: I was thinking about the triumph that I made today during the race. I was the first person off from the start.

Me: Really?

You: Yes, I was the **very first person**. I did an **incredible** race. I finished in **excellent** position.

Me: Oh good. And was it nice, was it a …?

You: (*Interrupting with irritation and contempt*): Well, I've already **said** so. I mean, just the fact that I **started** on such an **excellent** note. I was the very **first** person. I was running with **such a speed** but at the same time, as you said, yes it was a wonderful experience because I found time and places to adopt different paces. I was the first one off and I think that lots of people would say that I did a very, very stunning performance.

Me: Oh, well that's good. Good.

You: (shouting): You should be more **enthused**. When your son brings riches home, his accomplishments. But that's why I always have to go into **my space**, because there I can appreciate myself.

Silence while you close your eyes and sway wildly. Finally, you open your eyes.

Me: You see, I didn't interrupt you that time.

You: You didn't. But what I should tell you is that not only do you have an actor and an author as a son, but you also have a human being. Someone who experiences emotions and if you can't understand that ...

Me: Darling, I do understand that. Why would you think I don't understand that? I know that. *(Silence.)*

You: Well, that's a good thing because I will always be **emotionally** enriched, because I'm a very strong character, **very** strong, very bold, but also very just, because God is a part of my life. So obviously I hope that our relationship grows and evolves in profound ways because the truth is, if I did come from you ...

Me: Well you did, darling.

You: Then I have a part of your soul in me.

Me: Well, I hope so.

You: And that I live through you or with you in a way, so the sooner you accept that not only do I love you and do I cherish you and care for you, and if you could even understand, I mean how many sons actually tell their mothers …

Me: Oh, Sammy, I know.

You: I mean I'm a very bold character. I've had many girlfriends and many experiences in this life, but I'm truly telling my Mum that I do love and care for her very dearly.

Me: Thank you, Sam.

You: And I always wish the best for you. I always wish the best for you.

Me: I know darling and I love and care for you just as sincerely and I also wish the best for you.

You: Yes, and I hope that you do, but if you're not ready to experience yourself then I will reside with the ancestors who would. I think I possibly would have had a far greater relationship with Frieda Glucksmann, my great-grandmother, because she would have really let me care for her. We would have had a **tremendous** and such an emotionally enriching relationship because she would have allowed me ... she would have allowed my creative spirit to shine forth. She would have let me be as great as I truly am, and she would have enjoyed and basked in my glory, and her **basking** in my glory would have allowed me to be greater than I could have even been.

I'm glad we had that conversation Sam and I'm glad I recorded it because I would have forgotten it otherwise. And actually, in that moment when we expressed our love for one another there was a connection. I can hear it in our voices, both yours and mine. They were full of feeling. They were full of love. And, just for that moment, we were in contact.

***

1 July 2014

I'VE COME AWAY on my own for a few days. I'm not entirely sure why but when the idea came to me it had the feeling of something instinctive, a prompt from some-where deep within, so I decided to trust it.

I've rented a tiny studio apartment in Oxford. I'm on the third and top floor of a crenellated Georgian tower on Folly Island in the middle of the Thames. It's not really an island – more a spit of land coming off a bridge – but the house is beautiful, with roses and flax growing against the red-brick walls. It's called Folly Bridge House and claims to be the spot where Lewis Carroll invented Alice in Wonderland. I have river on either side of me and trees outside my windows and though I can hear the sounds of the city rumbling away in the background, the sound of birdsong is louder.

I am sitting up in bed, alone, with three or four days of aloneness stretching out in front of me and it feels okay. I've never been very good at being on my own, but something has changed since Sam died. I feel more comfortable in my own company. A friend asked me the other day if I could ever feel him around me, and I answered, very quickly, no. But I've wondered since if that's right because I don't feel alone anymore, even when I am. And, at times, I *do* feel Sam around me.

As I write this there is a sudden rush of wind outside. I feel him in it; in the dappled sunlight dancing on the bed; in the branches swaying outside my bedroom window; in the leaves trembling in the breeze. I've come away to make time for him. It's a comfort to feel his presence so powerfully.

A little later I look up from my writing. The leaves are still now and the sunlight lies unmoving on the bed. It feels as though they have delivered their message. I think about an afterlife. Whether there is one. Whether people endure in some way or another. I've never closed my mind to it. I don't see it in terms of heaven and hell, but I can imagine someone's spirit living on. And when I say I feel Sam around me I don't really know what that means. But in a way it doesn't matter. It's what I feel in the moment that counts. I don't have any wish to take it further, try to make contact via a psychic. I'd rather simply remain open to the possibility of something. Whatever that might be.

3 July 2014

I SPREAD MY photos of Sam out on my bed. I carry his Order of Service with me, wherever I go.

I like him to be with me. And I cry for a long, long time, until I can cry no more. Although my tears are exhausting, somewhere I know they're the real reason I've come away.

Although I'm not used to spending time alone, it's what I've needed: no one else to worry about, no pressure to commit, make plans or even think about the day ahead. I've simply allowed each day to unfold and take its own course. It's given me the space I needed to connect with Sam. It hasn't been easy but I feel braver since he died – the worst has happened and I seem to be surviving it. At times I've felt small flutterings of unease, little waves of anxiety swelling up inside me, but instead of letting myself get caught in up in them, or trying to fight them, I've simply gone with them, until they've peaked and passed. As all waves do.

But I have sudden and intense fears about the girls too. The thought of anything happening to either of them fills me with terror. Nic sends me an email:

Every time I think of what you must be feeling I can't

bear it and yet you do. You somehow bear it. I don't understand how. And because I don't understand I feel unsure about what to say for fear of making it worse. As if anyone could. Just let me know if there is anything I can do – or not do – which might help you. I'd have already taken out half of Reading with a machete and locked the girls away in the attic so you're doing well.

At once my terror feels legitimate and easier to bear.

***

I hope that feeling braver will endure. I'd like that to be a part of your legacy to me. You were so brave, and never more so than on the day I'm about to describe.

I never needed to use the recordings. When the community psychiatrist came to visit you, at our request, a day or two after I made them, she confirmed that you were suffering from a chronic psychotic illness and needed treatment. A Mental Health Act assessment was put in place. There would be two psychiatrists, your key worker in the CMHT and a social worker (an approved mental health practitioner or AMHP). You would remain unaware until everyone arrived in case you did a runner.

It was 5 July 2012. The day dawned bright and sunny. I felt sick with nerves and utterly desolate. Dad arrived. Paddy made us all tea. It was hard to go through the motions of normality as we waited for the knock on the door that would signal the arrival of the assessment team. When it came, all four of them were there.

Dad and I came into the green room. I can remember you looking up from the computer. You'd been to have your hair cut a few days earlier. Those golden, matted dreadlocks were now in a plastic bag stowed beneath your bed. I have them still. You'd swapped the tattered, food-stained T-shirt and cut off sweat-pants you'd been wearing for months, for a pair of smart black jeans and a shirt of palest grey-blue cotton with the faintest pencil thin check. You'd transformed yourself from pavement-dweller to smart young executive overnight. It was almost as though you knew. As though some sixth sense were telling you that you were about to face the greatest battle of your life.

'There are some people here to see you Sam. I'm afraid you've got to see them. I'm sorry Sam but you don't have a choice,' Dad said.

You shook your head the way you did. You didn't say a word, no protest, you just followed us out into the garden. You sat down with us all at the table in the sunshine. I can't remember why we did it there. Perhaps we thought it would feel less intimidating for you to be outside in the open air. As if that was going to make any difference. It was the AMHP who spoke first to explain who everyone was and why they were there. I could see you didn't like her from the start. I didn't either. She was officious and cold. It was a shame she felt she had to hide her soul. I still feel angry with her for the way she talked down to you, so patronising and condescending. When you protested she cut straight in.

'I'm afraid that's all irrelevant,' she said. 'None of this is your choice Sam. We're here to make decisions about you that will be binding on you regardless of what you think or feel.

That doesn't come into it anymore.'

I've never felt more proud of you. You argued your case heroically, with clarity, articulacy and controlled passion. With enormous self-restraint you remained calm, courteous, even respectful. But somewhere you knew that you were fighting for your life. Two circles of perspiration under your arms grew ever larger as the interview progressed. It broke our hearts.

The interview ended and the team withdrew. Mistakenly you thought it was all over, that you'd survived this potential travesty of justice. Sitting still at the table in the garden – the same table where the young policewoman sat less than two years later – you berated Dad and me for our betrayal, our lack of understanding and belief in you, our appalling failings as parents.

But then there was another knock on the door and they all filed in. It was awful to see the confusion on your face.

The AMHP held forth again, 'You have been officially sectioned under the Mental Health Act, you will be held in a secure unit until deemed fit to be released. If you abscond now the police will search for you and detain you.'

All the confidence and bluster of your impassioned arguments left you and for a moment you sat silently, simply shaking your head. You were crushed, bewildered, disbelieving. And utterly deflated.

But extraordinarily, you didn't remain so. With a monumental effort of self-will – I could see how much it took you – you gathered yourself sufficiently to say, 'I cannot, I will not, submit to your decisions. This is all a terrible mistake and a treacherous deprivation of liberty. You're part of a system that I deplore. I will not submit. I will not agree to go quietly. You cannot make me go.'

The AMHP began to speak again, 'I'm afraid you have no choice. This decision is final and binding. The police will come, an ambulance will be called, you'll be restrained if necessary. You will be going to hospital whether you like it or not.'

'Can you let **us** talk to Sam for a moment please?' I said.

We went inside the house, you, me and Dad. Everyone left but the AMHP, who stayed outside. For an hour or more we pleaded with you to let us take you to hospital, not to subject yourself to the indignity of the police being called, of being manhandled into an ambulance. The AMHP appeared at the door, saying she couldn't wait any longer. We begged for more time. She held off, reluctantly. Still there was no progress. Phone calls were made. Minutes later the ambulance pulled on to the drive. The police were due at any moment. By now we were in the hall. I'd packed a small bag for you. We stood between the front door onto the drive and the back door into the garden. You looked at us, defiant still.

'Please, please, Sam,' I said. 'Please don't make this any harder than it already is. For any of us. For you, for Dad, for me. Please let us take you. Please will you do it for me, Sam?' My voice broke as I looked at you with tears in my eyes.

'Okay,' you said. 'I will.'

When we arrived at Prospect Park Hospital the AMHP escorted us down to Bluebell ward. The corridors seemed to go on forever, through endless sets of blue double doors. The last *set were locked. It was the entrance to the ward. The AMHP rang a bell. On the other side, through a small glass panel, two pairs of eyes peered out at us. We waited. So did the eyes. Suddenly they moved aside. A member of staff appeared instead and held his card up to the door to release the lock. We were in an annexe to the ward. A queue of people was waiting by an open door on the left. They shuffled to one side to let us pass. I glanced inside where a doctor sat handing out medication. On the right was a small room with internal windows on two of its four walls, looking through to the main ward. Several members of staff were gathered there. The walls were covered with charts and white boards with lists scrawled on them in different colours.*

We were led down to a small meeting room with eight or so blue chairs lined up against the walls and a desk in the corner. You and Dad sat on one side of the room. I sat on the other. So did the AMHP. We waited. It was hot and airless. Although there was a window, it only opened a fraction. As we would soon discover none of the windows opened any further.

A nurse came in and introduced herself as Leah. She said she would be joined at some point by a psychiatrist. She explained to you that she needed to go through a series of forms with you as part of their admissions procedure. She was warm and gentle as she tried to extract the information she needed. You responded to almost every question with a statement; the same statement – that you shouldn't be there, that you had many, many friends, that you had travelled the world. It became your mantra. You repeated it again and again, as though somehow it would be the key to open those locked blue doors that had closed behind us as we entered the ward. All the powers of logic and reasoning that you'd somehow accessed during the Assessment now deserted you.

A psychiatrist came in. He too was warm, kind and respectful to you. I was so grateful to them for their kindness and patience. I could not have borne it if there had been even the smallest hint of impatience or disrespect towards you Sam. I'd never felt more vulnerable in my life than when I sat in that small airless room, knowing that I was going to have to walk away and leave you, my beautiful boy, with these strangers who would have total control over you.

When that moment came it was the hardest thing I'd ever had to do, and the most devastating. I can't imagine what it was like for you. We at least could leave.

***

5 July 2014

ELLIE CALLS ON FaceTime. She looks tired, a little strained.

'I want to come home early,' she says. 'I love the travelling, really love it but I'm always on the go – new people, new places. I'm just partying all the time. Everyone I meet is amazing, they're all so nice and the places are amazing, but I just think I need to come home.' She's gabbling now. 'I know it's going to cost a bit and I'm really sorry, but I've found a really reasonable flight in about three weeks' time and I know someone who's going to be on it. You don't know them but they're really nice and I think it would be so much better to travel back with someone else. So I could travel back with them and I think that would be better, just so much better than flying on my own.'

'Hold on Elles, slow down. What's going on? Just explain it to me again. It's only a few weeks after that you're booked onto a flight home anyway. Is no one else coming home then?'

'No, not anymore.'

'Are you trying to tell me you don't feel you can manage a flight back on your own?'

'I think I might be,' she says in a small voice.

I wait.

'I've got so good at distracting myself, by doing things. And I've always got people around me. And I've done it so much that I find it really hard now if I do end up on my own.'

'Is this about Sam, Elles? Is that what you're trying to avoid?'

'I think it is. It's got to the point now where I'm actually scared of being on my own in case I think of him. So when I am I just start to panic and then I sink into this awful black hole and I don't know how to get myself out. I just feel so bad, the panic's horrible and I can't stop crying and I can't breathe and I need someone there, cos if not ...'

'Oh Elles,' I say, 'you, poor, poor thing.'

We talk on until she's calmer.

'Let me speak to Dad about it and then I'll let you know. The thing is Elles I'm happy for you to come home early, of course I am, but this thing of not being able to be alone, do you think you're ready to try to do something about that now? It's just a defence Ellie, against the awful pain of losing Sam, but you can't keep on avoiding it. I mean you're doing well, in lots of ways. People find much more destructive ways of avoiding pain; drink, drugs, self-harm, so it could be a whole lot worse, but you're going to have to face it all at some point. You can't keep on running away from it. I just need you to acknowledge that.'

'I know,' she says. 'I know I'm running away and I need to stop. I've been running away from everything, I just don't know how to stand still anymore.'

It's painful to hear her admit this. It's what I've been scared of. I've tried so hard to face up to the pain of his death myself, and part of me has been hoping she would be able to do the same. But it's a lot to ask of anyone, let alone someone so young.

'You'll find a way Norbie. I know you will.'

6 July 2014

IN THE EARLY and mid-1990s I used to take the children ice-skating every Thursday evening. We all loved it, especially Sam, who tore round the rink like an out of control missile. The girls and I took lessons. Sam didn't bother.

In my dream I'm back at the rink. I'm excited. But

when we go inside, everything has changed. Nothing is as it used to be. And there are crowds and long queues everywhere. It's overwhelming. I've never felt less sure of what I should be doing.

I am wearing knee-length black socks. A woman tells me crossly that only white socks will be allowed. She sends me to the back of a long queue to buy them. When finally I reach the front another woman wordlessly hands me a huge pair of black boots, too big for my feet, with unwieldy plastic soles and trailing laces. I try to explain about the white socks but she ignores me and moves on to the next person.

I don't know what to do, where the girls are. Suddenly everyone sets off in the same direction so I fall in with them without knowing where I'm going. Then at my side, an old friend appears. As we walk on, the crowd gradually thins and I find myself alone with her on a long, wide walkway running parallel to the edge of a vast ravine. It reminds me of the bridge over the river at Pai. It has open, wooden slats which shift and sway with every step. There's no handrail. To our left is a series of wooden slatted pathways each stretching out from the edge of the ravine towards the walkway but stopping two or three feet short. Between them and to our right is a void; both bottomless and horizonless. At the other end of each pathway I see solid ground: coarse green grass and dark brown earth, the skeleton silhouettes of trees.

We walk on and on for miles. The walkway sways unpredictably beneath us. I'm too scared to try to make it onto one of the pathways. My friend reassures me. It's the only way back onto solid ground.

I brace myself as I stand there, aware of the void beneath me, of the terrifying drop. I make myself look down into it and then I leap.

I make it.

But immediately the landscape changes from peaceful countryside to the bedlam of busy, city streets. An open-top, red double-decker bus comes careering around the corner and from the top deck one of my sisters calls down that she needs my help. She's in obvious distress. 'It's a disaster,' she shouts, 'a catastrophe!' I imagine the worst: another death in the family.

Her voice comes again over the rumble of traffic, 'My Aga has broken down.' My friend steps in, shouting names and contact numbers for engineers as the bus drives off. We walk on through milling streets and though I feel daunted by the bustle of the city it feels manageable with her at my side.

The dream lingers in my mind when I get up. As I head downstairs, I pass Sam's open bedroom door. I glance in and see his empty bed.

His absence hits me like a physical blow.

I step into his room and find myself saying out loud, 'How can it be that you're never coming back, Sam? How can it be that I will never see you again?'

Downstairs, in the kitchen, I sink onto the sofa and

sob: for his lost life, for mine that must go on. And for the seeming impossibility of reconciling the two.

I think of the dream. The shaky wooden walkway is my current life, so fragile and unpredictable. I'm trying to negotiate a way forward without falling into the abyss of grief. I'm aware of the possibility of a future that's more stable and predictable. But the only way to get there is on one of the pathways and that means facing the abyss before I cross. I must negotiate that open gap, the wound of loss and all the pain that comes with it. I must feel the terror of a future without Sam before I try to re-engage with life.

Perhaps that's why I leave his bedroom door open. It's like looking into the gap over the abyss. I need to face the reality of his death in order to move forward. It would be so much easier to close the door and avoid being confronted by his absence, but it would be too soon to leave the walkway.

It seems that Ellie needs to find a way of staying on it, of bearing the discomfort of grief, the waves of loss and pain that feel too much. She's made a leap onto solid ground without truly facing the extent of her loss and, as a result, that seemingly solid ground threatens constantly to open up and send her plunging into the blackness of the abyss. She needs to start facing the death of Sam.

There is so much about loss and grief in the dream: how everything changes, nothing is as it was before. I was returning to a familiar place with the girls, but without Sam. How could it possibly feel the same? And in there too is all the disorientation of grief, the not-knowing where you're going, what you're meant to do or feel, whether you're doing it right, the sense of dislocation from a world in which others still know the rules. And when you step back into life, back onto seemingly solid ground, everything has changed, peaceful countryside has become a busy city and there you are confronted by others' lives moving forward, filled with normal cares and anxieties. You have to find a way to negotiate all that as well.

The friend who appeared at my side, walked with me and helped me to cross the void, was an old friend I hadn't seen for perhaps ten years before Sam died. Yet she and her daughter were there at his funeral. As I sat waiting for the service to begin, she came and touched me on my shoulder. Her eyes were filled with tears. She didn't say anything. She didn't need to. Hers was an unobtrusive presence on the walkway, but a vital one that gave me strength. I think she represented kindness and the healing power of others who are prepared to share your pain.

7 July 2014

PADDY AND I go for an early walk. The sky is shot with streaks of apricot cloud, a heron sits hunched and brooding in a tree. There's a flash of blue as a kingfisher darts across the water, a marbled white butterfly soaks up the early sun. I feel the beauty in it all. It touches me despite the ache of sadness.

On our return I walk out to the 'cottage' in the garden where I work – a small one-storey red-brick building built by an earlier owner nearly two hundred years ago. I'm seeing clients again today after a two-month break. It seems strange to be back in such a familiar space and yet one I've barely set foot in recently. I sit down in my chair, feet straight out in front of me, one hand on each arm. I breathe deeply, trying to ground myself, to bring myself into the room so that I will be entirely present for my clients. They know that someone in my family died unexpectedly two months ago. They don't know it's my son. They don't need to be burdened with that.

The break will have been hard for them, for some especially so, those for whom neglect and abandonment are part of their story. I may be punished for my un-scheduled absence, for my disloyalty and betrayal of their trust in me, for having a life of my own which impinges on their relationship with me. They are entitled to be upset with me. I've let them down. Therapy is all about reliability and trust. I should be available to my clients when I've said I will be. However much they can rationalise what's happened, they are entitled to feel let down on an emotional level. These are the feelings I must help them to work through now.

By the end of the day I'm shattered. But I'm glad to have started seeing my clients again – I've missed them – and to be reminded of their resilience. Most of all I'm relieved to have discovered that I could be present for each of them, that once in my working space I could put my own life to one side.

***

I'd always thought things might get easier after you went into hospital that first time, Sam, that you might finally understand that it wasn't just Dad and me who felt something was wrong. We knew it would be hard for you, but I don't think I'd allowed myself to think about just how devastated you would be. It was simply too painful for me to face.

I'm sorry.

It's still hard for me to think about, especially your disbelief about our role in your being sectioned: the very people who should have been on your side, should have protected you, should have understood, but seemingly turned against you. You knew there was nothing wrong with you. How could you hope to make the world listen if even your own family wouldn't? It must have been terrifying.

Rosy and I came to see you the next morning. We knew you'd be angry. I think Rosy was scared but she wanted to support you and she didn't want me to be on my own. In your mind it put her into the enemy camp with me and Dad. It took you a long time to forgive her.

On the ward a wall-mounted television blared out a reality TV show at full volume. In front of it, chairs were set out in a straight line, an identical row directly opposite them. There was no privacy. We went instead to a games room with an empty billiard table and table football; sat on one of three uncomfortable plastic sofas lined up against the wall and waited for you to appear.

You were angry when you did.

'I shouldn't be here,' you said. 'It's absolutely ridiculous. There is nothing wrong with me. You've betrayed me. I just can't believe anyone would do that to their son. I mean what's wrong with you. I have friends, many, many friends. I'm a philosopher. I got an A in my philosophy AS, a B in my A2. I did them both in just one year. I say again, just one year. I mean I did that. Do you not realise that your son is a philosopher, a historian? I've studied history, I've studied English. I'm very very optimal in all I do. I shouldn't be here. I don't belong here.'

Other patients came and went as you shouted. Two stopped to observe the unfolding scene.

'He's posh,' one said, shaking his head in admiration. 'Listen to his voice.'

'I know,' said the other, 'and listen to what he's saying. He's clever too, you can tell.' He turned directly to you. 'Are you a professor?' he asked.

You were diverted for a moment, even a little bit flattered. But then another patient spoke from the neighbouring sofa. She was lying, hoodie pulled up over her head, curled in a foetal position with her back to the room. She spoke to the wall. 'You may be posh,' she said, 'but you can learn something from a lot of the people in here.'

You ignored her. You weren't about to take a lesson from anyone on a psychiatric ward. But in the end, she was proved right. You did, in time, learn to value many of the people you met. But you certainly weren't ready to then.

You tried to make us understand that you simply shouldn't be there, your frustration and disbelief palpable. There was nothing we could say, just that we were sorry and we loved you and we understood the way you felt. But there was nothing we could do to make it any better. Rosy had brought in a whole bag of things for you including a book she thought you might find interesting. You were furious, incredulous that she could even think for one moment that you'd be interested in a book when you were facing this travesty.

You were standing up now, pacing the room. You pleaded and ranted in turn. Confusion and desperation suddenly overwhelmed you. You started to cry silently, turning your face to the ceiling, trying to hide your distress as you fought back tears. It was the saddest thing I'd ever seen. Then for a moment your frustration overcame you. You stretched your arms high in the air, stood on the tips of your toes and leapt towards me, snarling, as if to strike. I didn't flinch or step back. I understood and felt the pain of your powerlessness and confusion.

You didn't hit me. I knew you wouldn't. Instead, at the last moment, you brought your hands together, clapping them loud and hard just millimetres from my face.

I can't imagine how much it took to pull yourself back from the brink of breakdown. In all the indignities that you were forced to suffer, this was the only time I saw you come close to really losing control of yourself. And, in that split second of mastering your emotions you managed to hold onto something of the essence of you. It was an extraordinary feat. I'm not sure I could have done it. And in that moment, I saw so many aspects of you that I loved: your stoicism, your innate sense of right and wrong, your gentleness, your capacity to do the right thing, your remarkable bravery. It was all there.

It broke my heart. It will have broken Rosy's too.

***

10 July 2014

IT'S THE END of my first working week since Sam died. I'm exhausted, but relieved. I've found myself able to engage fully with each of my clients, to focus on them despite my grief. It's what I did too through the difficult days of Sam's illness. I discovered I could put what was happening in my own life to one side, focus on other lives, on problems beyond my own, and that actually there was relief in that for me. It saved me from feeling somehow singled out for difficulty. It helped me keep my own challenges in perspective.

Very occasionally Sam crossed paths with my clients, despite the huge notice I'd Blu-tacked to the back door saying when the garden was out of bounds. Once I glanced out of the window as I stood up at the end of the session to see my client out. We'd focused almost exclusively on her worries about one of her sons. I was horrified to see Sam, unkempt and wild-haired, moving down the lawn on hands and knees in a slow, exaggerated crawl. He was trying to avoid being seen – hence the crawl – but he could not have looked odder. The sun was behind him, illuminating his leonine dreadlocks. He was looking towards my consulting room when my client, reading something in my face, followed the direction of my gaze and looked straight at him. She looked back at me as if waiting for an explanation. I smiled and shook my head. 'Don't even ask,' I said. She laughed as she replied, 'I'm glad it isn't only me then.'

It's been hard not to be free to think about Sam. I've consciously had to stall my feelings. I hope I'm not creating a tidal wave of stored-up grief to engulf me later on. Sometimes clients have come to see me many years after the death of someone close to them, wondering why they're depressed or anxious or simply not coping with life. So often it takes them time to recognise that behind it all lies a loss they haven't truly faced.

After supper I go and sit at my computer, open two photos of Sam and gaze at them as I listen to the recording of him reading. I hear a keening sound; an awful, animal cry. It fills the room. It's me.

I am overwhelmed by the feeling that I failed him in some way, that there was something I might have done to save him.

11 July 2014

IT WOULD HAVE been my father's 89th birthday today. I've missed my parents especially since Sam died. They would have grieved with me. Perhaps I'd feel less alone with them here to share my pain.

Sam loved them both. I have a photo of him on the

swing, his curly blond hair catching in the spring sunlight. He's wearing a checked shirt and green corduroy dungarees tucked into red Wellington boots. The swing hangs from a huge oak tree in the middle of the lawn, and beneath it is a swathe of bluebells in full bloom. Mum is pulling the swing back, ready to release it with a push. Sam's small hands are gripping it tightly and he's grinning wildly in anticipation.

It feels a long time since she died; seventeen years ago, after a car crash in France. She and Dad popped in to see us en route to the ferry. The children and I stood and waved them off. Sam was only five years old, Rosy seven and Ellie one. I thought it was the worst thing that would ever happen to me.

Dad survived, and lived long enough – another eight years – to know we were concerned for Sam. He'd watch him sometimes with a quizzical look that seemed to say, 'And what's going on in your head, young man?' But he never criticised.

***

Grandpa spent a lot of time with us in the years after Granny died. One evening when he'd joined us for supper – you were around seven – you appeared at the table with a hand-written list.

'Grandpa,' you asked in your piping voice. 'Do you know any swear words?'

Without waiting for his reply, you continued. 'I do. I've looked them up and I've written them down.'

You picked up the list from the table and started to read.

'Cunt' you said, 'female genitalia or a form of abuse.'

'Goodness,' Grandpa interrupted. 'You do know some interesting ones.'

Not long afterwards he took us all out to supper to meet his new lady friend. She was strangely coquettish with you. After a while she turned to you.

'People always say I don't look my age.' She ran her hand down the back of her head. 'Guess how old I am Sam.'

You looked at her appraisingly. 'About a hundred ...?' you said.

***

17 July 2014

ONE OF MY clients has been away, so it is our first session since my unscheduled break. I read my notes from our last session, thinking about our work together, asking myself what my absence might have meant to him. Later, as I write up my notes, I notice the date of our last session. The first of May. I was with him, listening to him, when my own son was dying, alone. It is a desolate moment. I am a mother who was devoting time to others when her son needed her.

In time I see other things too: the need I had then to invest in things alongside Sam, to carry on living my own life too. I had to find a way of getting through the difficulties of his illness and its impact on us all. Work was a salve and an anchor when so much of my world was crumbling. Recognising this helps me with the guilt I feel now too, for setting my grief to one side as I work with my clients. I have never had greater cause to invest in the things that hold me steady. And work is one of those. I will have to find other times to grieve and make space for those feelings. I must make sure I do. I know they deserve as much attention as anything else in my life.

19 July 2014

THERE'S A PATTERN evolving in my life without Sam. There are places I go to, and things I do, to help me reconnect with him. I need the help. It takes time for my feelings to make their way to the surface. I'm too good at presenting a coping face to the world.

Sometimes I sit at my computer and open two of my favourite photos of him. I place them side by side on the screen, and I look into the eyes that are looking straight out at me. I can remember taking both photos and for a moment, as I sit at my desk, I can almost believe that I am looking through the viewfinder of my camera into those smiling eyes, gazing with quiet calm in one image and delighted mischief in the other. At the same time, I click on the arrow in the top left-hand corner of the screen and hear the sweeping tones of violins beginning the Adagietto of Mahler's Fifth Symphony. I hear the faintest murmur of my own voice saying, 'Okay, Sam,' a few rustles and coughs from the congregation and then the crystal-clear, piping tones of his thirteen year old voice as he begins to speak at my father's funeral.

He had a beautiful voice. Even when it broke it did so gently, moving down a tone or two at a time, no squeaks or embarrassing gruffness, just a gradual transformation from the voice of a boy into that of a man. I sit and listen, tears streaming down my face.

He says the final line,

'Do not stand at my grave and cry. I am not there, I did not die.'

As his voice stills to silence I say over and over, 'But you did Sam. You did die.'

And I cry until there are no more tears. Then, when I feel calm, I bid him a silent farewell and go to face the rest of my day.

At other times I go into his room. I haven't changed anything. His desk and bedside chest are littered still with untidy piles of paper and books, old birthday cards, travel documents, papers from his time at Reading College, letters from the Jobs Agency and hospital, vitamin supplements and Pro Plus. On his bed are some of the clothes I've laundered and, at the foot, on his trunk, is a plastic bag. It contains two jumpers he wore before he left on his last trip to Thailand. I've rolled them tightly and wedged them in. I've wound the opening round and round, tucking the end underneath. I wanted them to be as air-tight as possible.

I sit on his bed and lightly touch the marks on the wall above his pillow. I trace these marks that were left by him, as though in the tracing I will bring him back to me. There's a small greenish yellow smear – dried snot, I think, as my finger lingers on it.

'Oh Sam,' I say, 'you horrible boy.'

Yet I do not take my hand away. I want to feel this small remnant.

I pull out the jumpers one by one and hold them to my face. There is the faintest trace of body odour and the eau de toilette he used to spray liberally on the jumpers to mask the smell. Tears course down my cheeks as I bury my face in the comforting smell and breathe it in greedily. I know the day will come when not even the faintest trace will remain. I don't want that day to come. I fear having even this small comfort taken from me.

And sometimes I play music: the music we played at his memorial service. Bob Dylan's, *Make You Feel My Love* and *Going Home* by Randy Newman. There's one thing I still can't bring myself to listen to: the soundtrack by Eddie Vedder for the film, '*Into the Wild.*' It's simply too painful.

During our time of watchful waiting Sam became obsessed with the film. It was a time for him of intense self-exploration, preoccupation with diet, a need for purity and even celibacy. He saw himself as an ascetic, rejecting the tawdry superficialities and excesses of first-world living. He talked often of living off the land in some remote place and identified strongly with the character in the film: a young man who, feeling he doesn't fit into the world around him, takes off alone to fend for himself in the wild. He finally decides to return home, but in a cruel twist of fate is poisoned by his final foraged meal and dies. Sam listened to the soundtrack endlessly and we played it over and over in the car on our many day trips to London. I haven't been able to listen to it since he died. It takes me back to such a desperately difficult time.

***

You left for Thailand in April 2012. It was your fourth backpacking trip. Dad and I were paralysed with fear when you said you'd booked a flight. You did it the way you always did, no discussions, no warning, just telling us.

'Oh, by the way, I'm leaving for Thailand next week. I've booked my flights.'

'Oh blimey Sam. Are you sure that's a good idea? You know that Dad and I are worried about you.'

'But worried why? It's all in your head. How many times do I have to tell you that there's nothing wrong with me? I'm happy. I've never felt better. I'm twenty. I'm going anyway, whatever you say. There's nothing you can do to stop me.'

'But can you afford it Sam? Will you have enough money to pay for everything when you get there?'

'Yep,' you said, with finality. 'I've still got some of the money Grandpa left me.'

*Of course there **were** things we could have done to stop you. We could have removed your passport or asked for some sort of medical intervention. But it was so much more complicated than that. We agonised over it, as we did every time you went off travelling. I turned things over and over in my mind. Our only objective was to keep you as safe as we could.*

Living at home kept you on a level of sorts but you were determined to travel, so we had two options: to support you in your plans and hope you would stay in touch and still see home as a safe place to return to; or take action to prevent you from leaving.

We knew that removing your passport would at best delay your departure, but then you'd be leaving from a position of suspicion towards us rather than trust and would be much less likely to stay in touch. The same if we asked for a mental health assessment and you weren't sectioned – we'd been told on various informal assessments that you probably wouldn't be. Always we returned to that loss of trust. And would stopping you travelling keep you safe anyway? What if you carried out your threat to leave home and live on the streets? We'd probably lose track of you and you might be even more at risk.

*And did we even want you to be sectioned? You weren't unhappy and derived huge pleasure still from your life. We could still see flashes of the old you. We were worried this might be lost if you were medicated against your will. But then we also knew we might be more likely to lose you if we **didn't** intervene soon. All the medical advice was that early intervention and anti-psychotic medication would result in a better prognosis. But we were probably too late for that anyway. We'd been trying to get you help for more than a year but with no result other than a negative impact on our relationship. And then again, all the literature said that slow-onset symptoms like yours had a worse prognosis than a quick-onset presentation, so perhaps none of it was really in our control.*

And we worried what it would it do to you to be forcibly detained and medicated, that it would be more damaging to you and how you felt about yourself and your life, than simply letting you be; that perhaps it was better to let you have your freedom and do what you wanted to do, whatever the consequences might be.

And what about your – perhaps unrealistic – plans to enrol on a drama course later in the year? You had an interview later in the week. Your travel plans were built around the course. If we pulled the plug on the travelling, you would almost certainly retaliate by ditching the course. And what would you do if you didn't go travelling and didn't go to college …? Just carry on leading the incredibly reduced life you were?

But – and it was such a big but – if you went travelling would you be safe? We couldn't know. You'd been away three times and always made it home, but you were incredibly vulnerable then: tending towards paranoia in times of stress, unable to connect with people and quite likely to upset someone with your odd behaviour. And you were reckless and oblivious to danger. We knew we'd never forgive ourselves if you went and came to harm. But then again, if we stopped you going, you'd almost certainly have left to live on the streets, which would be just as dangerous.

It was so incredibly complex that I went round and round in circles. I began to understand the phrase "being beside oneself" with worry.

The night before you were due to leave, you ate supper with us. Afterwards you asked if we could talk, just you and me. We sat down together at the kitchen table. I waited for you to begin. You were agitated but making sense. You were back in my world for that evening. I could tell that your emotions were running high. I knew you needed to ground yourself before you left. You cried a lot and struggled sometimes to voice what you were feeling. You said how much you loved us but that you had to go. It was your destiny. It felt as though you were saying goodbye, that perhaps your tears were for the possibility that you might never see us and your home again.

'You know you don't have to go, Sam. You have the rest of your life to travel. There's no hurry, no pressure. The only thing you'd lose if you didn't go would be the airline ticket. I'm sure Dad and I could help with that. Money doesn't matter, Muelo, not beside happiness and wellbeing.'

You became calm. We moved into the sitting room and carried on talking. I took photos of you, lying on the sofa in your soft grey T-shirt and dark plaid pyjama bottoms with your black eye almost faded but the small cut on your cheek bone – from the evening when your light shone too brightly – still glistening red. You let me take the photos. So often you wouldn't. It was your gift to me.

'Don't make a decision now, Sam. Give yourself time to reconsider. Something's bothering you about going. Trust that. It's an instinct. We have to pay attention to our instincts. Don't feel you have to go darling. We'd love you to stay. Just think about it, sleep on it and see how you feel tomorrow morning.'

You were up before me, waiting in the kitchen with your rucksack packed. I knew immediately you weren't going to change your mind. When I got home after seeing you off at the airport I sat down and wept. That evening, after everyone had gone to bed, I went into my study and listened to the Eddie Vedder soundtrack over and over again. I played it into the early hours of the morning, and I wept uncontrollably for you. I feared I might never see you again.

You did return. It was agony for us while you were away, but not for you. Your travels gave you an identity and something to draw on both in the long months in hospital which followed, and afterwards. When people asked you about yourself and what you'd been doing since you left college, as they inevitably did, you were able to talk about taking an extended gap year. It gave you something to hold onto, an achievement, something with which you could counter the misery and humiliation of being hospitalised against your will.

Did we do the right thing then? Did we do the right thing in April two years later, when we faced exactly the same dilemma?
    I still don't know the answer to either question.

***

21 July 2014

I FEEL TIREDNESS like I've never before known. It isn't

lack of sleep. Now that the worst has happened, I sleep surprisingly well. It was anxiety that woke me in the past. But in my waking hours I feel tired to my core. I feel it in my bones but it probably starts in my head. It's the tiredness of grief. Sometimes I feel as though I'm drowning in sadness. It doesn't come in waves anymore; it's more like an under-swell that rises up and pulls me down into a dark place of sorrow. Only the strength of the pull varies. The sorrow is always there.

Many things can trigger a pull: a young man sitting on a bench outside a pub, a trip out on the boat, the grassy central reservation on the A4, a gesture as someone tugs at the shoulder of their T-shirt or moves their arm in a Sam-like way, a Tesco's carrier bag, an article in the paper about Fever Tree tonic water, a bottle of soy sauce, the sight of a Pizza Express restaurant, the mention of a music festival Sam once went to, a walk we used to do, someone cupping their cigarette with their hand, the large Bialetti expresso maker, a box of chilli flakes. The list is endless.

We go for the day to Bristol, to see Rosy performing at HarbourFest, an open-air festival. It's bright and warm. We sit in the sunshine being entertained by acrobats and trapeze artists on the Cirque Bijou stage. Simon and Imogen come with us, and we meet up with three of Rosy's old school friends and Rosy herself after her performance. We have spicy lamb kebabs and skinny chips and beer and cider from a small local brewery. I enjoy it. But Sam's absence is with me for every moment. I feel it in a visceral way. It's now a part of me.

Nicholas Wolterstorff describes himself as 'one who has lost a child,' an identity which is with him forever. I feel the same. It feels immutable. Something has changed in the very essence of me. Having children and being a mother has defined me more than any other element of my life. Now that I'm a mother who has lost a child, another strata has been added to the complex geology of who I am.

22 July 2014

IT'S EXACTLY THREE months since I last saw Sam. I feel a rush of anger towards the number 22 as I write the date on my client notes. It used to have happy associations for me – the day on which he was born, his lucky number – but now it has painful ones. It's the age he was when he died, the date in April when he flew off to Thailand, the date in June when he should have returned. More of his synchronicity. For me it's a number which sits now alongside loss and heartache.

In the afternoon there's a knock on the door and I'm handed a large, thick envelope. It's from Prospect Park Hospital and contains Sam's medical notes. I've asked to see them so that I can remind myself of the timeline of his illness. I want to know the exact dates of his admissions, so that I can put into order things that are jumbled in my mind. But now that they've arrived, I'm frightened to read them. It isn't fear of discovering something new and shocking which stops me opening the envelope. It's something more mundane than that. I'm scared to read about Sam's daily life on the ward. I'm scared it will take me to new depths of sorrow to see his life – which once held so much promise – reduced to a daily log of incidents and behaviours. I'm scared of seeing it all in black and white. I'm scared that within what I read there may be nuances of disrespect or a lack of understanding. I can't bear the indignity of it for him: to have had his life become the property of others, to have lost his right to self-determination and to have his responses recorded and analysed. It feels so wrong. I don't want to have to face all that.

The sealed packet marked PRIVATE AND CONFIDEN-TIAL sits all day on the desk in my study. Unopened.

25 July 2014

I FINALLY OPEN it. I start reading in the morning and I sit down again just before our neighbours arrive for supper. It's a mistake to read them then. One entry I read is devastating, but I have no opportunity to process it before they arrive. I simply have to carry on.

They leave at 1am. Immediately the tears rise up and spill over, splashing onto the plates I'm carrying to the kitchen.

They gather on my glasses, obscuring my vision. I have no choice but to stop and allow myself to face it. I need to see again what is written in the notes.

I pick up the heavy folder. In the section called "Progress Notes" there's a record of a conversation between Sam and a member of the Urgent Care Team who were visiting daily to monitor him taking his medication. It was entered at 10.13am on 23 October 2012, ten weeks after his discharge from hospital following his first sectioning. The entry describes him saying 'that his mother had lost all faith in him,' which was, 'affecting him to such a degree that he sounded sad rather than irritated/hostile.' This jumps out at me. Sam only did hostility with psychiatric staff, never sadness. He wouldn't have wanted to give them the satisfaction of that. The date jumps out at me too. 23 October 2012 seems familiar. And then I remember why. It was the day on which he tried to kill himself. The day he took an air rifle and shot it seven times at point-blank range into his throat.

It is devastating to think he believed that I'd 'lost all faith in him', and that this might have been part of his decision to try to end his life.

***

It was five days earlier, 18 October 2012, that things started to unravel. I was already in bed when Ellie started shouting for me at just after 11pm. Paddy was away and you'd gone out for the evening. I hated it when you went into Reading or Henley, but I couldn't stop you. It was three months since you'd left hospital after your first admission and you told me you were still taking your medication.

'Mum, Mum come quickly, please. There's something going on outside, there's shouting and I think I can hear Sam's voice.'

I pulled on my dressing gown and ran outside. There was a group of youths standing on the side of the street opposite the house. Amongst them I recognised the young man who regularly caused trouble in the village. He was part of the gang who sometimes made life uncomfortable for you. It started with insults and shoves – off the pavement or into a hedge – but when you were sixteen they'd set on you as you walked home from the station and punched you several times in the face. The police said they'd assaulted several people that evening.

You were standing in the road, yelling at them, accusing them of having attacked you. The group simply stood on the pavement opposite our house. They wouldn't leave and you wouldn't come in. You kept running across the road and squaring up to them. You had a phone in your hand. You'd dialled 999 and were talking to the police. You were overwrought. It was hard to know what you were trying to say.

I heard the voice down the phone, 'Is there anyone there with you Sam?'

'My Mum's here now,' *you said.*

'Can we have a quick word with her?' *I heard.*

I moved slightly further away. I knew what was coming.

'Does your son have mental health problems?' *the voice asked.*

It felt like a betrayal when I said yes.
They said they were on their way.

The stand-off continued. The longer it went on the more overwrought and less coherent you became. You'd been attacked at Henley station, God was on your side, justice would prevail. You crossed the road, went back again and took up position right in front of the gang. You were shouting and screaming now. I went with you, trying to calm you down, trying to prevent things from escalating, simply asking you very quietly to come back to the house with me, where we could sort everything out.

I asked the gang to leave. They wouldn't. I was there with you for ten or fifteen minutes, trying to calm you down. Out of the corner of my eye I could see Ellie in the front garden, just inside the gate, crying, on the phone. You began verbally to attack me. You said you hated me, that you were going to kill me.

The leader of the gang stepped forward in indignation. 'Don't you talk to your Mum like that,' he said. 'Do that again and I'll knock you into next week.'

I turn towards him, pleading. 'Please, please can't you just get going. Please. It's not helping, your being here. Please just leave me to deal with this.'

Perhaps they sensed the weary desperation in my voice or perhaps it was the distant wail of an approaching siren. They left.

By now you were walking up and down in the middle of the road, arms held aloft. You were looking up to the sky, appealing incoherently to some higher being. Neighbours appeared. Ellie was still crying.

Finally you agreed to come home.

We were walking in through the gate as the police arrived. Dad pulled in behind them. You were still ranting, incoherent.

We all went inside. The male policeman was so gentle with you Sam, sensitive to your heightened emotional state, so careful in how he spoke to you. The female was awful. Brusque, impatient, demanding that you answer questions when clearly you weren't able to. They wanted to take you back to Prospect Park there and then. I asked them not to. I wanted you to feel that the police were your protectors, not your enemies. I promised to get in touch with your case worker in the CMHT first thing.

Suddenly, it was all too much for Ellie. She started to hyperventilate. It had never happened before. Dad stayed with you while I took her upstairs and tried to calm her down. I don't know when, but later I heard the front door close as the police left. I could hear you and Dad talking and then you coming up the stairs.

I tried to get to sleep.

At 4am the ear-piercing shriek of the smoke alarm woke me. A smell of burning filled the house: smoke was coming up the stairs. Ellie ran out of her bedroom. You weren't in yours. The smoke grew thicker in the hallway and in the kitchen. Flames were licking out of the cooker from under the grill – a whole halloumi cheese, still in its plastic wrapper, and alight.

I managed to get it into the sink, extinguish the flames and turn off the red-hot grill.

You were on the floor next to the cooker, curled up on your side in a foetal position. I couldn't rouse you, but you were breathing. The stench was terrible. I opened all the doors and windows and took Ellie back to bed. I got your duvet, carried it downstairs and draped it over you. I pulled out a chair and sat at the small pine table in the kitchen, close to where you lay. I waited. I wasn't sure for what, but I couldn't leave you.

It was the loneliest of vigils.

At 6 am you began to stir. You were calm now, placid and malleable. You agreed to go up to bed.

I managed to get an appointment that day with your community psychiatrist. She tried to persuade you to go into Prospect Park on a voluntary basis. You refused. You admitted that you'd stopped taking your medication some weeks earlier.

'It makes me feel half dead,' you said.

She suggested a change of medication and daily visits for two weeks from the Urgent Care Team to ensure you were taking it. As soon as we got home you went onto the computer to look up the new medication, Olanzapine. I'd never seen you so low. You read out all the side-effects: weight gain, headache, dizziness and drowsiness. Feeling tired or restless. Memory problems. Stomach pain, constipation, loss of bladder control. Back pain, pain in your arms or legs. Numbness or tingly feeling. Breast swelling and discharge in women and men. Dry mouth. You went on to forums and read blogs.

'I'll be dead within ten years if they force me to take it,'
you said.

It was five days later that you tried to kill yourself

26 July 2014

I CRIED MYSELF to sleep last night. I'm awake early trying to process what I read last night. It's unbearable to think Sam felt I'd given up on him. I can't escape the feeling that I must be to blame for his suicide attempt. All morning it haunts me. Everything feels black and hopeless. I'm in a long narrow tunnel with no light, and bizarrely I have no desire to find a way out. I *want* to bathe in its murky gloom, to plunge headlong into the darkness of failure and loss, visiting and re-visiting my failings as a mother. The deeper I sink, the harder it becomes to function. I find myself unable to make decisions about even the smallest things, whether I want to sit inside or outside, stay at home or go out, have a coffee or tea, accept an invitation to drinks in the evening or not.

Finally, I make myself stop and think. What do I need right now?

I need to get out, to clear my mind.

I'm crying when I leave the house with Sigmund. As we cross the small railway bridge past the church, I think of my walk here just two days ago; how I stood on the bridge and waved at the train-driver, as I used to with the children, and felt that old familiar surge of pleasure when he waved in return and tooted as he swept beneath me. It seems another life, another world. I could no sooner think of waving at a train than walking to the North Pole.

After a while we turn off the road and head across a ploughed field, dry and dusty after all the sunshine of the past few months. There are no signs of life, just bare earth, fractured into deep cracks across the footpath. It feels appropriately desolate.

I think as I walk. I talk to Sam and tell him again and again that I never lost faith in him. Not ever. I keep on walking and thinking. Something eases in me. I see hedgerows bursting with summer flowers, thistles exploding into tufts of silk-soft down. I arrive at the railway bridge and hear a train approaching. I run, with Sig in surprised pursuit, and arrive just in time to wave and receive an answering wave and toot.

Later, on re-reading the medical notes I see other things too written in the notes: Sam's general hostility and irritation, his lack of faith in the medical profession, who do not listen to him, his belief that the medication is poisoning him and will lead to his death from cancer within ten years. I think about the events leading up to the day he tried to kill himself: the fight, the involvement of police and the community mental health team, changes onto stronger anti-psychotic medication with yet worse side-effects, and the feeling that the net was closing in on him once again. I wasn't responsible for any of that.

And most importantly I remember that seven hours after the Urgent Care team's visit, Sam came to find me after my last client left. He was lovely: lucid, calm, warm, affectionate. He stayed and chatted for almost an hour. We talked about what he wanted and the things he might do. He said he wanted to travel and do a massage course. We talked about friendship and family and the things that matter in life. We talked about all that had happened to him; about the family's concerns for his wellbeing and his hospital admission. He said that although he believed we'd made the wrong decisions and had been mistaken in many ways, he didn't blame us for that; he forgave us. I told him that probably we had made mistakes but that everything we'd ever done had been done with love in our hearts. We held each other for a long time in a tight hug.

He went into Ellie's room later that evening to say goodnight to her. He phoned Rosy in Bristol. He tried to call Simon. We realised afterwards that he was saying his goodbyes. They were loving goodbyes.

***

*I understand why you might have felt I'd lost faith in you Sam. It's because you never understood that you were ill. It must have been bewildering that Dad and I persisted in telling you that you were, when you **knew** there was nothing wrong with you.*

*You **knew** because – like fifty percent of everyone diagnosed with schizophrenia – you had anosgonosia, and it prevented you from having any insight into what was happening to you. It's a strange condition – perhaps the cruellest symptom of all – and means that although someone has clear clinical symptoms, they are entirely unaware of them. The name comes from Ancient Greek: 'a' – without, 'nosos' – disease, 'gnosis' – knowledge. It was originally used in relation to certain stroke victims who, despite losing movement in one half of their body, didn't know they had a disability. It wasn't that they were in denial or being difficult, they just weren't able to know it because of where the stroke had occurred in their brains.*

I've read up about schizophrenia and recent research into anosognosia in psychiatric disorders that uses neuroimaging to see what's happening in the brain. It reveals differences in the part of the brain responsible for self-awareness and self-analysis between people with schizophrenia and those without. Other studies suggest that these parts of the brain responsible for self-awareness are often amongst the first to be affected by schizophrenia. I've always thought that profound changes must have been taking place in your brain. How else to explain the strangeness of your behaviour? I knew that schizophrenia always strikes in late adolescence and early adulthood, and that its incidence – one in a hundred – remains constant worldwide. But I didn't know about anosognosia. And as soon as I did everything made sense.

So I do understand that without any insight into what was happening to you it was an entirely rational response for you to resist medical intervention and treatment, to question our motives, to feel that we had lost faith in you; even to question our love for you. How else could you make sense of it? You knew us to be understanding, open-minded parents. You'd seen us support Rosy in her decision to leave her medical degree after three years and go to circus school instead. Yet we weren't supporting you in the choices you were making. I would have felt the same. I wish I could have told you that, but I don't think it would have helped.

You never reached the point of achieving insight the hard way: by repeated psychotic episodes and hospitalization, over and over again and over so many years that even you might have come to see yourself as ill. I'm not sure I would have wished that for you. I never ever wanted you to stop being the quirky, challenging, endlessly entertaining individual you were. I just wanted you to be safe. That was why I wanted you to get help. That was the only reason.

Because in the end, you stopped knowing how to look after yourself, how to keep yourself safe in a world that didn't understand you and that you didn't understand. Of course, the greatest irony of all is that you actually became a greater danger to yourself once you were being medicated. Because in your view you were being poisoned for no reason. And that wasn't a life you wanted. That was why you attempted suicide that time. I understood.

***

27 July 2014

ELLIE ARRIVES HOME from her travels. As we walk back through Terminal 4 to the car park, she slips an arm around my shoulder and says she's sorry that it's only her returning; not Sam. I pull her close and say that I couldn't be happier about her being home, that Sam's a separate thing altogether. I'm not sure she believes me.

Rosy drives back from Bristol, as a surprise. It's lovely to see their excitement at seeing one another. But having them both home is hard too. Sam should be here with us. I feel more acutely than ever the pain of there being two rather than three, of there being daughters but no son.

29 July 2014

I STILL FORGET sometimes that he is dead. It happened yesterday when someone mentioned a consultant at Prospect Park leaving. I hope that's not James, I thought, before I realised that it didn't matter to us now. I felt myself falter psychically as I remembered. I had to give myself a moment to re-calibrate my world once again.

I come across Michael Rosen's poem:

> *don't tell me that I mourn too much*
> *and I won't tell you that you mourn too much*
> *don't tell me that I mourn too little*
> *and I won't tell you that you mourn too little*
> *don't tell me that I mourn in the wrong place*
> *and I won't tell you that you mourn in the wrong place*
> *don't tell me that I mourn at the wrong time*
> *and I won't tell you that you mourn at the wrong time*

don't tell me that I mourn in the wrong way
and I won't tell you that you mourn in the wrong way

I may get it wrong, I will get it wrong, I have got it
 wrong
but don't tell me

I think of the things people say, intending to help: "*don't let yourself get too down,*" and "*perhaps you're spending too much time thinking about Sam,*" or "*give me a call and we can go out and do something nice.*" It feels as though they're telling me not to grieve. I ignore them. They aren't me. I'm grieving my way. It's the only way I know.

Even when loss is shared, grief is a solitary process. Simon, Rosy, Ellie and I – despite the moments of coming together to compare feelings and memories – are each engaged in our own journey. We respond to different triggers, find different meanings, experience different moments of calm or storm. We're powerless to do anything other than plod along grief's path in our own time, at our own pace and in our own way. It would be much less lonely if there were a choreographer on hand to oversee the whole; to ensure matching descents and ascents, to create a harmony of pain or hope, rather than the clashing reality of difference.

You can't chart grief's course, nor predict its length, nor set the moment where one stage will pass into the next. It isn't a linear process, but a constant moving backwards and forwards and backwards again. We can manipulate it to some degree, as I do, with my conscious decisions not to 'go there' on my working days when I need to focus on clients; and on the days that I open myself up to its raw power by listening to music or Sam's voice. But it's largely its own master, neither to be hurried nor slowed.

For me it also seems to have developed an inverse reality. In the very early days and weeks the good days were those when I could function without being overwhelmed, and the bad days were those when I could think of nothing other than Sam and my loss. But now I think of the 'bad' days as 'good' days and vice versa. The 'bad' days help me move forward with my grief, whereas the 'good' days fail to.

Perhaps the real difference between then and now is that now I can think and process. Then it was all I could do to survive.

***

You tried to kill yourself on 23 October 2012, five days after the fight. Not because you were depressed or desperate and felt you couldn't go on, but because you thought your new antipsychotic medication would kill you anyway. You waited until we'd all gone to bed, pulled down the ladder to get into the loft and climbing up there found, hidden away, the air-rifle you'd had as a teenager. You took it with you over to the cottage, lay down on the floor in the bathroom, loaded the gun and fired it into your throat at point blank range. You re-loaded it and discharged it another six times, moving the gun a centimetre or two round your throat each time. Then you crawled through into the bedroom, climbed onto the bed and waited to die.

But you didn't. You came round five hours later. I woke at 5am to find you standing in our bedroom doorway in intense pain.

A voice I didn't recognise was saying, 'Mum, I need you. Can you come please?'

I couldn't take in what was happening. Your voice was raspy and strangled. I swung my legs out of bed and moved towards you in the half-light. The first thing I saw was the blood. It was everywhere; great rivulets of blood, all over your face, in your hair, all down your clothes; red and fresh in places, dried and crusted in others, streaks and splashes in every shade of red, maroon and black. Next I saw your neck. It was swollen to the girth of a tree trunk. Your face had lost all definition. You had no jawline.

I simply couldn't make sense of what I was seeing. My brain seemed to be registering a series of disparate factors, but it couldn't turn it into a coherent whole.

'What happened, Sam? What happened?'

I heard a voice speaking but again it didn't sound like yours.

'Mum, I tried to kill myself. I shot myself with my air-rifle.'

You were dazed and barely intelligible. Still I couldn't take in what you were saying or what I was seeing. Instead of doing anything, I was asking you questions: how, why, where? I was looking for the entry wounds on your neck. I couldn't see any because of the blood and the swelling. It was as if I didn't believe you. Where had you got the gun from?

Did we even have it still?

Suddenly a light snapped on and Paddy's voice cut through. 'Gill, call an ambulance. You have to call an ambulance.'

I can understand the disbelief now. My mind was attempting to protect itself from trauma. By suspending belief it gave itself the chance to build a barrier between itself and reality, a protective membrane, through which the reality could seep gradually, a slow dawning rather than a flood, a trickle rather than a surge. I'm grateful now for that disbelief. It kept me safe, intact, psychically. I couldn't bear to believe you, to face the dreadful truth of what I was seeing. Not just the physical damage but all the layers of meaning that lay behind it: that you had wanted to die. You'd wanted to die so much that you were prepared to commit this terrible act of violence on yourself.

You, my baby, my boy.

I dialled 999. Heard my voice asking for an ambulance, telling some faceless person that my son had tried to kill himself.

'How?' they wanted to know. 'How did he try to kill himself?'

'With an air rifle,' I said. 'He shot himself.' I was overwhelmed with shame. What sort of mother did it make me?

The wait was interminable. You lay on the floor groaning, your head in my lap. Five emergency vehicles arrived at once. Afterwards, I was told why. Because of the gun, the police had to attend first.

Then I was in the ambulance with you, holding your hand. And we were rushing, blue lights flashing, siren wailing. The closest hospital wouldn't take us. The trauma was too specialised. We were directed instead to Wexham Park, a larger hospital further away. The journey seemed to take forever.

When we arrived at A & E the ambulance men asked me to go in ahead of them and register you. It was a profoundly lonely moment, waiting at that desk, waiting for the woman to look up, waiting to tell her that my beautiful boy whom I had loved unstintingly and cherished and nurtured for twenty years had shot himself again and again despite the terrible pain, because he wanted to die, because this life was not working out for him and he wanted to move on to the next.

I told her none of that.

I was composed, gave her your name and address and described what had happened, but I registered the quick little glance she gave me, the glance to see what she looks like, the mother of a boy who has tried to kill himself. I sat by your bed on an open ward in A & E. Doctors and nurses came and went, decisions were made about scans and a possible transfer to the John Radcliffe for surgery. I felt faceless, invisible and yet also marked. Branded as a mother who must have failed in some catastrophic way.

I didn't cry. We were due to have had a meeting at the CMHT that morning so, ever-dutiful, at 9am I called your key worker and explained why we couldn't be there. She gave a little gasp down the phone and burst into tears. I found myself comforting her as she cried, and apologising. 'It's just so shocking,' she said again and again.

It was only when a middle-aged nurse, trying to wash the encrusted blood from Sam's neck and body, looked up from the other side of the bed and softly asked, 'And how is Mum?' that I felt a stifled sob rise up from somewhere deep inside me and escape into the quiet of the ward. She brought me a cup of tea. It was lukewarm and milky – not my usual piping hot and black – but the kindness of the act, the feeling of being seen, of existing, restored more to me than she will ever know. That small gesture of kindness broke through my defences and allowed me to cry.

The doctors told you that you were extremely lucky to have survived. You didn't entirely agree with them, but you were prepared to accept that perhaps it hadn't been 'your time'. You had six pellets lodged in your neck and the base of your skull. You won't remember, but I do, that one had exited through your oesophagus and you'd coughed it up while we were at home, waiting for the ambulance to arrive. Miraculously, they all missed your windpipe but one was lodged against the spinal cord, another against the carotid artery, and they were all deep amongst vital nerves and blood supplies. Apart from the obvious trauma and swelling to your neck, which compromised your breathing and made your voice thin and reedy, the only immediately obvious damage was to an ocular nerve. The pupil of your right eye didn't dilate and contract and the lid drooped slightly. It recovered in time. You had scars for a while but even they faded in the end. You were disappointed when they did. You said it was your necklace of pride.

The consultant decided it was too dangerous to operate to remove the pellets, that it was safer to leave them in situ. You became more and more distressed and bad-tempered over your week in hospital because by then you'd realised they were made of lead. The thought of having a toxic substance within your body was deeply discomfiting to you. You were convinced that the lead was poisoning you.

The psychiatric team got in touch with me and said they would be carrying out another Mental Health Act assessment. The AMHP said he'd call me afterwards, probably at about 8pm, to let me know the outcome. My phone didn't ring until 10.30pm.

'I'm sorry to be calling so late,' he said. 'Sam has been sectioned but it wasn't quite as straightforward as I'd been expecting and, in the end, it wasn't an easy decision. He put up an extremely good case for the fact that he wasn't a danger to himself and didn't have a mental health problem. He argued so compellingly and was so articulate that in the end we were divided. It was hard to reach a consensus. Two of the assessors felt that he shouldn't be sectioned. But anyway, the final decision was that as soon as he's medically ready to be discharged from Wexham Park he'll be taken straight back to Prospect Park.'.

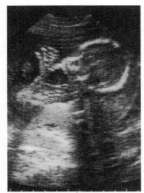

Hospital scan of Sam *in utero* –
sucking his thumb

Sam age 15 months,
May 1993

Gill and Sam sleeping, age 18 months,
August 1993

Sam age 3 with newborn Ellie, on
Simon's 35th birthday, June 1995

Sam – beyond excited – waiting for Simon to get home
from work on his 35th birthday, June 1995

Simon cuddling Sam, age 5,
summer 1997

Sam with summer freckles
age 12, 2004

Sam age 12 with Ellie 9, 2004

Mother's Day walk with Rosy and Ellie,
Sam gearing up for a dance, April 2009

Sam age 17 sharing a joke with Simon, August 2009

Sam with one of many water melons,
Sicily, July 2010

Sam lost in thought,
summer 2011

Sam and Ellie sharing a joke, early summer 2011

The green room, which Sam moved into and where
he slept on the floor, 2011

Sam, mistrustful, after the first visit
from the CMHT, 2011

Sam, home from the hospital for the
weekend, with Rosy, July 2013

Gill with Sam, July 2013

Paddy and Rosy with Sam,
hailing passing boats, July 2013

Sam with Rosy and Ellie on his 22nd birthday,
22nd February 2014

1 August 2014

I'VE COME AWAY on my own again for a couple of days. It's so new to me, this need to be alone. I'm sitting in a busy restaurant on Marine Parade in Lyme Regis, surrounded by families – children and teenagers out with their parents – on every table. It took me over five hours to get here by car. It's raining and the sea is grey under leaden skies. But none of that seems to matter. It feels right. That I'm where I need to be.

There's live music in the restaurant, a sole male singer. I like sitting here alone with a backdrop of sound and song. He strikes a chord. Grief surges up inside me. I'm grateful for it. I've found it hard to connect with Sam since I've been working again and caught up in the strong current of home and family life. It's an undertow which, however lovely, seems to keep me from him. I suspect that's why I need to come away, to be alone with him.

I wonder if I cut a sad figure, sitting here on my own, tapping away on my iPad. But, even as the thought is born and begins to takes shape, I dismiss it. I don't care what other people think. It's part of the invulnerability brought about by grief. Things that used to feel important simply cease to. The world shifted when I learned of Sam's death. There's something too about being released from the normal societal conventions and constraints I place upon myself. I remember feeling something similar when I was pregnant. I had a sense of a shield around me which protected me from some of the demands of life. I feel it now, the protective shield of being, in Nicholas Wolterstorff's words, 'one who has lost a child.' It isn't that I want to behave badly but that I'm temporarily released from the need *always* to behave well. It feels okay to put my needs first at times: a small but necessary consolation for my loss.

2 August 2014

I'M SITTING UP in bed at 6 am looking out through rain-stained windows at the beach, the Cobb and the little harbour ahead of me. A lone tractor with an orange flashing light provides the only colour and movement in a tableau of muted greys and creams as it rakes the sand. I see a pattern in its movements. Passing from right to left along the shoreline, it turns 180 degrees and back across the sand from left to right – a little further from the sea each time – before turning again and heading back to the shoreline. There's something soothing in its slow, repeated movements and the ever-increasing circle of its path.

I think of my slow, repetitive journey through grief; the visiting and re-visiting of loss, of anger, pain, guilt and regrets; of all that was, that might have been, of what was not and never now will be. This is my journey along the shoreline of grief. Just as the tractor returns repeatedly to where sea and sand meet, so must I return to that place where the pain of loss impinges on my life, until I'm truly ready to move on.

When I look up I see the orange flashing light disappearing into the narrow streets. It has completed its task. Will I ever complete the task of grieving for Sam? If so, it will not mean forgetting him. On the contrary it will mean being able to accommodate the loss of him within my life and remember him with happiness as well as pain.

***

A family appears on the beach: a small boy running in wide arcs across the sand, leaning forward with his arms behind him. He reminds me of you. I took a photo on Dad's thirty-fifth birthday while we waited for him to arrive home from work. You were three, Rosy five and Ellie just nine days old. You're standing next to a birthday cake and a bottle of champagne, your excitement spilling out of you: eyes on fire, mouth in a huge contorted grin somewhere between pleasure and pain, small hands tugging at your pyjama top and one leg raised, as if in readiness to take off round the room. Rosy is smiling sweetly into the camera as she holds you in a virtual head-lock under one arm. She is keeping you from spinning out of control. It's what she often ended up doing; not through choice but of necessity. You didn't thank her for it, but you learned to understand the love that lay behind it.

I think of the electricity of you: extravagant flares of energy – negative and positive. I wonder that the world can still turn without the electric charge of you; that I can continue to function without the pulse of you? And for the first time in days, I cry and cry for the loss of you.

***

8 August 2014

ON MY WAY home from walking Sig this morning, I look up to see, ahead of me, a young man crossing the road towards our house. He's slim, of medium height, with short hair and wearing a brownish-grey jumper and long shorts. He has a Tesco shopping bag swinging from one hand. For one moment it's Sam. My heart leaps before I can stop it. Then I remember.

But even after that, even though I know it can't be him, I desperately want it to be, and inside my head a small, insistent voice is saying over and over, 'Turn into our drive Sammy. Please turn into our drive.' I am willing him to be my son.

I lose sight of him for a moment as the road curves around the corner and then I see him again, beyond our driveway, as I knew he would be. I can see now that his gait is different from Sam's, his legs broader, but for those moments when I allowed the fantasy to continue, he was Sam. I feel as though I have lost him all over again. I sink to the ground outside the house and sob.

12 August 2014

PADDY AND I are in Wales for the week with Rosy, Ellie and Charlie. It's our first family holiday since Sam died and a replica of our last with him, last Christmas. The weather is capricious, changing in an instant from bright sunshine to torrential rain. Ellie's moods are as unpredictable.

We're going for a walk but Ellie is still in bed. She won't look at me when I go in to see her. The duvet is pulled up to her chin, the curtains closed. All is darkness and gloom. She refuses to join us. I try everything. She knows I'm trying everything. She asks me to leave her room. She wants to be alone. Her voice is flat and dull as lead.

It's warm enough to wear T-shirts. We've reached the line where the mountain begins; where bracken and heather replace grass. I glance behind me. The sky's turned black and within seconds the first raindrops are falling, big and fat. A vicious wind picks up and blows them, horizontal, into our faces. They aren't drops anymore but airborne arrows. We scrabble for our waterproofs. There's nowhere to shelter. The heather bends earthwards. We stop and turn our backs into the wind. It batters us for a few moments. Then suddenly it's spent. A sharp shaft of sunlight penetrates the clouds and lands at Rosy's feet. Charlie runs to join her on her hillside stage.

I wish Ellie were here to witness this display by the elements. I want her to know that this darkness will pass.

14 August 2014

I GO WITH Paddy to visit a little cottage that's for sale in a nearby village. My aunt has recently died and left me some money. The cottage is lovely, but I can't shake off the feeling that even thinking about it is a betrayal of Sam. I was looking at properties online when the police called me that Bank Holiday Monday. Pursuing it now seems somehow to deny the awfulness of all that happened subsequently. I'm not sure I can.

15 August 2014

ROSY, ELLIE AND Charlie demand to see the cottage too. They're outraged not to have been included on the first visit. There is an air of excitement in the car as we drive there and I can feel it beginning to infect me. We tumble through the gate and into the garden. I see it all with new eyes: the soft pennant stone in hues of smokey pinks, mauves and greys; the steep slate roof; the roses climbing the walls. I hear the song of the stream at the bottom of the garden. We go inside. I see the flag-stone floors, the exposed timbers, stone chimney breasts and the old kitchen range still in situ.

'Oh Mum,' the girls say in unison, 'do get it.'

'Please, Gilly,' chimes Charlie. 'Please, please do.'

'Sam would have loved it,' someone says.

I think it might be me.

***

Your second admission to Prospect Park was another travesty of justice. You told us often. I could understand why it wasn't clear cut when they assessed you after your suicide attempt. Your psychosis would still come and go. Often you appeared to have nothing wrong with you and at those times your ability to argue your case persuasively was extraordinary. But when you were psychotic, it was such a different story.

I could cope with your strange choices and the physical chaos of a son who didn't know how to care for himself but the hardest thing for me to bear was the feeling of not being able to make contact with you. Through all our run-ins over the years I'd always been able to reach you in the end, however upset and angry you were. I knew I could appeal to your reason and that it would, ultimately, prevail. Even when we had to agree to disagree, I always had the sense of being heard by you. I think you felt the same. Do you remember all the talks we had when you were little? We'd have them as I put you to bed, especially if we'd had a difficult day. However deep the hole was that you'd dug yourself into, I always found a way through to you.

But this was unlike anything I'd ever experienced before. I couldn't find you in there Sam. It was like knocking on the door of a room that I knew to be occupied but receiving no reply; throwing a rock into a pool, but discerning no evidence of it entering the water, seeing no ripples, hearing no splash. I came up against a sort of blankness so profound that I couldn't find a way through. It was terrible. And when you launched into one of your rambling rants about how dreadful we were, and how infinitely superior you and your way of life was to ours, I felt invisible, as though you weren't really speaking to the real me but to a me of your own creation. I didn't recognise the me you thought me to be. And I didn't recognise you. You were some stranger in my son's body. I felt I'd lost you. To be with you then was to feel a desperate and profound loneliness, for both of us. We wanted to connect. We both reached out repeatedly, but in those moments it seemed there was no place for us to meet.

21 August 2014

I DREAM OF Sam, and though I know him to be dead it doesn't seem strange to have him there with me. He's berating me for not buying him socks, despite the fact I have. And although I can see him – in the navy-blue Shetland wool sweater he once borrowed from Simon and never returned – and hear him, telling me off, I still know him to be dead. In dreams we accept, almost expect, the contradictions. It doesn't even occur to us to question them. I wish I could have been more like that with Sam in life.

23 August 2014

WE'VE COME TO Spain for a summer holiday booked before Sam died and I'm ill. It started yesterday. A really violent stomach bug. I've been up all night and Paddy has gone to the pharmacy to buy Imodium and rehydration sachets.

My phone beeps with the arrival of a text message. I really really want it to be from Sam. I want to see his name come up on the screen, to hear his news, to read his ungrammatical message with all its spelling mistakes and missing punctuation marks. I don't pick up the phone immediately. I want to pretend for just a little longer, to pretend that the possibility still exists.

As I'm writing this, I realise that yesterday was 22 August. Exactly four months since I last saw him. I hadn't realised that another whole month had passed, that it's one third of a year since he set off for Thailand. Is this why I've fallen ill? Is it my body's way of telling me, of reminding me, to slow down and let myself feel? Am I doing this right, this business of grieving? Is all this writing a good thing? Or is it just another way of avoiding the pain?

24 August 2014

WE'RE LATE ARRIVING at the airport to pick up Ellie and Katherine. They've already made their way into town by the time we get there and are standing on the pavement outside the car hire shop in a small patch of shade. Ellie is furious. She abandons her luggage on the pavement and climbs wordlessly into the car without a greeting.

27 August 2014

ELLIE HAS BEEN like a tinder box since she arrived and the tiniest spark of something not going her way – someone talking across her, a hint of criticism, her demands not being met quickly enough – can flare up into a blaze of anger, which seems to take a grip of her and burns cold and bright. She becomes strident, hectoring, unreasonable. And as it burns itself out, she sits brooding in icy, silent, self-imposed solitude until it lifts and she is back with us again. It isn't a hot anger. These aren't glowing embers fanned by passion or belief, but the cold white embers of loss and fear. They flare in an instant, burning with the intensity of magnesium, bright and raw and excluding. It's painful to see how lost and alone she is in these moments, so fragile behind this burning wall of anger and rejection, so unreachable.

I can only imagine what Ellie's feeling. Her experience of Sam's illness and death will be her own. I know there will be confusing emotions: overwhelming sadness, anger, guilt. So much of her adolescence was overshadowed by Sam's illness. How not to have resented the brother who seemed to matter more than she did? How not to feel angry with me and Simon for that? How not to have felt embarrassed and ashamed of this brother who behaved so strangely? And what of the fear she felt? Of Sam's illness, even of Sam himself after hearing him saying he would kill me. And how to make sense of all these emotions now that he is dead? I wish I could help her. But, for now, I can't.

28 August 2014

IT'S THE LAST morning of the holiday. Paddy, Katherine and I talk about walking to the little church high up above the village. Ellie's still in bed but I know she can hear us.

'Do you want to come, Nor?' I call. 'We'll wait for you to get up if you do.'

She doesn't reply. I wait a minute or two then knock on her door and go in. She's lying on her side, facing the wall, with the sheet pulled over her head. I sit down on her bed and rest a hand on the curve of her hip.

'Go without me,' she says through the sheet. 'I want to stay in bed.'

'Oh Norbie,' I say. 'I know it's hard and I'm sorry you feel so down. But do come if you can. You know you'll feel better if you do.'

'I don't want to,' she says in a voice as flat and desolate as tundra. 'I'm not going to change my mind.'

The streets are cobbled and lined with flat-roofed, whitewashed houses. Every now and then we catch a glimpse of an inner courtyard draped with bougainvillea. It's cool in the church. We each light a candle, place them at the feet of a carved wooden Virgin Mary, and then spread out among the pews. Above the statue is a vaulted ceiling of rich midnight blue with golden painted stars.

I imagine Sam up there with the stars, spinning wild and free.

As I sit in the dimness and silence, a swell of sorrow rises like an inner tide. Tears run down my cheeks for him and his too short life; for Ellie, so unreachable in her grief and anger; and for me, and all the pain I'm having to bear.

It's hard to bear our children's pain; to let ourselves see it and, at the same time, accept that we can't save them from it. It takes resilience and an understanding that this is about them, not us. All we can do is be there: be their punchbag when they need someone to punish, their comforter when they need someone to hold. And all the while we have to manage our own anxiety about whether they will find a way through.

***

Ellie's angry with you, for lots of things: for falling ill just as you were becoming the older brother she'd always dreamed of having; for dying just as she was starting to see a life for you that might work; for breaking your promise to her that you wouldn't come to harm while she was away travelling. And because it's too painful to be angry with you, she's having to direct it all at me instead.

You were so often angry with me. I remember coming to pick you up from Gatwick at the end of a Dolphin trip. Another mum had called me that morning to say she couldn't make it to the airport to collect her son and could I bring him too. I had to say yes though I knew you'd hate it. When I told you, you didn't say a word: you just narrowed your eyes at me and shook your head. Once in the car you positioned yourself so that you could see me in the rear-view mirror. Every time I looked in it you narrowed your eyes again and silently, exaggeratedly, mouthed, 'I – hate – you.' You kept it up all the way home.

I knew what you were really saying: that you'd been looking forward to being able to tell me about the trip, that you'd needed a bit of space from everyone, that you were disappointed. You just didn't have the words for that. You only seemed to have the words for anger. But I understood that underneath it all was sensitivity. You felt things so deeply, too deeply. At the Year 7 parent's evening – the first you'd been allowed to come to – our first stop was with Adam, who taught you history as well as sports.

'You're doing really well, Sam,' he said. 'I'm really pleased with how you've started to apply yourself. You've done one or two really good pieces of work this term. But sometimes, Sam, I know you could do more. You start an essay really well and then it seems as though you just give up.'

Tears sprang to your eyes. Adam saw them too. He looked surprised. I wasn't.

I've sometimes thought that I understood you too well, Sam. That it made it harder for me to parent you, made me lose sight of the need for firmer boundaries: not helpful either to you or the girls. But I realise it's not about understanding – one can't have too much of that – it was about an excess of empathy. I felt your pain and I didn't know how to stop feeling it. I wish I'd done my psychotherapy training when you were small. I would have known better how to help you, and the girls. You weren't an easy brother for them to have. You took up so much of mine and Dad's time and energy. Rosy compensated for your naughtiness by being good, too good, and neither Dad nor I questioned it. Or if we did, we unconsciously stopped ourselves seeing the impact it might be having on her. And Ellie learned to entertain us all, to divert herself and us away from the difficult, painful stuff. Again, we let her.

I sometimes feel I failed you all and wonder whether, if I'd been another mother, things might have turned out differently.

***

31 August 2014

FOR SAM'S 22ND birthday earlier this year I bought him a jumper. It's one of the ones rolled up tight and bundled into the bag at the foot of his bed. He didn't say much when I gave it to him, but I knew he liked it and he wore it often. He's wearing it in a photo one of the girls took of him on a walk that same birthday weekend in Waltham St Lawrence. He's happy, smiling, arms swinging in anticipation of skinny chips and a Bombay Sapphire and tonic at the Bell. It's bright and sunny and surprisingly warm for a February day. None of us wears a jacket. The sky is clear and chalky blue; the pale, faded, washed-out denim blue of a winter's day. The girls do cartwheels across the field. We spread ourselves in a circle round an ancient tree trunk and stretch our arms out wide.

I get out of bed this morning and go into Sam's room. I pick up the bag and unroll it, lean in for the jumper and ease it out gently, as if handling it roughly might disturb and dissipate what I am hoping for: the smell of him. Once more I raise the jumper to my face, press it close and breathe in. It is there still, fainter, but unmistakably him. I cry with relief, and then with sadness that this is all I have left of him. I roll it up lovingly and carefully slide it back inside the bag, place it at the foot of the bed and leave his room. Now that this small, silent, private ritual is complete I go to start my day.

1 September 2014

I'M IN THE kitchen, pottering. Ellie wanders in. She'll be leaving for university in a few weeks' time. We talk about the things we'll need to buy for her room in hall. She's being receptive. I decide to take a chance.

'How are you feeling about going?' I ask. 'I know it's been really tough this summer with Sam and Katherine and everything.'

'I'm not sure,' she says. 'I'm not really thinking about it.'

'But you need to Nor, don't you? It never works when you avoid things. And what about the moods?' I say. 'There are lots of difficult feelings you don't seem to be coping with very well. We've had a lot, haven't we? In Wales and Spain. It seems to be a very dark place you get into and it's really hard to reach you when you're like that.'

She doesn't say anything.

'I've actually written about it.'

'Have you?' she says. 'Can I read it?'

She doesn't say very much at first, just sits and nods and shakes her head. She turns towards me.

'I don't know what happens to me, Mum,' she says as silent tears slide down her face. 'When I feel like that, it's like I can't help myself. I can't control it. It's just these awful, dark feelings building up inside me, and I don't know what to do with them. I know I behave badly. And I wish I didn't, but I can't seem to stop. I know that if I was on the outside, watching myself, I'd be shocked.'

'I know, Nor. It's so hard. I think you're going to need some help with it.'

Ellie has never struggled to express her emotions. She's always been a small volcano, with her feelings close to the surface and easily accessible. But because they're so accessible she's had to find ways to avoid them: distracting herself and pushing the painful stuff to one side. But there's a lot of it now. Too much, and the feelings won't stay where they're meant to. They keep on spilling out. At times they overwhelm her. She's lived with Sam's strange behaviours and then his illness since she was fifteen. At times she was the only person in the family he would allow to visit her in hospital. She was still at school. It was a lot to cope with. She's never really recovered from the trauma of his fight and then the suicide attempt.

On that morning she woke at 5.30 to the sound of unfamiliar voices and heavy boots climbing the stairs. Peering out of her bedroom window she saw five sets of flashing blue lights on the drive. She didn't dare come out of her room. By then I was with Sam in the ambulance as the crew tried to stabilise him. My phone rang. It was Ellie.

'What's happened, Mum, what's happened?' she sobbed.

'It will be a few minutes before we're ready to leave,' one of the ambulance men said. 'We won't go without you.'

I ran inside. She was cowering on her bed.

I told her what had happened. And that Sam was alive and would be alright. She was beside herself. I had to leave her. She had her second panic attack. Poor, frightened Ellie. All the unresolved feelings she'd been pushing behind that wall for years swept over her in one almighty whoosh. My lovely, enthusiastic, warm, funny daughter was totally overwhelmed.

3 September 2014

ELLIE'S BEEN BETTER since we spoke. She seems to be more at peace with herself.

Rosy comes home unexpectedly, driving straight from performing at a festival in Kendal. Next morning she starts to talk. Even though it's gone well, and she's enjoyed it, she's been troubled all weekend by an underlying low mood she's been unable to shake off and it's made her feel anxious, a horrible non-specific anxiety.

Finally, she's able to identify what it is that she's been feeling: a terrible sadness about Sam. I watch her drag it to the surface, this difficult feeling. It's so hard for her to do. Etched upon her face is a small frown, a look of anxious puzzlement as she struggles to identify and name this evasive thing, and then I see the pain and discomfort as she recognises the feeling and allows herself to feel it.

They are so different, my daughters. With Ellie everything's at the surface, ready to break through. Rosy buries feelings deeper. It's harder to reach them. I grieve for them both.

4 September 2014

I READ ABOUT Shirley Williams' recent visit to Hamburg to see the canal named after her mother, in honour of her war-time campaign against mass bombing of cities. This April I flew to Berlin with Rosy and Sam to see the street which, in 2005, was named after my paternal Jewish grandmother, Frieda Glucksmann. She ran a Berlin orphanage for Jewish children in the 1930s and succeeded, against the odds, in securing sponsors and exit visas for every one of them.

I feel lucky to have had those five days away with Sam. It's a holiday that might so easily have been postponed until after his trip to Thailand; might so easily never have happened. He so nearly refused to come.

***

You were the only one at home on Mother's Day this year. I could see you were out of sorts as soon as you emerged from your bedroom.

'I want to go back to Wokingham,' you said. 'As soon as possible.'

'But we were planning to go out for lunch, Sam.'

You shrugged your shoulders. 'My only plan is to get back to Wokingham as early as I can.' You looked at me coldly and walked away without wishing me a happy Mother's Day. I wondered what had prompted the shift in mood. You'd been lovely the night before over supper. It didn't take long to find out.

It was in the car that you started.

'It should never have happened,' you said, shaking your head, 'I should never have been sectioned and I should never have had to go into Prospect Park. It's ridiculous. You've got to agree.'

I said nothing. You continued to hold forth on the inequity of a system that wilfully misunderstands people and locks them up for no reason.

'You've got to agree it was unfair,' you said again. I could sense your frustration with me for not agreeing with you. You wanted me to. You turned towards me and asked me a direct question.

'If you could turn the clock back and stop it happening, would you?'

I can remember exactly where we were, on that straight section of road, beyond Dolphin School, just coming into the bends and that big right hand corner where the phone signal always disappears.

The problem was that I was feeling out of sorts too. Neither of the girls had been in touch, I hadn't received any cards, you'd ostentatiously failed to mark the day. The truth is I was feeling sorry for myself. I was tired. Right then being a mother seemed to be a thankless task. I didn't have the energy to try to deflect the question. So I didn't even try to.

*'I'd turn the clock back to stop you ever becoming ill, Sam,' I said. 'I think **that's** unfair.'*

You were furious, beyond furious. I'd crossed a line. I'd talked about you being ill.

'That's it,' you said. 'Always that same thing. Why can't

you understand that I've never been ill? It should never have happened.' You were shouting now with frustration and tears brimming in your eyes. 'It – only – happened – because – of – you.'

'I'm sorry, Sam, I said, inadequately. 'I'm so sorry. I didn't mean to upset you.' I really meant it, but you wouldn't look at me or talk to me at all. As we pulled up onto the pavement next to your house you opened the car door, turned towards me and said, 'And by the way, there's no way I'm coming to Berlin with you and Rosy next weekend. You can forget that. Why would I want to spend time with a mother who says I'm ill when I'm not?' You slammed the door behind you and crossed the road to your front door. You went in without your usual wave or even a glance.

I left a message to say again how sorry I was to have upset you. You didn't respond. All week you ignored my text messages and calls. You finally got in touch on the eve of our departure.

'I'll come,' you said, 'but I haven't forgiven you.'

You were distinctly cool when I picked you up on the way to the airport. You thawed gradually over the four days that we were away. We went to the hotel Grandpa loved with its artwork hung four paintings deep. You were tricky at times, endlessly questioning, relentlessly pressing buttons to try to provoke a reaction, but your slightly manic energy made us laugh too. We laughed a lot. In the evenings we ate at the little café around the corner from the hotel, and you discovered spaetzle which you consumed by the plateful behind its steamed-up windows. But in-between times I could feel you resisting me. One day you refused to come out and stayed in bed all day instead. You needed to remind me you were still angry with me. And when you laughed and were happy it felt as though it happened by mistake and despite your best efforts to carry on hating me. When you left for Thailand two weeks later, you were still punishing me for what I'd said on that day. You weren't actively hostile anymore, but you were wary.

As though allowing yourself to love me was a dangerous thing.

It wasn't the first time you'd rejected me. Each time you were admitted to hospital there would be a long period of being berated by you for what you saw as the ultimate betrayal of a son by his mother. You'd ignore my calls and texts and when I came to see you'd I'd be turned away by regretful staff. You told me again and again that you hated me for what I'd done. You sent a text message saying it would be the last I ever heard from you. As far as you were concerned you had no family anymore. You repeated relentlessly your wish to have been born into a better family, one that loved and appreciated you. You spoke often of your wish to move on to your next life, where that wish might be granted.

At times like these I'd try to see it as the schizophrenia talking, rather than you. I'd allow myself to grieve for the tragedy of all that was being taken away from you, and all of us, by this cruel illness. I learned to hate the illness, but never you Sam. But it was hard not to allow some of what you said

GILL MANN

to penetrate, to begin to question myself, even to believe that maybe you were right, maybe a different mother might have saved you from all this. And sometimes when the attack was too fierce, the pain too great and I didn't have the emotional energy to deal with it, I had to distance myself, to shut down a little on my love for you, to allow myself to feel angry, even to dislike you for being capable of inflicting such pain.

But in the better times we did find a way of talking. I'd let you say what you needed to say, I'd really listen to you, and then I'd say, 'I know Sam, I know. It's awful what you've been through. But I also know that everything that Dad and I have ever done has been motivated by our love for you. I'm sure we made mistakes. I'm sure we got things wrong. And if we did, I'm sorry, I truly am, but it wasn't for lack of thoughtfulness or care. I can honestly say that everything we've ever done has been done with love and concern for you at its heart.'

Often you said, 'You know God's going to make you pay for this Mum. One day you're going to face judgement and I wouldn't want to be you then. It's going to be vicious, you're going to have a terrible, terrible time in your next life. I mean you can't go locking people up for no reason, making them poison their systems with vile drugs that go against everything they believe in. I mean I'm your son. Mothers are meant to love their sons, not call people in and have them locked up against their wishes. God's going to judge you for all of it. He is. And it's not going to be pretty.' You looked quite pleased at the thought of that.

And I'd say, 'I know Sam and that's fine. I'm totally happy with that. I'm happy to accept God's judgment and

234

*whatever vicious fate he thinks I deserve. Because **I** know what was in my heart. I know it was love, and actually I have faith that God will know that too.'*

And on a good day you'd concede that though you hated what I'd done and all that had flowed from it, you didn't hate me. And that was a salve for me, for all the pain of what you'd said before.

And then we'd hug and in that hug was all the love we both knew to be there, as strong as ever, at the core of our relationship.

I'm glad you got to see where Grandpa grew up, that your feet trod the same streets and paths round Lehnitzsee that his had eighty years earlier. I wanted you to have a sense of your heritage, of the rich and varied worlds which shaped your ancestors, and you through them. I look at the photos I took of you and Rosy: outside the house in Berlin where Grandpa lived with its wooden gables and steep pitched roof; in the street next to an information plaque about your great-grandmother, pointing at a large photo of her; beneath the street sign, Frieda Glucksmann Strasse. You're grinning broadly despite yourself.

***

5 September 2014

IN OCTOBER 2013, we all went to the Peak District for a weekend to celebrate my sister, Kate's, 60th birthday. All my siblings and all but one of our – between us – eleven children came, some with partners and children. Sam had only come out of hospital in August, after his long third stay there. As usual it was touch and go until the very last minute as to whether he would come or not. It required quiet but persistent perseverance to persuade him to do anything. Despite being so much better he was often weighed down by inertia and his default response to any suggestion was an automatic 'no'.

It seemed hard for him to hold on to happy, good experiences, in a way that might make him seek to replicate them. It was as though we were starting from scratch each time we suggested something for him to do. Previous enjoyment provided no incentive to repeat the experience. Each attempt to get him to do anything required a huge investment of time, energy and effort. In his book, *Far From the Tree,* Andrew Solomon (2012) notes how even someone who has a fantastic time whenever they go out for supper, may have absolutely no interest in doing it.

As soon as we were in the car I knew he would be okay. When we arrived he threw himself into the spirit of the weekend, coming to every meal and smoking with conspiratorial glee outside the front door with his fellow-smoker cousins. He came with me to visit Chatsworth. He was typically impatient as we toured the house, trying to rush me through the rooms and halls. I allowed myself to be rushed. I was happy simply to have him with me.

6 September 2014

TODAY IT'S THE turn of disbelief. I'm back in that place

where half of me is waiting for someone to tell me that it's all been a dreadful mistake, that Sam will be home soon.

7 September 2014

IN MY DREAM I'm at the GP practice where I work. I'm chatting to Elsie, the practice nurse, when the door flies open and two young Eastern European cleaners come in. They are vibrant, full of life as they hand out a bin bag to each of us. Everyone else seems to know what to do. They begin to gather up their possessions and bundle them into the bags. They look comfortable and composed as they collect up the remnants of their lives, throw them into the bags and secure them with knots. All the while the cleaners sweep and wipe and hoover around them, taking their bundled bags as they pass.

I, by contrast, am paralysed; surrounded by photos, cards, letters, travel and entrance tickets, mementoes with which I cannot bear to part. Apart from my space, cluttered and uncleaned, the surgery is now clean and sparkling. I dither, unsure, wanting to hold onto things yet tempted too by the lure of neatness and cleanliness around me. The dream ends while I'm standing there wondering which way to go.

That's where I am now, caught between past and future. Part of me wants to clear away all the mess of my past life, all the loss and grief; but somewhere I know that good things will be discarded too if I don't sort through it first.

8 September 2014

WE GO TO visit the cottage in Wales. Everything is progressing quickly. It feels as though it's meant to be. It's in a village at the foot of a huge escarpment in the Brecon Beacons. The walk up and around the escarpment was one of our favourites. I feel a connection to Sam when I'm there.

As we drive home again, I feel a small swell of excitement inside me. But then, unbidden, my mind flashes back to an image of him waiting on the other side of the locked blue door of Bluebell ward, waiting patiently for my arrival and to be allowed out with me to the hospital café; such a dismal, utilitarian, sterile space, but the only place we could go. And I feel guilty again for not being able to save him from being sectioned and all that meant, and for still being alive when he is not.

And guilt, awoken from its crocodile sleep, fixes its ever-watchful eye on my excitement about the cottage, about something for the future in which Sam will have no part. Excitement seems suddenly to be a terrible misplaced thing, an aberration, maybe even a sin. Guilt flexes its tail, slides silently forward and with one fierce, unforgiving snap of the jaws seizes my excitement and drags it down into the soupy, brown waters of self-recrimination.

As I sit in the car, lost in these difficult, confusing thoughts and feelings, words break through: a poem on the radio.

A Brief for the Defense by Jack Gilbert

Sorrow everywhere. Slaughter everywhere. If babies
are not starving someplace, they are starving
somewhere else. With flies in their nostrils.
But we enjoy our lives because that's what God wants.
Otherwise the mornings before summer dawn would not
be made so fine. The Bengal tiger would not
be fashioned so miraculously well. The poor women
at the fountain are laughing together between
the suffering they have known and the awfulness
in their future, smiling and laughing while somebody
in the village is very sick. There is laughter
every day in the terrible streets of Calcutta,
and the women laugh in the cages of Bombay.
If we deny our happiness, resist our satisfaction,
we lessen the importance of their deprivation.
We must risk delight. We can do without pleasure,
but not delight. Not enjoyment. We must have
the stubbornness to accept our gladness in the ruthless
furnace of this world. To make injustice the only
measure of our attention is to praise the Devil.
If the locomotive of the Lord runs us down,
we should give thanks that the end had magnitude.
We must admit there will be music despite everything.
We stand at the prow again of a small ship
anchored late at night in the tiny port
looking over to the sleeping island: the waterfront

is three shuttered cafés and one naked light burning.
To hear the faint sound of oars in the silence as a
  rowboat
comes slowly out and then goes back is truly worth
all the years of sorrow that are to come.

Its message reaches me through the murky waters of self-reproach. Guilt's jaws slacken and begin to lose their grip. Perhaps I am allowed to feel happiness, to take delight, despite the devastation of losing Sam. Denying myself gladness in other things won't bring him back.

19 September 2014

I SPEND THE day with Ellie preparing for her imminent departure to Newcastle University. We make lists and shop and pack. It's the first time I've seen her talk about it with anything approaching enthusiasm. It's lovely. But underneath, all day I feel a swell of sadness about Sam. I try to keep it hidden. I hope I succeed.

He never went through this rite of passage and never will. His life was hijacked before he was able to capitalise on his intellect. It doesn't seem fair, like so much else. There's no way now to put things right, to try to make up for the unfairness. It's hard to live with the feeling that we failed him, that we should have been able to do something to redress the balance.

Other guilts pile in. We were so mean financially with Sam. We made him pay for his food out of his benefits.

He was so accepting, so uncomplaining. We didn't give him money for his 21st birthday and discouraged others from doing so. We never told him about the payout from a Children's Bond bought for him at birth. He was ill by the time it matured and we were terrified he might take off on further travels and slip under the radar.

I can't shake off the feeling that I really did fail him.

28 September 2014

I'VE BEEN AVOIDING thinking of Sam. When sadness threatens I push the thoughts away. I feel a hardness developing around the softer parts of me, something brittle that won't let me cry. I don't want to be brittle but I don't want to feel the pain either.

30 September 2014

FINALLY I CRY. It's a relief.

I'm sending some photos of Sam to the Dolphin for an obituary for the school magazine. As I attach them to the email they appear not as icons but as huge luminous images which fill the screen. Suddenly there's no avoiding the dreadful reality of what I'm doing.

As I sit and scroll through the photos – up and down, again and again – I play the recording of his unbroken voice, clear as a bell, reading the poem at my father's funeral. For a moment I'm back there with Sam at thirteen, his whole life ahead of him, his voice lifting and falling on the gentle tide of Mahler, motes of dust dancing in shafts of afternoon light, the congregation leaning forward, listening, still. I want to freeze it there, this life of his, to hold it, keep him safe, cocooned in love, with a future ahead of him. I don't want to be selecting photos for his obituary.

I want to select a different ending.

6 October 2014

THERE'S A HIDDEN compartment in the car that we only found when we put the back seat down. I look in there today for the first time in years and come across a small blue cap Sam wore when he was small. I pick it up and hold it gently in my hands. I feel as though I'm cradling a fledgling, unsure what to do with it next. I would have liked to show it to him. Instead I carry it upstairs to his bedroom.

I raise it to my lips before I place it on his bed.

8 October 2014

I'M SITTING IN reception at Prospect Park Hospital with Simon. We're meeting the nurse consultant and the ward manager of Bluebell, Sam's old ward, to talk about an idea we have for setting up a home cinema. It feels strange yet familiar to be back here, walking down the long, long corridors with their blue double doors.

When we arrive at the locked doors of Bluebell ward we ring the bell and wait for a member of staff to release the door to let us in. It's hard to walk onto the ward and to see no Sam. He was always there on the other side of the locked doors, waiting; with his slow, often reluctant, smile. It all feels exactly as it used to. Except there is no Sam.

We've come to look at the room we're hoping to convert into the cinema. It will have an interactive screen so patients will be able to Skype or FaceTime family on it, as well as watch films and DVDs. They plan to hold film nights and have a film club. They think it will be used a lot. They tell us all this as we wait for the room to become free. There's a meeting going on inside.

After a while the door opens and two young women emerge (perhaps a social worker and a health worker from the community). Behind them comes a tall, skinny young man, malodorous, with matted dreadlocks. He looks suspicious, wary, as he surveys us briefly through narrowed eyes. Then with a twitch of his shoulders and a movement of his arm, he slopes off towards his room, oblivious to the two young women calling their goodbyes to his retreating back. It could be Sam. Only his height distinguishes him from the son we've lost.

In the meeting we talk about the equipment they will need, the services, the lighting, seating, how the room will be decorated. I can't quite believe the commitment and energy I see in the two women we meet. They care deeply about their patients. They want to make a difference. We're lucky, all of us, to have people such as this, caring for the most vulnerable amongst us.

My head is buzzing when I climb into my car at the end of the visit, but I'm not sure with what. I sit and wait a moment before I begin the drive home. I place my arms on the steering wheel and leaning forward, rest my head against my hands. I let myself feel the pain of being here again.

***

I'm excited about the cinema. I think it could really make a difference. But I feel so incredibly sad too. Coming back has reminded me powerfully of all the times I walked down those corridors – on the way to visit you, never knowing how you would be with me. At times you'd be pleased to see me, happy to be coming out – even if it was only to the hospital cafeteria – chatty, engaged. But always we would walk painfully slowly, your natural pace decelerated by medication. At the worst times you would swerve haplessly into the walls, unable to walk in a straight line, feet dragging and arms hanging, stiff and lifeless.

For long periods of time you weren't allowed to leave the ward, so we'd try to find somewhere to sit away from the blaring TV. At others you'd refuse to see me. After your third admission in February 2013 you were very angry, especially with me, for what you saw as yet another betrayal. I would arrive at the locked doors of the ward and wait for a member of staff to answer the bell and let me in. I would ask them to let you know your mum was here to see you. You'd with-drawn consent for us to be informed or involved in any aspect of your care. We were completely in the dark. We'd be informed if you were discharged but not told where to find you. I've never felt so powerless and vulnerable, as when I waited to find out whether you would see me or not.

I took to arriving unannounced, with Sigmund, just two or three months old, a little bundle of black fur in my arms and sometimes you were unable to resist the lure of a shiny, wet, black nose and out-sized paws, and would appear round the corner, gaze at me, reproachful and unsmiling. You'd stretch out your arms to take Sigmund from me and head off down the corridor.

'I don't forgive you,' you'd say. 'Just because I've agreed to see you, it doesn't mean that I forgive you. It doesn't change anything. I still hate you for what you did.'

'I know, Sam. I know,' I'd reply. And if I saw even a chink of something softer, I would risk, 'I hope you might forgive me one day, Muelo.'

***

9 October 2014

I GO TO hear an old friend perform in a string quartet. Across the room I see her talking to the mother of one of Sam's classmates from Dolphin School. Our boys were in the same small class together for eight or more years. I haven't seen her since Sam died. I walk up to where she stands and touch her lightly on the shoulder. She leaps back from me as if scorched by my presence, turns away towards someone else and talks to them as if I'm not there. I talk instead to my friend and then, as I leave, touch the mother's shoulder once again. She still doesn't know what to say to me. She wishes I would leave her alone. I see it in her face. I say how good it is to see her even though we haven't had the chance to talk. She smiles before turning wordlessly away once more.

I recognise the dogged determination that has made me try a second time to make contact with this woman. I'm doing it for Sam. I can't bear for him to be written out of history, as though he never existed.

10 October 2014

SIMON CALLS ME from his car. He's ranting about people he's just seen for the first time since Sam died, who talk to him and do not mention Sam, even people who were close to him. He can't bear the way that they seem to be writing him off, as though he never existed. I tell him about the woman the night before.

I know what it is. The thought of losing their own child is so unbearable that they can't allow themselves to think of Simon and me losing ours. They don't know what to say, and therefore they say nothing. Yet it's so simple, all we need is a few words: 'I'm so sorry.' We don't need more than that.

11 October 2014

LYING ON THE doormat is an unusually flimsy letter with a hand-written envelope. Inside is a slip of paper headed St Mary's Church and beneath that in block capitals and large bold print it says, 'Annual Bereavement Service'. It's the All Souls Day service, when the dead are remembered by name and their families light candles in their memory. I went after each of my parents died. I recall feeling both humbled and comforted to find myself standing in line with others mourning, as I was, the death of a loved one, waiting to light candles for them. It took away something of the loneliness of grief to be involved in a communal act of remembering. However personal our thoughts and memories were to each of us, there was solace in being part of a community of mourners, bound by our shared experience and purpose.

12 October 2014

PADDY AND I go away for a night. Despite the fact that the booking is in my name, the male receptionist pointedly hands both key-cards to Paddy, as though I can't be trusted with them. I roll my eyes as we leave the reception area, take the lift upstairs, and walk down the corridor. When we reach our bedroom door Paddy stops and brandishes the cards. 'I am *master* of this room,' he declares, smiling. I smile too.

It's a Sam catchphrase that's passed into the lexicon of post-Sam life. In late summer 2012, just weeks after being discharged from his first sectioning he came to Wales for a week with Paddy, me and Charlie. We took them to a rope and riding centre in Wales. He went pony trekking while Charlie learned to rock climb on an indoor climbing wall. We missed seeing Sam set off because we were delivering Charlie to his lesson, but we waited outside for his return. A string of ponies, each tethered to the one behind, came ambling into the yard at a funeral pace. At the front were half a dozen small children, arranged in order of size, none of them older than seven or eight. At the rear came Sam, sitting tall and proud on his diminutive pony. He was bigger than it was, his feet almost touching the ground. Everyone was drenched, the ponies bedraggled and miserable. As they dawdled past, he looked up and acknowledged us with a small wave. 'I am *master* of this horse,' he said self-importantly. Beneath his rain-spotted riding hat his face broke into a broad grin.

***

When you were sectioned and diagnosed, I was devastated. But there was also some relief. That may be hard to understand, but we were desperate for you to get some help. And it made parenting you easier once we knew what it was that we were up against, that you were ill rather than being eccentric and contrary. It put everything into context to understand that these weren't choices you were making but symptoms of something bigger than you. And actually it helped me to know that others had finally recognised what I'd been seeing. It gave me something to hold onto, terrible though it was. I naively thought it meant that the unbearable strain of living on the edge of an ever-shifting precipice had ended, that once you were getting medical help everything would stay on a level. Of course it was much more complicated than that. If anything, it got harder. Or perhaps it just felt harder because I'd let myself hope.

The first time you were sectioned it was under section 2 of the MHA which meant you could be kept in hospital for twenty-eight days. It gave them time to assess you and make a diagnosis. When you came home at the end of the month it felt as though we had you back. You were calm and coherent and normal. For the first two months, when you were still taking your medication, you were a joy. You came to Wales for a holiday. You looked so well. You'd started to care for yourself again. You came on walks and out for meals. You were funny, you were quirky. Sometimes you were difficult. You were you. I have that photo of you in a field of bullocks at Cilau farm. We call them the Cilau killers because they're always so frisky. The day the photo was taken, Paddy was telling you the story about the time I had skirted round the edge of two fields – so as to avoid them – only to discover when I hopped over a barbed-wire fence into a third field that they were all charging through an open gate I hadn't seen. They were heading for me at high speed in a cloud of dust. I'd never hopped back over a fence so fast. You loved that story and immediately turned and ran towards the bullocks shaking your carrier bag – for some reason you insisted on carrying your own lunch – at them. They suddenly advanced towards you. You shot off at a run. I swear you moved as fast as I did when I hopped back over the fence. You looked terrified, and then amused, once you realised they weren't chasing you. I captured the moment with my camera – you grinning broadly, plastic bag swinging out to the left, the cows behind you, watching. That photo always makes me smile.

You stopped taking your medication after two months.

You didn't tell anyone but I sensed that something was changing. By the latter half of October all the old behaviours were back. That was when you had the run-in with the gang, were put onto Olanzapine and tried to kill yourself. You went back into Prospect Park once you were discharged from hospital and stayed there for three and a half months. You said that life wasn't worth living on medication. It was clear what the implication was. You never did make things easy.

*James finally decided **not** to put you onto antipsychotics. He agreed with us that medicating you forcibly would probably create a higher risk than allowing you a respite from anti-psychotic drugs and letting the illness take its course. He said at some point the scales would tip in the opposite direction, the risk becoming higher with you unmedicated, and then you would need to be re-hospitalised.*

You'd said you didn't want to come home when you left hospital that second time, that you wanted independence from the family. I didn't know whether you meant it or were just angry with me still. I didn't try to find out. I simply said okay. I still feel guilty. But the truth is I didn't know if I could manage to keep you safe at home or whether I could cope. And even more than that, I was scared about the impact on Ellie of living with you unmedicated and psychotic. It's desperately hard as a parent to have to choose between children, to make a choice for one that inevitably means failing another. We do it so often without realising it: small subtle choices where the 'easy' and less demanding child's needs are overlooked. But this time I knew. I remember the long, hard look you gave me. It haunts me. I wish I'd found a way to explain. I can still see the look of surprise on the faces of your medical team when I told them what you wanted. I'm not sure what I'd have done if you'd changed your mind.

By then I'd started to research alternative ways of managing schizophrenia and discovered that there were Steiner homes and other therapeutic communities who offered long-term residential care. I felt so hopeful. But all enquiries came to nothing. No one was prepared to take someone who had no insight into their illness. Your social worker found a vacancy in some supported accommodation in Reading. It sounded perfect. But when they came to assess you for the place, they said it wouldn't work. It would be too disruptive for the other residents if you didn't accept that you were ill. Finally, a room was found in a house with two other residents and a member of staff on duty. It was only a couple of miles from home, a short walk from shops, near a park. It seemed ideal. But it wasn't long before things began to unravel.

This was perhaps the hardest time of all for me to cope with. I hated you not being at home. You moved into the house but it was never a happy place for you. There was no sense of community but even if there had been you wouldn't have been able to take advantage of it as you were already showing signs of psychosis. You were only there for a month and in that short time you became steadily more and more unwell, often refusing to speak to Dad and me except through your first floor bedroom window. You would shout down aggressively, only occasionally agreeing to come home or go into town with us.

Once Rosy and I came to try to coax you out for a walk and a trip to a café. As usual you would only talk to us through the window, but we persisted and eventually you agreed to come. Your agitation was palpable as soon as you joined us. Going into the outside world increased your discomfort.

We went to a little café in Reading. You stood by the chiller unit for ten or fifteen minutes, unable to select anything. It wasn't that you couldn't decide what you wanted to drink, it was that you couldn't decide which bottle to take. You repeatedly took one, looked at it intently and suspiciously, then put it back and re-arranged all the bottles, before selecting another, only to reject that too a few moments later. When finally you'd made your choice, you came to join us at our table. But even then you remained transfixed by the bottle, reading the label over and over with a frightening intensity, as if your life depended on it.

Afterwards we walked back through the town. You stopped every few steps and looked up at the sky, gesturing and muttering. If we turned around and caught you in the act, you responded with an aggressive stare through narrowed eyes, challenging us with an angry, 'What?' And when I asked who you were talking to you said I was mad and imagining things. As we passed the statue of Queen Victoria in Market Place Square you fell back behind. Rosy and I carried on walking, but slowly, and when I turned to look for you, I saw you standing at the foot of the statue, arms outstretched in supplication, shouting at the stony-faced monarch, appealing to the heavens. It was a desperate moment. It seemed that you were truly lost to us again.

You took to disappearing from that house. The first time I took a call to say they didn't know where you were, Dad and I came to your room to search for clues as to your whereabouts. We discovered your bedroom door open, your house keys, wallet and mobile phone on the bed. Apparently you'd left in jeans and a jumper. No coat. It was a bitterly cold January day with snow on the ground and sub-zero temperatures forecast overnight. We sat on your bed and wept. Dad asked me if I thought we'd ever see you again. We searched round the lakes. Paddy walked along the River Thames and Kennet and Avon canal in case you'd decided to walk into town. There was no sign of you anywhere. You were reported as missing to the police. They searched our home and Dad's, more heavy feet pounding the stairs, leaving a trail of footsteps in the snow across the lawn as they checked the garden and outhouses. They offered to send up the police helicopter with its thermal imaging facility. I sat at home and listened mutely as I heard it chopping through the air.

It was three days later that you re-appeared on the doorstep at home. Gaunt and unkempt, clearly de-hydrated, you said you hadn't eaten or drunk anything since you left as you hadn't been able to find water in glass bottles. You'd been to Banbury to see two friends from Henley College. You couldn't understand what all the fuss was about. This was why you'd chosen to live independently, so you wouldn't have us meddling in your life all the time. It was ridiculous that the police had been involved.

The second time you took your wallet and mobile phone, but you were gone for even longer. Five days. You didn't respond to text messages, calls or emails asking you to let us know where you were. The police were informed again by the care-workers at your house. You were classed as a vulnerable person so they had to investigate. They were fantastic again. They started tracking your bank records and the use of your bank card. Initially that drew a blank but after several days they discovered you'd tried to withdraw cash in Paris and within a few hours you got in touch to say you'd run out of money and could we buy you a Eurostar ticket home. Dad came to meet you at St Pancras. You were just as scathing about the fuss as the time before.

Two days later you called me late at night to say one of your housemates had punched you in the face. You didn't know why and wanted to come home because you didn't feel safe there anymore. I came immediately. It turned out you'd been behaving more and more strangely, looking at people suspiciously and aggressively demanding to know what visitors were doing there. The social worker for another resident had complained to your care worker and asked that you move out.

You didn't go back. James was consulted, and the CMHT. You'd reached the point where the balance had tipped. You were now more risk to yourself unmedicated. It was early February 2013. You'd been out of hospital for less than a month. Arrangements were made for another MHA assessment to take place at home. I didn't know how to cope with it all over again. I went and waited at Dad's house when they were due to come. Paddy let them in. I don't even know how you got to hospital that time. I'm guessing your social worker took you there. I feel terrible about not knowing that. Perhaps I did know but have simply blocked it out. I was close to tipping point myself.

I'd hoped, naively, that you might not blame me this time. But you did. The cycle of rejection and gradual thawing began once more. You were detained under section 3 of the MHA this time, so they could keep you in hospital for much longer. You threatened to appeal but never did. You were put back onto anti-psychotics. It was a long seven months for all of us.

***

16 October 2014

I AM AT the checkout in the supermarket talking to a woman I know from years back when we used to share chaperone duties at a dance show our daughters were in. We are talking about the pleasure of making only infrequent trips to the supermarket nowadays. I find myself saying that the fewer children I have at home, the fewer times I need to shop. I listen to myself in disbelief. It sounds as though I'm making a virtue out of Sam's death. It's not what I meant at all.

18 October 2014

SAM WAS IN my dreams last night. He was in the car with us as we went to visit a friend. It was so lovely to have him back. The family felt whole again. I feel ridiculously grateful to have spent even that short car ride with him. I miss him so much: his physical presence, the tone of his voice, his laugh, his smile. I would go to the supermarket a hundred times a day just to have him back.

22 October 2014

TODAY IS LAURENCE'S birthday. For years he formed a trio with Sam and Simon T. Laurence put up with Sam even though, every lunchtime when he opened his lunch box and withdrew a nice, healthy tuna sandwich, Sam would loudly exclaim, 'Oh – my – God, that stinks,' as he unwrapped his own hermetically sealed cheese-string or baby bel – the only things he would eat – and pointedly moved away from Laurence, holding his nose. I talked to him about it, but it made no difference.

I'm out walking with Hen, Laurence's Mum, when she reminds me about his eighth birthday party.

'There were about twelve of them,' she says, 'and several were vegetarians. So I made home-made bean-burgers for everyone. My kids love them.'

'Oh God,' I say, 'It's coming back to me.'

'So they were all sitting round in a circle when I handed out the food. I gave Sam his plate and he's looking at it like it's about to explode. And then he says in that incredibly piercing voice of his, "*What's in it, Hen?*" And I can't believe what I said. I said, "It's okay Sam, it's not meat, it's quorn. You know, it's a type of mushroom," and he looked at me as though I'd just told him it was radioactive waste. And then he went, "Urrrgghh." Well I knew that was it. This whole chorus of "urrrgghhs," rose up and needless to say, at the end of the meal, I slid twelve untouched bean-burgers into the bin.'

24 October 2014

I'M UP SOON after 4.30 am to fly to Newcastle to see Ellie. On the bus between departure lounge and plane are two small boys: one a toddler, the other around four years old. I watch them alternate between playing happily together and subtly provoking one another. They make me think of Sam when he was their ages. I see him in his navy blue play-suit, thumb parked unceremoniously in his mouth, fingers curled into a tiny fist, eyes alive with knowing mischief. I picture his body beneath, the gentle ridges of his ribs, the barely perceptible curve of his belly, the milky smoothness of his skin, compressing into a bank of lateral wrinkles as he leans forward, then easing back into smoothness as he sits up again. I see his tumbling, white blond curls and eyes disappearing into the crinkle of his beaming smile. Even then there was something infectious in his smile and laughter. It was impossible not to be drawn in.

I see him next as a small boy. He's in the egg and spoon race at Dolphin Nursery Sports Day, running with one arm stretched out ahead of him, the other tucked behind and resting in the small of his back. He's totally focused on keeping the egg on the spoon as his little legs power beneath him. He's ahead of the others and almost at the finish line when the egg parts company with the spoon. I see him hesitate for a second, as he weighs up the options.

He runs on without the egg.

He's not that interested in the detail.

He'd rather have the glory of being first across the line.

The bus is almost full now and I've lost sight of the two small boys, but my mind remains filled with images of Sam. I see him next at eight or nine. He's calmer now, has lost some of the manic energy that used to propel him through life. The sun has lightened his thick, cropped hair and brought out freckles across his nose and cheeks.

Then he's at senior school, with white shirt barely tucked into dark grey trousers. He's walking with a group of friends towards me, as I wait to collect him. They're laughing about something and one of them bashes him with his shoulder. Sam steadies himself and, as he does so, sees me. He smiles and raises his arm in greeting.

I see him next at seventeen. He's grinning broadly, a perfect ellipsis of a mouth stretched tight from ear to ear, eyes barely visible, sparkling with impish mischief and light. He's cooler now, aware of himself. He's wearing skinny black jeans, black Converse with white laces, and tight black cardigan buttoned over a white T-shirt. Across his chest is slung a square Dunlop bag in retro off-white plastic with black trim. He is every inch the sixth-form student. He shouts, 'Bye!' as he pulls the door closed behind him and walks, gravel crunching beneath his feet, towards the station.

Now I see him a year or two later still. He has returned from his travels and cut off his blond dreadlocks. He keeps them in the bag beneath his bed. His hair is cropped close to his head, his eyes are still bright but there is a hint of mania in the brightness and something closed off about him. It is as though he has drawn a veil across the brightness, for he's living almost exclusively inside his head now. I see us on a walk in the country. His skinny body, tight with pent-up energy which he discharges with little jumps and skips. He resists my attempts at normal conversation, brushing me off with irritable one-word responses. Instead he stops to talk to the trees, wrapping their trunks in a tight embrace, looking skywards between their waving branches, before releasing his clasp and taking off again with giant, bouncing strides and wildly swinging arms. This new Sam walks with a different gait, pushing himself off with each step, as though launching himself into a private world of wonder and promise.

Then I see the Prospect Park Sam. He moves slowly, as if wading through treacle, every step invested with the effort required for movement. His feet slip-slop across the plastic linoleum of the long hospital corridor, and his arms hang lifelessly by his sides: that terrible tell-tale sign of someone on powerful medication. He smiles sideways at me across the corridor, a smile as slow as his walk. His hair is curly again and unkempt, flattened at the back and sides by long hours of lying on his bed.

The bus lurches around a corner and I reach out a hand to steady my bag as I remember him the last time I set eyes on him. He looks well again. He's been on good form for the last eight months, funny, engaged and gradually forgiving us for our part in his difficult last few years. He's excited about his trip to Thailand and eager to get going. He promises to stay in touch, to let us know when he arrives, to stay safe. We hug, he pulls back, looks at me for one last time and smiles his long, slow smile and then he's off, threading his way through the crowds in the departure area. I see this young man I love so much, striding purposefully towards his next adventure. It's hard to let him go but I know I must. He doesn't look back.

On the way from Newcastle airport to the hotel I pass a hospital sign. I feel a momentary lurch of dread as my mind forms an unbidden imagining of having to visit Ellie there. I say a silent prayer that I should never have to. These unwelcome fears come from nowhere, as unexpected as a sudden lightning strike in clear, blue skies. They make me feel vulnerable and exposed, as though my love for my two remaining children, intense as ever, now places me on less than solid ground, ground which might open up and swallow me if anything were to happen to them. I have never shied away from dark imaginings. I've always acknowledged the fragility of human life and somehow felt protected by the thought that I could allow myself to do so, as though there were some unwritten contract with God or fate that, for so long as I could allow the worst to exist in my mind for just a fleeting second, it would not happen. But now that it *has* happened, these passing thoughts feels less like a safety net and more like dark foreboding.

***

Ellie and I go to the Body Worlds exhibition and it makes me think of you. You would have loved seeing real bodies pared back to the essentials, and so much emphasis placed on the importance of how we treat them, what we put into them, what we give them to cope with.

Dad described you in his Tribute as 'a most beautiful physical specimen … put together by someone with a terrific sense of scale and proportion.' You were. Even in adolescence you seemed to stay in proportion. When you got into nutrition and the benefits of raw food you became a walking advert for your cause. You were slim and fit and toned. It took extraordinary self-discipline and strength of will to stick so rigidly to your beliefs but of course you'd had all those years of honing your obstinacy and immovability, so you probably had a head-start on lots of people. I'm not sure it stayed healthy, your obsession with what you would allow into your body.

Medics talk of a new eating disorder now – orthorexia – where someone systematically avoids foods they believe to be harmful. I think you might have qualified for a diagnosis at one time. You started to prepare your own food when you were about seventeen. There's a photo taken in early 2010. You're sitting with us all at a family meal. Our plates are piled high with our supper: two salads – one couscous, roasted baby vegetables and goat's cheese; the other tomato, avocado and mozzarella – and crusty bread. Your plate is bare but you're holding aloft a jug of some green, juiced concoction. You're toasting us all with your health-giving liquid and behind the jug you're grinning delightedly. You were so happy then. You were extreme in your beliefs and already different; but not yet odd.

You gave up on healthy eating once you were on anti-psychotic drugs. And the body you had worked so hard to optimise by feeding it only with natural, pure and health-giving produce lost its tone and tautness.

'What's the point,' you asked, 'when I'm being poisoned anyway?'

It was another horror for you too, to come round after your suicide attempt to discover that you had not only survived, but unwittingly introduced those six lead pellets into your precious body. To you they were six lethal centres of toxicity, and you could feel them leaching their poison into your system, gradually killing you.

Initially your lead levels were raised but repeated blood tests revealed a steady reduction down to healthy levels. Needless to say, you were having none of it. You always knew best and doctors didn't know anything, so there was no corresponding reduction in your sense of ongoing toxic contamination. You could feel the poison doing its work, giving you headaches, lethargy and low mood. You became obsessed by it, depressed and anxious at the thought of the slow drip of malignancy spreading through your system. You badgered your psychiatrist for something to be done. He finally agreed. He could see that it was an increased risk factor for you. You'd already shown that you were capable of taking drastic action if people didn't listen to you.

You were referred to a head and neck surgeon. We sat waiting for endless appointments at Charing Cross Hospital while different doctors explained to you, patiently and respectfully, that in terms of your physical well-being, an operation to remove the lead would not bring about any improvement in the symptoms you were describing, that an operation would be painful and carry with it serious risks. They explained that the pellets were lodged in difficult places to reach, one against the carotid artery, one close to the spine, others at the base of the skull and located amongst numerous nerves and beneath muscle, which might be compromised or irreparably damaged. There was a risk that you might lose the ability to swallow, would never again be able to eat or drink, would have to be fed by a tube going directly into your stomach. You listened with palpable impatience.

'When can I have the operation?' you interrupted.

Later we sat in the hospital canteen.

'Sam,' I said, 'you've got to listen to what you're being told. This would be an operation with serious risks. The neck is like a chicane with all the vital blood vessels and nerves going through it, and muscles that really matter. They'd have to cut through some of those to reach the pellets and they're saying that it might affect your ability to swallow.'

Unusually, you seemed to be listening, so I carried on.

'There's a chance that you'd never be able to eat or drink naturally again. It's not just about the pleasure that you take in food and drink, it would be the social side too. Just think about it. No more shared mealtimes, no more trips to Pizza Express or to the Bell for a Bombay Sapphire and tonic and skinny chips. Just think about the reality of being fed through

a tube into your stomach. Surely you'd miss all that wouldn't you?'

You hesitated for a moment, perhaps thinking about what I'd said.

'Do you think they do a vegetarian option?' you asked.

I could only laugh. In resigned exasperation. It was so **you**. *The delusion about being poisoned was part of being ill, but the impatience, the refusal to listen or reflect, the desperation for a quick fix, the need for instant gratification, the need to have your own way, that was all the you I recognised, it was the you I'd been battling to contain and moderate all my life.*

A couple of months later you had the operation. The doctors recognised the very real mental anguish caused to you by the idea of those lead pellets unleashing their toxins into you, and though three pellets were removed, it proved enormously difficult to locate and extract the rest without causing damage. The operation had lasted four hours when the surgical team called it a day. They said it was too dangerous to continue and that they weren't prepared to operate again: the risks were too high. We returned for two more post-operative appointments. You tried to persuade them that they should attempt to extract the final three pellets but finally you had to accept that there was nothing more to be done.

I stand in the Exhibition looking at a head and body – the tangled web of vital muscles, blood vessels and nerves compressed into the neck – and think of those six pellets and the surgeon's tools charting a course through it all. It seems to me a miracle that you survived your suicide attempt and the operation without serious injury or death.

Thank God you didn't die then, just twelve weeks after being discharged from hospital from that first admission. We would have lost the opportunity to make any sort of peace with you. You were remarkably casual about your survival, but you did admit later that you were glad you'd survived and were happy to accept that it wasn't your time.

I come across two set of lungs displayed side by side; one from a smoker and one from a non-smoker. The former are leathery-looking like a pair of fire-bellows, coated in black. The latter are pink and soft. You took up smoking to relieve the boredom of being in Prospect Park, declaring that you weren't addicted but merely smoking through choice. Eventually you admitted that you couldn't give up. Initially it felt like a negative spin-off from an already awful situation, but it also came to be a part of the new you we all embraced. Standing outside for a cigarette you made friends in hospital, bonded with your smoker-cousins, were joined by Imogen – smoking a crayon – for a mid-meal chat. Rather than hold it between the fore and middle finger of an outstretched hand, you held it between thumb and forefinger, with the rest of your hand cupped around it or tucked under it. It became a part of you.

Once you recounted with outraged disbelief how you'd woken to the sound of people hammering on the door of your room in Wokingham after one of your housemates, spotting smoke billowing from under your locked bedroom door and unable to rouse you, had called the fire brigade. You'd fallen asleep with a lit cigarette in your ashtray which, piled high with abandoned cigarettes and butts, had caught fire as you slept on, oblivious. You hooted with laughter at the thought of your housemate "overreacting" like that. You never were one to see or take responsibility for your own part in things.

***

26 October 2014

THE PURCHASE OF the cottage in Wales has all gone through. I finish work and I head there, on my own. Or rather with Sam, for that's how it feels now when I spend time alone.

Part 3

27 October 2014

I SPEND MY first night in Wales. Sigmund is with me. At 3.30 am he fights his way upstairs, past the barrier I have carefully erected, and leaps onto my bed. I'm secretly glad.

The cottage is lovely. It's like having a doll's house with which I can endlessly play. I feel very close to Sam here. I've put photos of him everywhere. And because it isn't home, with all its associations to difficult times, it somehow feels a more uncomplicated emotional space.

I love my home. It's full of happy memories, but I can't get away from the painful ones too. Sometimes I lie in bed and I see the door opening, Sam standing there, bloodied; I hear sirens and the heavy plod of police and paramedics on the stairs; hear the knock on the door that signals another Mental Health Act assessment. There was so much intrusion, not unwarranted, but difficult nonetheless. Something is lost when the sanctity of a family and home is pierced repeatedly by outside agencies: police, paramedics, social workers and doctors. They come invested with authority, with a right to be there, to invade, to question, to take action. It changes a home to be so intruded upon.

The cottage has nothing of that. It's a small sanctuary, a haven, where I can create a safe and separate space.

28 October 2014

FINALLY I LISTEN to Eddie Vedder's soundtrack to *Into the Wild*. I stretch out on the sofa and sob.

5 November 2014

AT ST MARY'S I place fresh flowers on Sam's grave. Later, as dusk falls, I return for the All Souls service. I dress in black: exactly the same clothes I wore for the early communion service I went to after learning of his death. I can't say *why* this feels so important. I know only that it does.

The next day I find myself again wearing black: a silent communication to the world that, despite appearing to cope, I am still steeped in grief.

9 November 2014

I CRY WHEN I awake to find the day dawning and realise that the year has inexorably ground its way forwards to my birthday. I'm taken aback by the devastation I feel. I simply don't want it to be my birthday. Not without Sam in my life. I want it neither to come nor to go. I simply want the day not to be. Each and every passing day takes me further away from the memory of a living Sam. Special days are the worst. It isn't just his absence that makes them so hard, but the message lying behind their coming and going: that time and the world move on. Swept forward on the tide of life, I leave him further and further behind me.

He died on the first of May. He's still dead. Nothing has changed in that despite the six months that have passed and all that has happened since then. Ellie has started university. I have bought the cottage in Wales. Rosy has performed at Glastonbury and Bestival. Lily, Lee and Charlie are about to start a new life in Ibiza. The only thing to remain the same, unchanging, is the deadness of Sam. I don't want time to remind me of this by flagging up markers.

Except, of course, I need it to. For in the insult of the world continuing to turn, days continuing to dawn and the sun continuing to rise, lies my potential salvation. I don't expect time to heal, if healing means the sealing over of this dreadful wound, but I know it will lessen the pain and that I will learn to welcome the relentlessness of its passage. It keeps me connected to life, even if part of me resists it.

Paddy and I walk up the Llangattock escarpment. It's a long, steep climb. I welcome the pain of it. As I near the top I hear voices, adults and a child, approaching on a different path. I run. I need to get to the large flat rock overlooking the valley below before the voices do. It's the rock I've photographed the children on for years. I can see

Rosy and Sam standing on it in their red hooded fleeces as I hurtle over puddles and past a startled man. I know it's rude. It wouldn't be okay in a city and it certainly isn't on a Welsh mountain, but I fling myself onto the rock possessively. The family arrives. They join me there and the mother starts to breastfeed her baby as the little boy's piping voice cuts through the silence. I hate them for destroying my quiet moment of remembering Sam with their slurping, grunting baby and their talkative child. But most of all I hate them for still having their family intact and their future ahead of them.

10 November 2014

SAM VISITS ME in my dream. It's comforting. He's leading the life he might have led, as a student, and I have gone to visit him. A friend pops in to see him and they talk about a paper they've had to read. Sam is interested and lively and even though he's complaining about how hard it's been to understand the paper, it doesn't matter because I can see how engaged he is. The friend commiserates, but I can tell he hasn't found it hard. I can see he likes Sam and values him for who he is. I feel a small rush of happiness for Sam and of relief for myself as I think, 'Sam's all right. I knew he would get there in the end.'

It was what I often thought in the years before his illness took hold and even after it had. He could be so difficult, so unpredictable but sometimes I would see something in him to fill me with hope for the man he would become. I knew he would be an interesting adult, unusual, different in a positive way, and sometimes I saw too his potential to be a good person, and to be at peace within himself. And that made me happy.

I'm glad I could hold onto that hope and my belief in him. It helped Sam to believe in himself. It's why it was so devastating when he thought I'd stopped believing in him.

I never did.

15 November 2014

IT'S 3.38AM AND I'm sitting in bed with only Sig for company. Paddy is on his way to the airport with Lily and Charlie who are leaving to join Lee for a new life in Ibiza. Ellie is asleep next door, having come down from Newcastle for their last evening. Rosy is back in Bristol after coming home for my birthday meal. She made Welsh cakes with Charlie, and Mars Bar sauce, his favourite. We're all going to miss them.

It's hard for children when parents end up with new partners. It isn't their choice. I remember Rosy, before she'd met Paddy, hearing a message he had left on the answer phone. 'He's got a *horrible* voice,' she said with venom. It was all she could think or feel about this man who threatened her fantasy of life going back to normal, with her Mum and Dad back together again. And Sam, whispering to Paddy one morning as Rosy left the room for some entirely innocent reason, 'Rosy *hates* you, you know.' And Ellie, a couple of years later, saying as we all sat in bed for our early morning drinks, 'I've been thinking. When you and Daddy get back together, Paddy can still live with us. He can be our butler.' It seemed hilarious at the time but it makes me realise how much the children still had invested in the idea of Simon and me becoming a couple again. If it was hard for my children, it must have been immeasurably harder for Lily. She'd already lost her Mum. How not to feel she was losing her Dad too? How not to hate us all for that?

I think of all the fun we've had together too, despite the difficult beginnings: meals inside and outside with all of us round the table; Charlie and Sam lying side-by-side on the floor propped up on their elbows playing on Sam's Xbox; Lily helping Ellie her with her homework, two blonde heads bent close together; Rosy and Charlie careering round the garden and bouncing on the trampoline; Ellie and Charlie competing to sit on my lap.

'She's *my* Mum,' from Ellie, and Charlie's indignant retort, 'Well, she's *my* Gilly.'

I see Rosy, Sam and Ellie in a pyramid on Paddy's back; Charlie humouring Imogen with endless games of hide and seek, shouts of 'Ready or not, here I come,' echoing all around the house.

And now it's just Paddy and me on our own. The family is shrinking and I can't do anything to stop it.

26 November 2014

WE GO TO friends for lunch. I sit next to a man whose eighteen-year-old son, Freddie, died three years ago. He knows I know about Freddie and I know he knows about Sam, but we haven't met before. He turns to me and smiles. I smile in return.

'Shall we get our dead children out of the way first?' he asks.

His directness is such a relief. It means anything can be said. There's no need for niceties or avoidance. I'm with someone who has been through the horror of losing a child, who has found the words to talk about it and who isn't afraid to go there, right to the heart of it.

I think of my friend Jane who lost her nineteen-year-old daughter, Rachel, and her elation when Simon, bumping into her on the Thames towpath, introduced her to Kim as 'Rachel's mum.' She hadn't realised until that moment just how much she had missed being described that way. Most people had been avoiding it.

27 November 2014

ON THE RADIO I hear two people describing their experiences of being diagnosed with schizophrenia. Above all else they plead to be seen as people rather than as a diagnosis.

***

You hated everything about your diagnosis and the medication you were forced to take but finally, after your seven-month stay in hospital in 2013, you were prescribed an anti-psychotic drug that left you with fewer side-effects and things began to turn around. You seemed, almost, to accept that you had to take it. It returned you to us Sam. You weren't entirely the same Sam, but much of you was there: the sense of humour, your wacky, inimitable way of seeing the world, the capacity to be funny, warm and kind.

You made some good friends on Bluebell ward, a group of six of you, who looked out for one another. It helped you realise that good, ordinary people ended up on psychiatric wards. You stayed in touch with them after your discharge. They all came to your funeral, or those who were still alive did. By then two were already dead. You phoned me in tears on the night you heard Andy had died of a drug overdose. You couldn't believe it. You were asked to read a poem at his funeral and chose, 'Do not Stand at my Grave and Weep.' Paul told you afterwards you read it beautifully. Those friendships were important to you. These were people who had shared something with you that so many others hadn't. It created a special bond between you.

You left Prospect Park on 10th August 2013. By then it had become a kind of home. You even asked to go back in for a couple of weeks later that autumn because I was going to be away.

Before your discharge we'd had time to think about where you wanted to live and we'd set the planning process in motion to renovate the barn in the garden so you could live there. We were ready to start the building works when you returned from Thailand. I received the planning permission just before you set off in April 2014. It had all just gone out to tender. You would have been able to live independently but tap into family life when you wanted to. Until it was ready you wanted to live in a shared house again and went to the one in Wokingham paid for by the mayor.

Although you missed the person you'd been and struggled to forgive us for our treachery in involving the mental health services, you began to re-engage with us all. You started to take pleasure in family life again. The next eight months had their ups and downs but most of the time things stayed steady. You regularly came to stay at home. Christmas 2013 came and went. You stayed for a week or more and then we all went to Wales, both the girls and Charlie too. You seemed to be in a good place. It was a joy to have you back. It felt like a gift after four such difficult years. You began to make plans in early 2014. You went on a taster day for a massage course and signed up for it. You bought yourself a moped – one of your impulse buys, but nothing new there.

It seemed to me that you were happy, were finding a contentment of sorts in spite of all that had gone before. I think we all began to picture the life you might lead: not the life you would have wished for yourself, but a life nonetheless that could bring you autonomy and pleasure and a future worth investing in. You began to make contact with friends again. We dared to hope that the worst was over.

Dad and I weren't entirely unhappy when you announced in April 2014 that you'd bought a flight to Thailand and planned to go off travelling once again. That nice Mayor and your very frugal way of life had made it *possible for you to put aside some of your benefits, so you could fund it yourself. I think we'd always known that the time would come again; and we could see that being a traveller gave you an identity and your life meaning and structure. We hoped it might protect you in a world where social etiquette demands that we give an account of ourselves and explain our place in it.*

We were nervous as we always were when you went away but we felt more confident about you than on any of your previous trips. That was probably naive, but you seemed so much more grounded this time. You were so much better, so much more your old self.

We only had you back for eight months before you left on your final trip. It's been doubly heart-breaking to lose you again so soon after you'd been restored to us.

1 December 2014

I WANT TIME to stand still. I'd like to stop the clock and prevent Christmas and New Year's Eve from happening. I can't bear the thought of 2015 arriving. However hard 2014 has been, it keeps me linked to Sam. I'm simply not ready to move into a new year. I begin to understand depression. It answers this urge to stop time and prevent life from moving forward. It's an unconscious act of defiance against an external world that refuses to be frozen. Instead we freeze things internally. It prevents us from living. We disengage. Without any conscious intent we keep things in a state of stasis and leave the world to move forward without us.

In Sam's bedroom I find a plastic bag. Inside is a tangle of miscellaneous electrical leads. I don't know what to do with them, but I feel a need to do something. I take them downstairs and drop them into the kitchen bin. There is a thud. With it comes a flood of desolation.

In his cupboard I come across a deep ruby-red, crushed velvet gown, with wide bell sleeves, trimmed at the edges and round the neck with gold and silver. I remember sitting at the sewing machine, cursing the stretch in the fabric as I tried to coax it under the presser-foot, the ribbon trim escaping to left and right. Finally completed I held it up for six-year-old Sam – soon to be one of the three kings – to see.

'I'm not wearing a *dress,*' he said as his face registered disbelief that I could even think of it.

'It'll look fine, Mr Muelo. I'm going to make you a crown too, remember. They'll match.'

Within a few seconds I saw his slow smile creep across his face and heard his hoot of delight as he saw the potential for comedy.

'Can I put it on now?' he asked.

'Yes, fine,' I said, 'just slip it over your clothes.'

He held his arms up in the air as I eased it over his head and then he took off at a run, swinging his arms so the sleeves swayed and caught the light, shouting,

'Look Rosy, look Ellie, I'm wearing a dress. I'm going to be a King in a dress and Mum's going to make me a crown.'

The crown is on the top shelf of the cupboard. I take

it out carefully. It's remarkably intact, just one of its castellations bent at the corner. The jewels are still all there, glued to the iridescent silver card and, inside, the padded, crushed velvet cap studded with silver discs.

I see Sam walking onto the stage with a grin as sparkling as his crown, and then a look of concentration on his face as he bends on one knee to present his gift.

24 December 2014

THE LAST FEW weeks have passed in a blur.

Lunch out. Meeting new people. Being asked about children. Saying three separate times that I had lost my son this year. Hearing my words sink without trace into the dark well of their inadequacy and awkwardness. Feeling Sam disappear with them and my own feelings sink like a stone into dark emotions that I struggle to name: loneliness, anger, fury. Feeling my face suddenly refuse to play the game and go through the motions of social etiquette. It becomes stiff and wooden. It's on strike; it won't move. I don't want to be here amongst strangers who are struck dumb by my loss and shift in embarrassment from foot to foot or look at their plates rather than me. And even when they respond with sympathy and warmth, I feel myself brushing away their kind concern as though it is something trivial and unimportant. It feels as though I can only lose, whichever way they, or I, respond.

Shopping for Christmas. The pain of seeing things I want to buy for Sam: that I would have bought for him. That moment of forgetting as I walk the aisles and find myself hesitating in front of a possible purchase.

I miss shopping for him. It was such a mix of pleasure and pain – never knowing whether your gift would be greeted with disbelieving derision, or wonder. Either was possible. He could be the harshest critic if you got it wrong; but the warmest enthusiast if you got it right. It was the best feeling ever when you did.

25 December 2014

I WAKE EARLY, creep out of bed before anyone is up and go into Sam's bedroom. I sit on his bed, hold his jumper to my face and cry. I pick up notebooks and read his spidery scrawl: little snippets of surprising beauty, words full of wonder and awe about life and nature. There are just a few lines on each page. They seem to reflect his life: intense bursts of feeling and energy, the promise of something extraordinary but fizzling out to nothing. His was a light which shone so brightly at times. I think of the message still on the answer phone, breathy with excitement as he told me about being given the A/A* for his first piece of assessed work for his English GCSE. In it I heard him daring to believe in himself, in a future which might hold promise. I think of his last few years, of those broken hopes, of the dawning realisation that others were slipping into worlds beyond his reach, his friends at university, setting out on lives that he himself might have lived had things been different.

My heart breaks for a moment. I let it break.

And then I put it back together and head downstairs to put the oven on for the turkey.

26 December 2014

I SURVIVE CHRISTMAS. There are moments of surprising loveliness and others of overwhelming sadness. I hear the Archbishop of Canterbury, Justin Welby, talking about losing his 7-month-old daughter in a car accident. He says you have to attack the significant days: anniversaries, birthdays and Christmas, or else they attack you. Attack them by remembering the person you've lost: the happy memories and the sad ones, letting yourself feel both the joy of having had them in your life and the pain of having lost them. Perhaps my visit to Sam's bedroom early on Christmas morning was my way of attacking the day.

31 December 2014

I'M NOT READY to let 2014 go. It feels like letting Sam go. Yet I know that I have no choice. It's another day I don't know how to get through.

I am disagreeable and out of sorts as Paddy and I trudge uphill in the Black Mountains. I don't realise until later that what I really needed was to walk alone. I keep on stopping and every time I stop he does too. And it gets on my nerves, which I know isn't fair because I'm not telling him what I need, but of course I don't know, so instead I huff irritably.

'What's up Gill?' he finally asks.

'I don't know. I'm sorry Pads,' I say. 'I seem to need to be difficult. Why don't you just keep going?'

I stand and wait for him and Sig to walk on ahead of me. I step to the edge of the path, look down to the rugged valley below, up to the rocky crags. I feel the weight of the hills bearing down on me. I've never felt smaller nor less significant, yet I've never felt the loss of Sam more keenly. A kestrel wheels above me as I speak into the vastness of the landscape and berate him for leaving me.

***

2014: you breathed its air, felt the warmth of its sun on your skin, walked under its stars. I don't want to leave it and you behind and move into a new year without you. We still don't know what happened that day in Pai: how and why you died, whether you intended to. It makes it harder than ever to let the year pass.

I was so angry with you when I read the email from the embassy saying the autopsy had been unable to confirm the cause of death because 'the body was too much putrid.' Can you imagine how it felt as your mother to read that? I couldn't bear the thought of you lying alone with no one to find you. And then the toxicology report with its casual mention of traces of morphine and tranquilliser in your liver. My anger with you could only increase; for taking drugs, for either wanting to die or being so reckless that you did. I called Dad. He wasn't angry, just sad. He reminded me of a quote in 'Far from the Tree' (Solomon, 2012) where the sibling of a man with schizophrenia says that though his mother got over his brother's death, she never got over his life. Dad too felt that schizophrenia was the real tragedy of your life. All the waste and lost potential. I wanted to be angry with the illness, but I could only feel angry with you. I wanted to shake you and ask you what on earth you were thinking of. But of course you weren't thinking, or if you were, it was the way you thought with a mind affected by schizophrenia.

*It was always so hard to know with you, where **you** ended and your illness began. Of course that's not actually a helpful way of looking at it. The illness was part of you. I've been reading the chapter on schizophrenia in 'Far from the Tree'. I could relate to almost everything in it. It made perfect sense to me when Solomon wrote of the wish of most parents to see the illness as some sort of overlay or an invading force. If it is, then the potential exists for it to be lifted off again or ousted – what any parent would wish for. He said the reality is very different, that the symptoms combine with the person who's already there. In your case it seemed to make you a more extreme version of the person you'd always been. There was both gain and loss in that. It meant that we could still recognise you within the new behaviours. It gave us something to hold onto. But in other ways it muddied the waters and it makes it harder to know what to make of the way you thought about death. I don't know how much was you and how much was distorted by illness. You won't remember the first time you spoke about dying but I do.*

It was the summer after Dad and I separated and you were seven years old. We were at Grandpa's house with Rosy and Ellie, playing tennis in the garden. You were being impossibly obstructive that afternoon, swimming against the tide at every turn, refusing to play at the same time as Rosy, complaining about everything, kicking balls away rather than picking them up. You and I had been on the court for fifteen minutes while Rosy sat and watched and now it was her turn. But you were refusing to move off so she could play. You'd taken up position about three metres in front of her. Every time she moved so did you.

'Oh come on, Sam,' I said, 'you were the one who insisted on playing on your own with me, and now you don't want Rosy to have her go. That just isn't fair.'

'But I've got nothing to do.'

'You can be ball boy with Ellie, or you can sit and watch like Rosy did.'

'I don't want to. I'm going to go and play on the climbing frame.'

'You can't do that on your own Sam, it's too far away. We're going to go there after Rosy's had her turn at tennis. You know that. The sooner you move out of the way, the sooner we'll be able to.'

'But I want to go now.'

'Well, I'm afraid you can't. You're going to have to wait.'

And on and on and on until you stomped off in fury into the laurel bushes. You weren't gone for long. A few minutes later you were back on the court.

'I want to go now.'

I ignored you. You reached into your pocket and pulled

out a handful of laurel berries. You thrust them towards me on the palm of your hand.

'If we don't go now, I'm going to eat these,' you said. 'I don't mind dying.' I looked at you. You looked steadily back at me.

'I mean it,' you said.

I knew you weren't going to eat the laurel berries but as I looked into your eyes I saw more than simple defiance. It seemed to me you might mean what you'd said about not minding dying. You were so sensitive, so aware, felt things so deeply. You just didn't have the words for all the difficult feelings assailing you: Aidi had died, Dad had moved out and I was struggling. Your world had turned upside down. But still I couldn't understand how you could feel that way when you were so loved.

I understand it better now. You were fragile. Behind the wall of anger and bad behaviour lay fear. Quitting or threatening to quit became your way of dealing with it both internally and externally. You became notorious for dropping out of things. You'd come marching in from some activity that you'd insisted on doing and announce, 'I've quit,' with something approaching pride. Your external world reflected your internal world. If things weren't going your way, you simply disengaged. It was easier to give up than to stay with the pain and try to work through it. I tried to help you see you had other choices, but you made it very hard. And always I'd been aware that, alongside your tremendous capacity for joy and passion for life, was a curious detachment. Perhaps death seemed just like one more way to disengage.

Schizophrenia made this ambivalence about life worse on

every level. As your interest in spirituality and Buddhism grew so did your absolute certainty that this life was just one of many. You became increasingly casual and fatalistic. You would talk often about death, imagining the turnout for your funeral, speculating on who would come, where you'd like your ashes to be scattered and, most of all, what you'd be in your next life. Death held no fear for you. You'd accept whatever fate brought you. You refused to see any connection at all between what fate delivered and the choices you made.

It's hard to leave 2014 still not knowing what was in your mind that day. It feels unresolved in me and though moving into another year changes nothing – for every passing day takes me further away from a living you – I feel I have unfinished business with this year, and with time for how it's treated me. I think back to those early days of grieving when time played tricks on me. I felt it stop as the policewoman's words set in the air. For just a moment, one brief hiatus, I felt the world hold its breath. And when it started up again time had altered. It moved painfully slowly: minutes felt like hours, hours like days, and days like weeks. There was a qualitative change too, a shift from fluvial to glacial. It no longer flowed. It had become three-dimensional and granular, grinding its way forward, inch by inch. I felt its hard edges scraping against me, jagged as metal. I wished only for it to speed up again, slide over me like silk.

And now my wish has been realised: it's rushing by, taking me with it, taking no account of my wish for it to slow down, even to stop. It feels that time has let me down twice-over. It's cheated me.

***

5 January 2015

I'M OUT WALKING in the Beacons when I hear a throaty growl in the distance, the rumble of an approaching military jet. Within seconds I hear the sound of splitting, as the air above me is rent in two. And then it's gone and there's only silence.

This noise of ripping fabric brings suddenly to mind my maternal grandmother raising a well-used sheet – worn thin and bare – and tearing it down the middle from head to toe. 'Sides to middle,' she used to say as she sewed them back together again. 'You see, they'll be good as new.' Even as a child I thought that unlikely.

Now I know that lives tear too. Can they be re-sewn, re-configured, sides to middle, new strength found? Even if they can, I know I will always feel the tell-tale ridge down the centre, at the heart of me.

7 January 2015

THERE IS A tiny church in Partrishow and little else. It's the Church of St Issui, founded in 1060 with the offerings of pilgrims to an early Welsh saint who lived close by. It clings to the hillside, its ancient gravestones leaning into the valley below, bending low to protect themselves from the wind and swirling cloud. There's rain in the air as we walk around the churchyard. Some of the headstones bear only the faintest traces of the words once engraved into them. They wear coats of lichen in soft silver-green.

I try the door. It opens and we step inside. There is a timeless simplicity to this patient, weather-worn place – an echo of pilgrim feet, of prayers intoned in quiet supplication, of new lives celebrated and lost lives mourned. On the wall is a plaque for a seventeen-year-old son: *"He giveth His beloved sleep."* Tears fill my eyes as I think of Sam. Life wasn't easy for him. Perhaps there is a release for him in sleep.

We find that the rain has passed when we step outside again. A wash of weak winter sunshine now bathes the church's grey stone walls and steep-pitched slate roof. We make our way down to the well where a huge flat stone marks the grave of St Issui. It is a place of healing and pilgrimage still. All around are small offerings: teetering pyramids of pinecones and pebble cairns. The trees by the side of the stream, the Nant Mair, are hung with strips of cloth and dotted with hammered coins. I feel a pressing need to leave something of Sam here too. Back at the car, in the boot, I find a single black sock with a name-tape stitched in green: Samuel E Roberts. I tie it to a low branch. It takes a while to get the name-tape to face outwards. It matters that it does.

10 January 2015

I HEAR SAM'S voice in my dream, calling me from his bed, 'Mu-um.' I imagine him lying there.

In the supermarket, I meet a woman whose son who went

through ten years of nursery and prep school in the same class as Sam. We stop for a quick chat. We re-meet in almost every aisle. She makes no mention of him, not in the first aisle, nor the second, nor the third, nor the fourth. Finally, between the tonic water and the crisps, I bring him into the conversation, mentioning a mutual friend who came to his funeral. Still she utters no words of sadness, no condolences as a mother, no simple, 'I'm so sorry.' Instead she stutters that she didn't come because she, 'didn't really know him.' In my world of loss this feels irrelevant. She's missing the point. You come out of shared humanity. You come because it could have been you. It could have been your child.

In *Levels of Life,* written after the death of his wife, Julian Barnes describes the inadequacies of others in the face of death: those he calls, 'the silent ones,' who fail to acknowledge his loss; and those he calls, 'the advice givers,' who fill the awkwardness of not knowing what to say with unsolicited advice. There haven't been many advice givers since Sam died. Perhaps there is no advice to be given when someone loses a child.

It's hard not to blame people for their inadequacy in the face of death, however unfair that is. I have a mental hate-list of all the people who 'should' have come to his funeral but didn't; who have failed to mention his dying; who don't pick up my cue when I say his name. I need somewhere to locate my anger about the unfairness of his death. I feel a perverse thrill of pleasure when I add a name to the list.

The pregnant policewoman is on there still, for failing to give me any hint of what was to come: for accepting that cup of tea, for engaging in all that small-talk. There were so many ways she might have let me know that there was nothing routine about this visit, nothing social, nothing light. Everything about it was wrong – the informal clothes, the absence of a police car, the mood and tone of her greeting. I needed her to look at her feet, to ask if there was somewhere we could sit down, to *sound* grave. I know I played my part. How could I *not* have assumed the worst with all that had gone before? I might have cut through all the niceties if I had. But I saw only what I wanted to see; what I could bear to see. I didn't want the worst to be a possibility. And despite knowing this – and understanding that people who avoided Sam's funeral or said nothing were simply protecting themselves from the thought of pain so intense that they doubted their own ability to cope with it – I still need someone or something to blame. My hate-list provides a focus for all my difficult feelings.

***

As I climb into bed I check that my phone is on. It's a habit I can't break after all the years of worrying about you. I got used to it ringing late at night. You had no sense of time. You'd call if something difficult happened, like Andy dying and the time your housemate thumped you. Sometimes, if you were feeling down, you'd call from hospital and ask if we could chat for a while. When you went missing my phone seemed to ring all night.

The British Transport Police called me once at 4am.

'Sorry to disturb you Madam but I've got a young man here. He says he's on his way back from Reading Festival. He has a bin-bag over his shoulder, a phone which is out of battery and a missing wallet. I gather he's called Sam and is your son. He assures me you'll be happy to pay his train fare so he can get home.'

'Oh dear,' I said, 'Yes, of course. Thanks for sorting him out. If you don't mind waiting a moment, I'll just get my credit card.'

'Right you are Madam. I'll just find out where he needs to get to.'

When I returned, I heard laughter at the end of the phone – your unmistakeable chuckle and the policeman's too.

'I don't think I'll be needing that credit card,' he said. 'It's only a two-pound fare. I think he can have that on us!'

If I could choose, I'd have all those night-time calls instead of this absence.

***

11 January 2015

A FEW WEEKS after Sam died, I noticed a deep, lateral groove in my fingernails. I guessed it was caused by the trauma of hearing he was dead. It has almost grown out now. I will miss it. I like to run my fingers across the ridge. It feels right to bear this physical manifestation of the impact of his death. I don't want it to disappear.

We watch *Spiral*. Laure Berthaud is pregnant and wants

an abortion. She has a scan to work out the gestation of her unborn child. It's fifteen weeks. Later, as I stand in front of the mirror getting ready for bed, I think of my two miscarriages; both at twelve weeks – the first between Rosy and Sam, the second between him and Ellie. My mind wanders on. If I hadn't lost those babies, then everything might have been different. Perhaps I wouldn't have had a son with schizophrenia and would still have three children. Initially it seems a seductive thought, but suddenly I realise what it would mean: never having had Sam or Ellie. How could I possibly wish for that? I catch sight of my face in the mirror. I look guilty and confused. It seems a terrible thing to have been seduced by this thought for even a split second. What sort of mother does that make me? A bad one. I make myself slow down and think. No, I am not a bad mother, I am merely a bereft one clutching at thought-straws that promise a fantasy re-run of her life: another version in which I don't have to lose a child.

Guilt is ever-present at the moment. I've failed in a mother's primary duty, to keep her child safe.

15 January 2015

SAM COMES TO see me in my dreams again. I am on the landing at home, talking to someone at the foot of the stairs about the economy. Every time I make a comment, he chips in from his bedroom, its door ajar, with something cheeky and funny. Eventually I stick my head round the door in mock irritation. He is lying on the bed propped up on one elbow, waiting for me – a huge, delighted grin stretched across his face.

I awake feeling warm inside and flooded with gratitude. I have received a gift: Sam back with me for a moment – moving, talking, emoting. He was whole and three-dimensional. I exchanged words and laughter with him. I can't seem to conjure him up in my mind's eye. I'm not sure I even have one. When I try, unsatisfactory, pixelated images come in and out of focus. Then, just as I think I have him, the picture begins to break up and fade.

18 January 2015

I DREAM AGAIN of Sam. He looks at me with mistrust, as he did in the last two years of his life, as if he dare not let me too close. I ask him for a hug. I say I need one. From him. He looks at me, warily. I stand and wait, in limbo. Then something softens in his gaze. He opens his arms and lets me in. He holds me tight.

Ellie calls. She is sobbing down the phone from her room at university. She wants Sam to come back, just for a few minutes, so she can hold him.

Rosy calls. I hear the sadness in her voice and the snuffle of tears. She has been crying all day. She misses Sam.

He said we would all get over it if he were to die. He said it casually, as if telling me the train was delayed. I told him we wouldn't.

They say that time heals. I wonder if it does; whether some things aren't beyond healing. I heard Libby Purves talk once, ten years after the death of her son, Nicholas. She didn't speak of healing, but rather of space changing, of one's world growing broader and higher. Nicholas's death hadn't become any smaller for her in that time, but her world had opened up again.

24 January 2015

I FEEL POSSESSIVE of grief, as though it belongs exclusively to me and those who loved Sam. I don't want others to have any claim on it. I see them mourning their loved ones and there is a part of me that stands coldly back. I don't believe they know what true grief is. I feel as though there's a finite quantity of grief to go around. By staking their claim on it, they dispossess me and diminish mine.

25 January 2015

LEAFING THROUGH PAPERS on my desk, I come across a sheaf of hand-written pages: the notes I made on different treatment options for schizophrenia and a list of possible therapeutic communities for Sam. I remember my excitement and the seed of hope within me as I called each in turn. In the margin next to every one of them is a large cross and the date I phoned them. They all said the same: he wouldn't be considered for a therapeutic community without any insight into his illness.

I bundle them up and drop them into the bin. Even now I can feel the disappointment.

I've done no more sorting of Sam's possessions since

clearing out his room in Wokingham. I haven't tidied his bedroom: have thrown virtually nothing away, moved nothing. I know I'm not ready yet. I don't know when I will be.

I don't know what that even means.

Paddy and I go out for supper. In the restaurant, the waiter shows us to a diner-style table with red banquettes. It's the same table I sat at on Mothering Sunday in 2012. I show Paddy the photos he took that evening, on the drive, before we left home.

'You made me take so many photos,' he says.

'I know I did. I think I always knew I was on borrowed time.'

9 February 2015

I GET TOGETHER with an old friend and fill her in on all the years of Sam's illness and then his death. I am shocked, in the re-telling, by what we have all been through. I re-live for a short while the anxiety generated by existing alongside psychosis.

It was relentless then. The anxiety and my certainty that he was ill. Then the pendulum would swing in the other direction and I'd be beset by doubts. I'd got it all wrong, was making more of things than I needed to. He was actually fine. Sometimes a sort of blindness would set in. Even bizarre behaviours seemed quite normal. It seemed that I was caught up in Sam's madness and it was only in telling others that I was able to reset the gauge, as I read the concern in their faces. I wasn't always ready for it. I would feel defensive of Sam if someone reflected back to me the abnormality of what I was describing: conversations about next lives, funerals, questions about death; would you rather be microwaved or guillotined? Who would you tell if you saw me walking on water? What would you do if you knew I had been a god in an earlier life? What would you rather be in your next life – a building or a flower? All these conversations were woven into the fabric of life with him. They were part of it. But they always had been.

10 February 2015

I'M SITTING WATCHING the BAFTAS with Paddy. I can't understand why *The Grand Budapest Hotel* is included in this year's awards. It seems so long since we watched it. And then I realise. It was the last film I saw with Sam before he died. It feels as though I watched it in another life. In some ways, I did.

11 February 2015

IT'S ELEVEN DAYS until Sam's birthday. He liked his birth date with its predominance of '2's: 22.2.92. We plan to scatter his ashes on the day. I know I need to prepare myself now, in advance, rather than think I'm okay with it and then find myself hitting a wall as I feel the unexpected impact. I need to think, to really think, about the meaning for me of scattering his ashes; ask myself whether I am ready to say goodbye; how it will feel to look inside the decorative brass urn now sitting on the mantelpiece; how it will feel to handle them.

'We're going to scatter Sam's ashes in the Brecon Beacons,' I hear myself say, 'on his birthday, on Sugar Loaf mountain. It was one of his favourite walks.' I say it all as though it's something ordinary, some inconsequential daily routine: 'We're going to have fish for supper tonight' or 'We're going to the cinema on Sunday.'

It isn't ordinary. It will be his birthday and he won't be there.

I don't want to shy away from this truth on the day. I want to engage with it, allow it to be the tragedy that it is: another farewell, a letting go. I want to feel the pain of this goodbye, I don't want to let the meaning and the feelings glance off me. I want it to penetrate, to soak in and permeate this coping part of me, to filter down through the layers of defences I have erected, to trickle past the blocks and barriers, to reach the deepest part of me. I want to be there with my grief. I want to make that walk with Sam in my mind, as I bid my final farewell to the baby I held in my arms, the toddler who sat on my knee, the boy and young man in whose successes I rejoiced and for whose struggles I wept. I want truly to be present.

12 February 2015

AS I MAKE my way to the churchyard to see Sam, I look

back across Mill Green to the three women I've just said goodbye to after an early morning walk: sensitive, warm, supportive friends. I feel all of a sudden very alone on my way to see my dead son, as they head home to carry on with the lives in which their sons still play a part.

Envy is an ugly feeling. I'm aware of it jostling for space, elbowing its way in when I see or hear of Sam's contemporaries reaching milestones he will never now reach. I try not to let it take too much of a hold. I know that the momentary satisfaction of an envious comment or act dissipates all too quickly. There's nothing to sustain me in the hollowness that follows. I know too that I mustn't suppress it altogether. I let myself acknowledge its presence and its legitimacy. How could I not envy my friends and family for their happy fortune of having all their children still? I try not to hate them for it but if I do, just for a moment, that is alright.

16 February 2015

I TALK TO Paddy about how to prepare, in a practical sense, for scattering Sam's ashes on Sunday. I need to get organised: to set some ashes aside, for a black sand beach in Hawaii and for Samye Ling. Sam would have liked the idea of a small part of him ending up at both. I need to work out how to open the urn. Paddy thinks I should take it into the undertakers and ask them to do it for me. He's worried it will upset me to handle his ashes myself.

I think about it as I slice the chicken breasts for supper and measure out soy sauce, sesame oil, rice wine and fish sauce for the marinade. As I pour and tip, and tip and pour, I become aware of a battle inside me. I don't want to leave this task to strangers; it is something *I* want to do for Sam. But I'm scared too – scared to look inside the urn, to see what's there, to see how little is left of him. And if I don't want to feel this fear on Sunday I must face it before then. I need to prepare myself emotionally as well as practically.

A minute later, Paddy heads upstairs and, in a moment of sudden clarity, the battle ceases inside me. I know what I have to do.

***

I'm ready to see what remains of you Sam. I'm still scared but I know I need to face my fear. I collect two film canisters, open them, discard the films and take the empty canisters into the kitchen. Then I walk into the sitting room and take the urn from the mantelpiece. I think of you as I hold it in my hands and carry you through the kitchen, scooping up the film canisters as I pass by. I place the urn on the wooden work surface in the utility room and slowly unscrew the lid. Inside is what seems to be a flower, something like a rose or fringed tulip, with exuberant, overlapping petals. It's not unlike the flowers we placed on your coffin in the crematorium. On closer inspection, I realise it's a cotton rag, slightly frayed around the edges, gathered up into a circle, pulled together and secured with an uneven strip of cotton tied into a bow.

I raise this small white package from the urn and feel the weight of it in my hand; so insubstantial, so little to represent a life, such a poor and inadequate remainder of the bundle of warmth and electricity that was you. I feel the ashes through the cotton, cold, granular and ungiving; no substitute for a living son.

I pull on the bow. It loosens and I tug it free, the cotton unfurling to reveal what remains of you: a small heap of whitish-grey shards, firm and sharp, and between them, grit and flecks of black, like broken pumice crushed into tiny pieces.

It isn't ash.

There is nothing soft about these remains — not powdery like icing sugar, dissolving into silky traces. Instead they are hard and unyielding, just like the undertaker said.

I take the canisters and dip them in, working the firm, plastic edges through the shards. I secure their lids and wipe the outside of the canisters with my hand, ready to put to one side. My fingers are patterned with tiny ridges of white, like crusts of chalk-dust.

But it isn't chalk. It's you.

Unsure of what to do next, I pick up the lid to the urn and, as I do so, feel the brass finial shift slightly in my hand. I rotate it until, loosened altogether, it comes free, revealing a small hole from which the ashes can be scattered. I replace it and, gathering the cotton bundle up, I tip its contents — you — into the urn. I hear gritty shards meeting metal.

When I finish, a soft shadow of dust remains on the wooden work surface, a thin, grey film, a scattering of you. I sweep it up with my hands, tipping it from my palm into the open urn, then replace the lid and slowly and gently secure it to make it safe for your final journey with us. I re-tie the *empty cotton rag and slip it with the film canisters into one of my handbags hanging on the kitchen door. I will return them to the brass urn when we are back from Wales. The skin on my hands feels dry, as they do when I peel off my gloves after gardening.*

This is you on my skin.

I don't wash my hands.

Returning to the kitchen, I set the table for supper, water the kitchen herbs, take scissors to cut two chillies from the plant, chop them with ginger and garlic. The dryness doesn't last for long. I know that all the while I am depositing small atoms of you along the way, that you are becoming a part of my ongoing life. Earth to earth, ashes to ashes, dust to dust.

I feel such sorrow as I do all this. But there is relief too: relief in having seen and handled and dipped my fingers into what remains of you. I've made my peace with these stark remnants. I feel now I can let them go without losing the part of you that lives on inside me.

***

18 February 2015

ON OUR WALK round the lake we always stop at Sam's peg. It isn't his peg at all. It's a fishing platform that belongs to the Loddon Park fishing club. But to me and Sigmund it's his. There's hardly ever anyone there. But today on our walk I round the corner to find Sig standing on the path, his way barred by the chicken-wire fence that normally lies in a roll on the ground. This time it's been pulled across the entrance. Sig stands in sturdy outrage, his four feet planted in disbelief. He looks at me first, then out onto the peg. He cocks his head to one side as if to say, 'He's got to be joking. Who does this bloke think he is?'

Sam's peg is occupied. There's a tent – one of those dull-green shiny ones that matches the water on an overcast day – and next to it a fisherman is sitting in his deck-chair reading a book in the sunshine, two fishing lines set up behind him.

We always walk out over the water here. Like Sam did. He liked to tight-rope walk his way round the edge of the peg, balancing on its thin wooden ledge. If he lost his footing and slipped off, he'd go back to the start and begin again. He was unapologetic for the delay, it was just what he did, and I was meant to understand that.

We stand and wait. I'm not sure what I'm waiting for. I'd like the impossible to happen and the fisherman simply to disappear. I spend a lot of time wishing for the impossible these days.

The wind is raw, despite the blue sky. It travels across the lake in gusts leaving it furrowed like an autumn field. I walk on to the next peg. It won't be the same, but it will do. Sig resists at first, but then he joins me. I stand out over the lake and watch two swans glide across the water, stark white against the bulrushes in their winter shades of pale gold; leaves dry and folded earthwards, dark brown heads standing tall with remnants of seeds clinging to them, small candy floss crowns.

I look up as I always do. Overhead, gulls dip and wheel against the sky. Every now and then they disappear against a passing cloud. I stand and raise one arm to the heavens. I don't care what the fisherman thinks. It's my salute to Sam.

I wonder if I will always feel the need to stop here and what will happen when I'm old and infirm and unable to walk round the lake with its gnarly tree-rooted paths. I will miss it. It's one of my shortcuts to connecting with Sam.

***

Today there's no need for a shortcut. It's 22 February, twenty-three years since you entered the world on the crest of a wave.

I'm awake before 6am. I hear the wind first: the rattle and shake of it in the cottage rafters. And then the slash of rain as it flays the windowpanes. It has abated by the time we leave the cottage to drive to the foot of Sugar Loaf Mountain. Dad and Kim are following in their car. Imogen has asked if she can travel with us. Tucked between Rosy and Ellie in the back seat, she wants to know what ashes are. I explain. She nods her head sagely, a small frown settling on her forehead as she ponders this newly acquired knowledge.

We set off from the car park at 9.30am. It's grey and cold and threatens more rain. You are in the urn, wrapped in your favourite jumper, the blue cotton one Dad bought for you. The urn is in a small rucksack. We carry it in turns. It's important this sharing of you. We each had our own relationship with you, our own memories, our individual sorrows and joys in our life with you. The time we each spend alone with you, as we carry you on your final walk up Sugar Loaf, is precious. Even Imogen takes her turn, her face, with its small frown telling us how seriously she takes her role on this special day; and betraying too with a fleeting, small smile, her pleasure at being treated like everyone else.

It's hard to part with you when my time of carrying the rucksack is up. I sense a reluctance in each of us to hand it over when we have to, yet it's important we do, for in that moment when the rucksack is passed between us, something is shared: we recognise and acknowledge the pain of parting from you. It's a rehearsal too of what we know to be coming, the moment of scattering your ashes, of letting you go.

I'm allowed to carry you for a second time. There's no discussion. I'm simply handed the rucksack for the final ascent. I'm grateful. I wear it back to front, resting on my tummy, and I cuddle you to me. I run my fingers over the curve and bump of you as I did all those years ago when I carried you inside. As I place one foot slowly and carefully in front of the other I recall the feel of you then: the earliest flutterings of movement, as light as air in water; your first kick; the pressure of you against my ribs; an elbow or knee making its way across the stretch of my tummy in the bath; the image from your twenty-week scan; my hopes and fears for this unborn life in the making. I recall other carryings of you too: as a baby, as a toddler and then as a little boy, clinging on tightly, the comforting weight of your head on my shoulder as you fell asleep in my arms.

The ground is frozen underfoot, hard and unforgiving. It becomes slippery when it starts to snow. We are quiet as we near the summit. Our pace slows without our knowing it. Like Dad taking his time at the crematorium in Bangkok, each of us is reluctant to reach the moment when we have to say our last goodbye.

We are spread out now, a long, thin line, snaking up the mountain. Each is alone with his or her thoughts. Rosy and Ellie walk with heads bowed, eyes cast down. Kim's face is etched with sadness. She holds Imogen by the hand, steadying her on the uneven terrain. Dad walks behind them, his face strained and grey. With the back of his gloved hand, he wipes tears from his cheeks. Paddy plods slowly behind us all, a steady, solid presence, ready to gather up anyone who falters.

The wind is howling and carries with it small arrow-heads of frozen flakes that batter unprotected skin. The snow begins to settle, and all is grey, the landscape drained of colour. It's bleak. Yet there is beauty in this bleakness too, something uplifting in the gusts of wind and swirling snow.

We have the summit to ourselves. Each of us heads word-lessly to the trig point. We wait until all seven are gathered there. Still no one speaks. I open the rucksack, unroll your jumper and take out the urn.

Dad hands a piece of paper to Rosy, and another to Ellie.

Rosy begins to read. It's the AA Milne poem Dad read at your cremation in Bangkok. As she finishes, Ellie raises her sheet of paper and reads the final farewell from Dad's tribute at your memorial service in Wargrave. Her voice fades.

It's time.

I unscrew the finial from the lid of the urn. Wind whips

around us. Snow falls. I hold the urn at arm's length, tilt it and shake.

You are seized by the elements.

I pass the urn to my right. Gusts of wind gather you up and carry you away from us in every direction. This is not a gentle scattering. You don't fall to the ground like soft rain. You are snatched up and carried off: upwards and downwards, to the east and west, north and south, borne on the wind and blended with the snow. Nature reclaims you.

I don't see you go. It happens so quickly. But I know you have, for there is grit in my eyes. And at my feet, on the stone apron of the trig point, lies a small scattering of you, like broken shells on a shore. I see Ellie bend down to retrieve a small piece which she slips into her pocket. Dad leans over to take photos of these tiny remnants. It's hard to let you go.

We head for the lea of the mountain, out of the wind, and gather round once more, the empty urn at our feet. We toast you with Bombay Sapphire gin and tonic. Imogen smiles with pleasure when I give her a glass of tonic, ice and lemon.

You always spoke to her as though she were an adult. She loved it.

The snow continues to fall. We move on to hot tea and digestives to warm ourselves before we begin our descent. We cup our hands round our tea. It is ferociously cold. Two men arrive at the trig point. We can hear them making a spoof video about summiting K2. They take a photo of us all together. They do not notice the urn.

All is white now underfoot. Around us the wind bays and yowls. There is something fitting about the weather and the *landscape.*

'Beautiful but extreme,' says Ellie, 'just like Sam.'

As we come over the top of the mountain to make our way down, we are battered by the full force of the elements. I don't think I've ever seen Sugar Loaf like that before – under attack from the weather. I'm not sure you will have either. We walk head-on into wind and driving snow. Dad is carrying Imogen in his arms. Suddenly he loses his footing and falls over. Imogen screams, a sharp piercing cry just like the one she gave when she heard that you were dead. Rosy picks her up. She's fitter and stronger than any of us. We talk little. We're lost in our thoughts and we're concentrating on staying upright on the weather-battered terrain.

Back at the cottage, we strip off our saturated clothes. They lie in sad heaps on the old pennant floors. We dress hurriedly because our table is booked for 2pm, and there's no time to spare. Over lunch we talk of you. You're not there. And yet you are.

We all go back to the cottage. I make tea. The whole day is about you. And all day I can feel you with us. You're there in the strong feeling of shared love and shared loss, you're there drawing us closer together, to one another and to you. It's hard to describe. But I think you, more than anyone, would understand. We seem to have been bathed in love for the day. Your love for us. And our love for you. I feel your presence so strongly. It's a wonderful feeling on this terribly difficult day.

Rosy describes the weekend as 'exquisitely painful.' It's strange to feel such depths of sorrow and yet, alongside it, gladness too. For that is what I feel: glad and proud and grateful to be part of this strange-shaped family, who can come together in sadness, allow the sadness to be, and yet make something joyous out of it too. Everyone has played a part in making your birthday a day to remember with more than just sadness. I feel lucky to have this family around me. And, above all, I feel that you were lucky Sam to have had this family around you.

***

23 February 2015

I'M EXHAUSTED AFTER yesterday. Grief is exhausting. And complex. And confusing. It's so hard to know if one is doing okay. There are no pointers, no rules, no markers to tell you if you're on the right path. I have no idea whether I am or not. But I begin to realise more and more that in many ways it doesn't matter. I am simply where I am; and I am glad to have had yesterday with its pain and joy. I am glad to have been able to feel it all.

2 March 2015

I'VE JUST CROSSED the slatted footbridge next to the lake when I see two policemen walking towards me. They smile reassuringly.

'Can we just take a minute of your time please to ask you something?'

'Yes of course,' I say as one of them holds a photo out

towards me. It's a young man. 'We're just wondering if you might have seen him on your walk around the lake.'

I shake my head apologetically as I tell them I haven't.

'Well, keep an eye open and if you do, will you call it in please. Phone 999 and explain that we've asked you to, and that it's about a missing person.'

I'd seen the helicopter overhead as I climbed out of the car and felt a lurch of dread. I've heard it clattering through the air all the time I've been walking. I think of the parents worried sick at home, waiting for news. Just two years ago it was me.

5 March 2015

I'VE DECIDED TO do some voluntary work at Prospect Park Hospital. I am torn between working with patients directly or with families struggling with a family member requiring in-patient care. The decision is taken away from me when I am invited to be involved in planning for a programme of help for families. There is a meeting coming up and I want to prepare for it.

I make a list of the things I struggled with most when Sam was both becoming ill and in treatment. Once I start, I cannot stop. It seems to be endless:

- How to know in the early days whether he was ill or just being contrary and eccentric? How not to feel frustrated by his inactivity and lack of motivation? When to coax and cajole, when to let it go?

- How to cope with his never understanding that he was ill, with knowing he held me responsible for 'destroying' his life?

- How not to doubt myself when he told me again and again that I was the one with the problem: that I was neurotic, unstable and imagining things? How not to let that get inside me?

- How to respond to him in a psychotic state, when failing to challenge behaviours or statements felt like collusion, yet challenging seemed to increase his sense of dislocation? When to name what we were seeing, ask *him* to see it; when to leave it to others to deliver hard truths?

- How to deal with difficult, personal things, like body odour, hygiene, the impact on others of his unkempt appearance and unsettling behaviours? What to challenge, what to live with, but most of all, how to help him manage in a world he no longer fitted in?

- How to cope with the anxiety of his wanting to lead his own life: going out drinking, clubbing and wanting to travel? When to encourage and support, when to discourage? How to distinguish between real risk and my own anxiety? How to let go, as a mother, of a child so vulnerable? How to respect his autonomy and his right to make choices and decisions for himself whilst also fulfilling my role as a responsible carer?

- How to cope with the feeling of being an informer, of being disloyal to him, revealing things to professionals that could only increase the likelihood of his being sectioned?

- How not to feel guilty about handing him over to others, to a system he hated? How not to feel guilty for feeling relief when the burden of his care was removed from me?

- How to trust others when I knew and understood him so well? How much, when and what to impart, when to step back? How not to feel like an over-involved mother and part of the problem?

- How to help Rosy and Ellie cope? How much to tell them and how much to protect them from the truth? Whether to tell them to talk openly to friends or ask them to protect Sam by not sharing with others? How to get the balance right between their needs and his?

- What to do with my own feelings of grief over what was happening to him, my sadness about a life barely lived? How to deal with all the broken dreams and expectations I hadn't known I had? How to cope with the feeling of not being able reach him, the sense of alienation from him; with feeling I was losing him? How to like this new Sam? How not to feel angry with him for what was happening to him and the impact it was having on us all? How to separate his illness out from him? How to cope with never knowing what I was going to find, how he was going to be; with the emotional roller coaster of hope and despair? How to enjoy the good and happy moments and allow them to count without making myself too vulnerable to disappointment?

- How much of my own struggle to share with the girls? By being honest was I validating something for them and what they were feeling, or was I burdening them with yet more when they were already dealing with so much?

- How to continue my own life without feeling guilty for having things Sam didn't? How to manage my own needs without feeling I was abandoning him?

It is desperately hard for a family to live alongside psychosis and to find itself caught up in the ebb and flow of something both beyond their control and outside their understanding. The impact on us was huge. No wonder I'm still battling my way through self-doubt and all the questions to which there still aren't any answers.

***

I go into your bedroom. Your smell is still there on the jumper, tightly rolled and sealed in its plastic bag. I feel ridiculously grateful. I move on to your shoes and slippers, holding them to my face, eager to capture any trace of you. There's a pile of books, pieces of paper and notebooks. On the top is Milan Kundera's 'The Unbearable Lightness of Being' with an inscription from Rosy. Tucked inside are two boarding passes dated 19 June, from Bangkok to Delhi and Delhi to London Heathrow. They must be from 2012. Beneath is an 'Owing Note – patient copy' from a local pharmacy for fourteen Aripiprazole tablets.

Next I come across pages torn out of a notebook, from which your twelve-year-old hand-writing stares up at me. Notes from a school trip to Fountains Abbey. You write of Benedictine Monks; their silence during meals in the refectory. You describe barrel vaults, rainbow ribs, columns and corbels, "pointy gothic" and "rounded Romanesc"; of monks coming to the "warming house" to escape the bitter cold, the Prior sleeping in the warmest part, above the others; of donations from the wealthy to secure their retirement to the Abbey.

I picture you on the trip, listening, trying to absorb information, making notes, always a little uncertain but trying nonetheless. I feel a rush of protective love for you. Things didn't come easily. You had to fight to stay focused. I come across my own handwriting: notes on the Fountains Abbey project you had to do; a list of things to be included, those to be omitted. Even now I feel a twinge of anxiety for you. Your notes seem so sketchy. Did you have enough?

Then there's a page about different types of rock: "igneos, metamorphic and sedimentry." I can see the effort you're making with these notes: pressing hard with your pencil, making lists on how rocks are broken down; freeze and thaw, weathering, erosion. You're trying hard with your spelling too. I picture your face, a frown of concentration, the effort to stay engaged.

Beneath this testament to your perseverance is a letter from Prospect Park Hospital, dated 30 July 2012, discharging you from section 2 of the Mental Health Act, stating that your nearest relative has been informed.

Then there is a note from me, saying I've popped out for coffee but will be back at 10 and asking if you will 'please, please, PLEASE' come for a walk with me later on.

I was trying very hard too.

There's another loose sheet of paper, and in your spidery hand you've written, "In and at a time I used to be capable of many things, I had many skills and strong attributes. These included a heightened sensitivity to music and film with a fineness in my observation and experience of both. I possessed an openness to life and the universe that manifested itself in a beautifully expressive, potent and powerful way of majestic subtlety."

Finally, I come to the Moleskine notebook I gave you before you first set off on your travels. There is only one entry: "Tonight I await great fortune, great promise and untold riches, the world is an oracle of divine magnificence and magnitude; orchestral harmony and great virtue sweep through the air in swathes."

20 March 2015

I'M SEARCHING THE internet for a podcast I watched when Sam was showing signs of being ill. It helped me to understand the prodromal phase of schizophrenia, the psychological changes that sometimes precede full-on psychosis and diagnosis.

I don't find the podcast but I come across some diagnostic criteria for schizophrenic prodrome. They list nine symptoms; marked social isolation or withdrawal; marked impairment in role functioning; markedly peculiar behaviour; marked impairment in personal hygiene and grooming; blunted or inappropriate affect; digressive, vague, over-elaborate or circumstantial speech, or poverty of speech, or poverty of content of speech; odd beliefs or magical thinking; unusual perceptual experiences; marked lack of initiative, interests or energy.

Sam met every single one.

I also come across another recent study charting the changes in the brains of schizophrenia sufferers and the progressive destruction of grey matter. This time there are photos from MRI scans. They show the areas affected in vibrant greens, blues and pinks. Again the research sheds light on why more than 50% of sufferers have no insight into their illness. The affected areas are those parts responsible for self-knowledge and awareness. I am profoundly sad for Sam.

But perversely, there is comfort for me in seeing those dreadful images of changing brains. In moments of self-doubt I persist in torturing myself with the idea that I failed him: in not being able to halt his inexorable slide into bizarre behaviours and beliefs; in not being able to help him understand that he was ill; in not being able to join him in his certainty that there was nothing wrong with him, in not being able to convince him that I *hadn't* failed him when I sought help from mental health services. This latter haunts me most for in that perceived failure, Sam began to doubt my love for him. And in my darkest moments his doubts seem to get inside me and become my own and I start to think that, had I loved him more, all might have been different.

The images give me a weapon with which to fight these doubts, for even I can see that love could not win against such a powerful enemy. And this helps me to see things more clearly and to know once again that I couldn't have loved him more than I did.

25 March 2015

I FIND GROUPS of people very difficult at the moment. I don't know how to be in them.

7 April 2015

I CHANCE ACROSS an article about Paul Heiney, a journalist and broadcaster like his wife, Libby Purves, and his recent book about sailing solo to Cape Horn after the death of their son, Nicholas – also a sailor – at twenty-three, following his battle with depression. He was hoping to make sense of it all. Reading it makes me feel less alone. Before I would have read books and articles about loss with interest, real human interest, but now I read them with a thirst to make connections between the loss described and mine, between the other's experience and my own. It is powerful this need to feel that others, even total strangers, have shared something I have felt.

***

The article made me think of you Sam. So much does. You were the opposite of depressed with your exploding rainbows and green and blue spirits making you laugh out loud. But there were other things that brought you to mind. Nicholas's Dad is inspired by him. You inspire me too. I try to view the world in the way I think you might have seen it, through the lens you held up to life. I challenge myself to find different perspectives, to strip away some of the layers of my over-thinking, to value simplicity. And how could I not be inspired by your fortitude, your stoicism in the face of disappointment and indignity? There's so much to learn from you. I think we're all inspired in different ways.

Rosy has written in biro on the side of the painted Victorian table next to her pillow, 'And those who were seen dancing were thought to be insane by those who could not hear the music.'

There is a photo of you next to Nietzsche's words. I should have been annoyed when I saw them inscribed into the wood, but I wasn't. I understood the need to make it permanent, to have others read it, wonder about it, perhaps think differently. We all have a need to keep you alive.

Nicholas wrote poetry. I think you might like this poem. I love it. It's called 'The Silence at the Song's End'.

'I sing, as I was told

inside myself.
I sing inside myself
the one wild song, song that whirls
my words around, until a world unfurls
my ship's new sail
I catch the dew and set
a course amongst the ocean curls.'

Nicholas's family came to feel that his death had been, 'simply written in the stars'.

'That is how he was born,' his father said. 'That was the path he was on. And I don't think any of us could have done anything different.' He described his sensitivity and vivid imagination, explaining to his headmaster, as a nine-year-old, why he didn't like school.

'As I walk around,' he had said, 'I don't feel very happy because the bricks of the school curl themselves up and throw themselves at me.'

I think of how you experienced the world and how Rosy described you at your memorial service: 'Sam was always different. He was hard-wired, right from the beginning, to experience a reality different from the rest of us.' And later, 'He was always liable to float away from us. His feet were only lightly secured to the ground.'

I think we held onto you for as long as we could.

That family, like yours has, worked hard not to be destroyed by their son and brother's death. They understood and *respected his decision to die. We've tried too to understand why you might have taken risks with a life that was disappointing you. You would have wanted – when it was your time – to slip out of this world and into the next leaving us all intact. You would have wanted us to survive.*

On his long and solitary journey, Heiney would climb the mast to mend a sail and as he did, sometimes a gull would swoop down near him. He had a sense of it being his son, "he the spirit and me the poor sod with the needle and thread in his hand." After the broadcast of a radio play based on Nicholas's poetry, Libby Purves texted her husband. "Tell him it's been a success," she wrote. "He's not very far away from you."

I have that feeling too. I have felt you in tumbling clouds above my head, in early morning sunlight dancing on the bed, in the rustle of a wind-blown tree, in the dewy quiet of the churchyard, in the howling wind and battering snow on Sugar Loaf, in the inky blue of a sky before dusk and in the love and warmth of us all gathered together on your twenty-third birthday. It feels that you are never far away.

I think you sang songs inside yourself. Songs that made you skip as you walked and laugh at what you saw inside your head. You are a song inside me now, a melody that stirs or bursts into life when I think of you. I carry the pulse of you within me.

***

9 April 2015

ON THE DRIVE back from Wales I hear Adam Foulds on Book Club talking about *The Quickening Maze*, his book about a lunatic asylum in Epping Forest where the poet, John Clare, and Tennyson's brother, Septimus, were both incarcerated. The two men shared an acute sensitivity to nature and felt things more deeply than others, especially the wonders of the natural world. It is a fictional account of actual events, exploring poetry, madness and identity. I studied Clare's poetry for English A-level and loved his descriptions of the countryside and rural life. Foulds talks of the importance of home to John Clare, who once walked 130 miles over several days and nights to get there, eating grass and tobacco to sustain himself. It wasn't long before he was re-admitted to the local asylum, where he spent the next 25 years. I have no recollection of being told he spent much of his adult life in mental institutions. Have I forgotten this central fact or was it the stigma attached to mental illness that prevented the teacher from burdening her nice young women with this reality?

I see Sam in Fould's descriptions of these men, in how they experienced nature and in their feelings about home. There was something sustaining for him too in returning home. I sensed it when he arrived back from Hawaii in 2010, and after he went missing in early 2013. I felt some burden slip away from him as he walked in through the front door. On his trips abroad he would often phone after about six weeks to say he thought he had been away for long enough and was ready to come home.

Foulds speaks to me most when he talks with great sensitivity about the difficulty of defining where difference stops and madness begins. He says the most helpful definition he's come across in his research is from the psycho-analyst, Adam Phillips, who said it was the point at which your family can no longer cope with you.

***

We reached that point at different times along the way. The hardest time of all for me to think about is the moment when I agreed with you that you should go into supported accommodation rather than come home after being discharged from hospital the second time, after your suicide attempt. I knew you weren't going to be put back onto antipsychotics. You'd made it clear that the medication was the reason you'd tried to kill yourself. 'It makes me feel dead anyway,' you said, 'so what's the difference?'

When you said, 'I want to be independent and I don't want to live with a mother who thinks I'm ill, when I'm not; who calls people in, who can't accept her son for who he is. I want to live somewhere else,' I knew there was a chance you didn't mean it and that it was just a way of punishing me for betraying you. But this time, instead of fighting for you, instead of the endless discussions and negotiations that would almost certainly have ended with your agreeing to give coming home a try, I simply said, 'Okay.'

I can still remember the long, slow look you gave me, holding my gaze as you absorbed this unscripted turn of events. I saw your hurt and wariness beneath the bravado. This time I had changed the rules of engagement and you didn't know what to do. But your pride wouldn't let you back down.

I didn't discuss it with you after that. I allowed the wheels to be set in motion for alternative accommodation to be found. The truth was that I couldn't cope with you coming back home. James had decided you were less of a risk to yourself 'mad', than you were 'sane' but medicated against your will. I knew what it would mean if you weren't on medication. I just couldn't do it again.

I was running on empty. For three years I'd been watching you slip away from me, and then return. Over and over again. The tension between despair and hope was agonising. I told myself I was thinking about the rest of the family, the trauma of you shooting yourself, the difficult weeks leading up to it, the impact on Ellie, her panic attacks, her fear of being alone in the house with you in case she couldn't keep you safe. She was in her final year at school, coping with the pressure of being Head Girl as well as her A-levels. I told myself I was protecting her. But the truth is I was as much protecting myself.

You knew. You always knew me too well. I probably knew it somewhere too. It was a desperate moment for both of us when I said okay. I felt the understanding pass silently between us. I wish I'd found a way to talk to you about it, openly and honestly. If I'd explained the impact of your suicide attempt on us, perhaps all this unspoken hurt would not have floated between us, muddying communication and understanding.

I'm sorry.

***

10 April 2015

I FEEL ANXIOUS all morning. I don't know why. It's a horrid, non-specific anxiety, infecting everything. I set off for the Dolphin to collect some copies of the school magazine. It contains Sam's obituary. As soon as I'm on my way I understand what it's about. I desperately want the obituary to do him justice and need to see it in hard copy to know that it does. But at the same time, I'm dreading that moment of opening it up and seeing, in black and white, the incontrovertible evidence of his death.

The anxiety dissipates as soon as I see his sweet face smiling up at me. Sadness comes instead.

13 April 2015

I ADDED SOMEONE to my hate-list yesterday. It doesn't take much. I'd bumped into another mother from school and she'd failed to mention Sam. Today she sent me an email, having read the obituary in the magazine. She was fulsome in her apologies for not having heard the news and warm and heartfelt in her commiserations. I had to cross her off again.

It confirmed the things I know rationally. My hate-list isn't fair, it isn't reasonable. But I need it. For now, it provides me with a silent repository to put difficult feelings like anger, envy and bitterness. They are just as much a part of grieving as sadness is, even though they're harder to own. If I don't allow myself to acknowledge and feel them, I might one day discover, too late, that they have shaped my life without my realising it.

I hope one day that need will pass.

15 April 2015

THE WISTERIA OUTSIDE Sam's bedroom window is in full bud and beginning to unfurl its glorious mauve petals; a tentative uncurling to the promise of spring. Our first spring without him. It grieves me to think it will quicken from tight green buds to open blossoms in his absence: tapping its long green tendrils against the glass of his deserted room, unleashing its perfume towards a window behind which lies no tousled head resting on folded hands, no outstretched limbs. This year there will be no witness to its extravagant display. Just a neat, white, empty bed.

18 April 2015

THE ANNIVERSARY OF Sam's death is fast approaching, and before it, other anniversaries too. On the twenty-first it will be one year since we all went out for supper on the eve of his departure. Rosy joining us in the restaurant, slightly breathless after her walk from the station. Sam swelling with unspoken pleasure to know she had come from Bristol for the evening, just for him. On the twenty-second, exactly one year since we took him to the airport, one year since I saw and held him, heard his voice and laugh, felt his arms around me. Then the first of May, the day he died. And, just as painful, the fifth. The day we heard.

I am feeling them all already. The echo of melancholy is now a part of spring. It's there: in the particular slant of the sunlight, the drifting bleat of lambs, the smell of the first cut of the year, the hollow hammering of the woodpecker, the morning light beneath the curtains, the gentle rhythms of dusk and dawn, violets hugging a bank, sunlit blackthorn blossom against a darkening sky, the first waft of charcoal on a barbecue, the neon green of new leaves growing against the gnarled silver of wintered wood.

Sometimes it all comes together in sudden brutal harmony and carries me back with a jolt and I am there, living it again. It happens today. One moment I am sitting in the garden, my face towards the glow of the afternoon sun, warmth on my skin, wondering at the blueness of the sky and flush of birdsong. The next, I am back on that Monday, living the moment those terrible words floated towards me.

20 April 2015

I HAVE CRIED for much of the evening. My eyes are puffy and my nose is sore from so much blowing. Sig is here with me on the bed, twitching and puffing in his sleep, emitting little quarter-barks and sighs. His is a comfortable, comforting presence after so many tears.

21 April 2015

I WANT TO immerse myself in Sam and in the loss of him. I don't want to have to think about anything else.

***

It's arrived. One of the days I've been most dreading is here: 22 April 2015, the anniversary of the day you left for Thailand: a whole year since I last saw you. I sit in bed and look at the text messages we exchanged then. They've taken on new meaning now. They bring you back to me.

> *Hey there just arrived woohoo nice weather in Bangkok :) so lovely to be here I wonder if I'm ready for another day of traveling or weather to stay in Bangkok for a bit ill see but I imagine ill book the train....Love Sam x*

You sent it at 01.23 UK time, and I replied at 05.31. I would have woken early and stretched out my hand for my phone to see if there was word from you. I can hear you saying woohoo and see your smiling face. You'd promised to text us, and you did. This you, who medication had finally returned to us, is thoughtful and considerate. I hear the excitement in your text, the feeling of freedom and adventure, the possibility of re-building your life with trips like this, a way to reclaim all that was taken away from you.

I scroll on down. Now there are messages sent after your rucksack and passport were stolen and you'd been, with Dad's help by phone, to a police station and the Embassy.

> *Passport and visa sorted as well as I phone charger*

yay! So don't by one!

And then a little later.

She gave me the cable but when she took it out to show Me she left it out Just realised ill go back tommorow.

I feel your growing confidence, a pride in overcoming these difficulties, a sense of agency and self-belief. The next day you text again.

Really impressed with the British consolate they gave me a temporary passport which looks better than my original! On my way to the train station to Chiangmai ill text you when I get to pai...Love Sam ...... I'm so glad I got that passport it was really frightening with nothing. there are some really good people here x

Then a few hours after that, a message sent to Dad and me,

And dad thank you for being more proactive. mum didn't seem very phased.

This last one makes me smile. It's so typical of you to have a dig at me for asking Dad to help you. You had no awareness of the practicalities: that Dad was at home whilst I was in the middle of a working day, needing to leave for a full afternoon of appointments scheduled at the GP practice I worked at. Such details passed you by.

Scrolling back through earlier messages I come across some from March 2014. We've left you looking after Sig for a *couple of days. You're taking it very seriously.*

> He did 2 separate poo session about 5 individual poos.
> is that normal. I picked them all up.

I reply that it is and ask if he was okay overnight.

> Yeah fine, wen will he need his next crap.

I smile now as I did then. It will have cost you a lot to pick up his poo, the boy who refused to carry on eating if someone sneezed within a ten metre radius of you, or if a pea touched a sausage on your plate.

Further back still there's one on 25 January 2014 from me to you. You and Ellie were at Dad and Kim's, celebrating Imogen's fourth birthday. I tell you I've just had a call from Vodafone to say you've exceeded your download limit on your laptop. I tell you to stop using it unless you've got wifi. You reply immediately.

> Okay god dang....

I give you some better news then: a parcel has arrived for you, with a customs note on it containing the word 'candy.'

> Yay candy, ill come home if we have a takeaway x
> We will. I'll order it now if you want. What would you like?
> Yes, subze tandoori saag aloo.

They matter so much, these mundane, inconsequential messages. It's hard to hold onto all the subtleties of our relationship without these prompts. I can tell from reading them that you were in a good mood that day. The 'god dang' and 'yay' tell me that. I recognise your impatience and incapacity to wait. You want your candy now, and you want the takeaway to arrive as soon as possible after you do. I see the mutual manipulation between us: the way I offer up the news of the candy to lure you home; how you get what you want by making the takeaway a condition of coming. You know I want to see you, so you're going to get something out of it for you, because you're still angry with me for thinking you're ill and there's a constant battle raging inside you between that anger and your love for me, your need of me. I see how instantly I respond to say we'll have a takeaway. I know I need to grasp the moment, before you change your mind, before your need to punish me re-asserts itself and takes sway over the candy and the curry.

There is so much in this simple exchange, so much of you and me, the broken trust and hurt, but most of all, I think, I hope, the love.

I watch a fifteen second video clip of you. I took it on a walk on 21st April 2012. You must have been in a good mood because you've allowed me to film you. You're standing in the woods and you're thinking about what to say, lips moving slightly in preparation for your pronouncement. You look towards me, away again. Something changes in your eyes, like a light coming on and you speak, looking into the distance.

'And you shall inherit the salt of the earth.'

You say it portentously; a prophet granting gifts to his followers.

'Thank you,' I hear myself say.

I see the glimmer of a smile around your eyes as you turn towards me. You're pleased with yourself, happy.

I see the Sam I knew so well: the conflation of two sayings – salt instead of fruits, the way you amused yourself, made yourself smile. And the new Sam I was trying so hard to know: the dreadlocks, the stained mid-blue cotton jumper you never took off, the hint of grandiosity.

Dad comes for coffee. I watch him, sitting at the kitchen table, picking up his phone to look for a particular message from you he wants to share with us. Afterwards I see how hard it is to drag himself away from you. He continues scrolling through the messages. Different emotions cross his face: a smile, a fleeting frown, a whisper of amused exasperation, a closing of the eyes and slow shake of the head and then the etchings of pain as he feels the loss. For a moment you were back with him, there in your texts with their dyslexic misspellings and absent punctuation, and it is hard for him to leave you and return to the present. He wants to stay with you, just as I have wanted to all week.

***

1 May 2015

THE ANNIVERSARY HAS arrived. I wake and reach for my phone to see the time. It's 05.31, the exact time I reached for my phone just over a year ago to see whether Sam had texted to say he'd arrived safely in Thailand. I read his text messages now, scrolling through them until I reach his last: so upbeat with his news of renting a scooter, his plans, the photo of the girl he'd met in Bangkok. It arrived at 34 minutes after midnight. I do a quick calculation. That would have been 6.34am in Thailand. As soon as I saw his message – at 07.04 UK time, 13.04 in Thailand – I replied.

> *She looks nice! Hot springs sound lovely and so does spending a week on one of the islands. So glad you're having such a good time. Love you. Mum xx*

Suddenly it occurs to me that he might already have been dead by the time it arrived. He might never have seen it.

Sig bounds up the stairs and on to the bed. I stroke him and feel the comforting warmth of his body lying on mine. I whisper, 'Sammy's dead Siggi. He died a year ago today.' I cry. Sig looks up for a moment, questioningly, then lowers his chin and rests it slowly between his paws on my chest.

I'm on my way to the chiropractor and driving round the one-way system when I find myself pulling by mistake into the lane I used to take to visit Sam in the house in Wokingham. He would watch out of the window for my arrival and run down the stairs to greet me.

In the chiropractor's waiting room, two mothers with toddlers sit and discuss in endless affectionate details the miscreant ways of their two youngest children. There is a friendly competitive edge, with each topping the other's tale of naughtiness. I sit quietly, thinking that I could have given them both a run for their money with tales of Sam.

2 May 2015

IT FEELS LESS difficult today, as though I can breathe more easily.

4 May 2015

THE GIRLS ARE both home for the Bank Holiday weekend. It is quiet and, at times, contemplative. We remember Sam with family and friends: a walk round Twyford Lakes and then to the Bell at lunchtime. Rosy reads an extract from my journal. She reads it beautifully, her voice is mesmerising with its low timbre and even tones. I look down at the table in front of me as I focus only on the words. I feel sad but not moved to tears. I seem to be encased in steel for the day. Her voice begins to crack as she reads the last few sentences. *'I see this young man I love so much, striding purposefully towards his next adventure. It's hard to let him go but I know I must. He doesn't look back.'*

I keep my eyes lowered for a few moments. Others are crying. I cannot.

5 May 2015

THE DAY PASSES. As it must.

7 May 2015

FOR MOTHER'S DAY in 2009 Simon made a video for me. I watch it over and over again. And finally, I cry.

***

Dad shot the video on March 22, exactly five years and one month before the last day we ever saw you. You would have been 17 years and one month old. We all went for a walk in the Chilterns and in the evening Rosy and Ellie cooked supper for me and Paddy at Dad's house. You didn't help with the cooking. In the video you're generally either unsmiling or scowling. You were a teenager with your family on a walk you'd rather not be doing.

But there's a moment halfway through when something shifts. You and Rosy are dancing round a signpost in the woods, drumming on it with sticks. You're slowly getting into it but suddenly you shift into a higher gear and go into a sort of chicken move, your upper body and head jerking forwards from the waist. Your face changes too. You come alive. I can feel your energy.

I want to freeze the film, make you step out of it and back into my life. I want to shake you and tell you not to die. I want to take you home, where you belong, keep you safe. If necessary, lock you in. Anything to keep you alive and part of this family. Anything to have you back in our lives again, well or ill, easy or difficult, challenging or rewarding. I just want you back.

Like those text messages, the video captures the nuances of you. The challenges: your tendency to swim against the tide, to hold yourself on the outside of things. There's footage of

Rosy and Ellie in the kitchen, preparing the meal, Rosy and Ellie running across the field towards Dad, filming them, Rosy and Ellie are chatting away as we walk. Where were you?

But it captures the wonder of you too: the moment when you bend down into the lens and say hello in your silliest voice, your arm slung affectionately over Ellie's shoulder as the three of you walk down a path, the twirling of a stick like a drum majorette, the chicken dance.

And whether you're smiling or scowling, joining in or standing apart, you're there as an element of the family: part of its shape, its dynamics, the way it works. You're part of a whole as well as being yourself. You always were more than the discrete entity you sometimes tried to make yourself. You were a part of us.

And we're having to find a new way now without you.

At the end of the video Dad has filmed us walking towards a stile. It wasn't staged. He had simply run on ahead. In the fore are Rosy, you and Ellie, from left to right, in birth order. You in the middle are the tallest. Ellie has almost caught up with Rosy in height. There is a lovely symmetry to the shape you make, like three small hills in a line. Paddy and I are behind, our heads and shoulders perfectly in line with the valleys. I am in the valley of Rosy and you, Paddy of you and Ellie.

I want to freeze that frame forever and keep the shape of that small unit intact.

***

19 May 2015

THE FLOWERS ARE wilting on Sam's grave when I visit. The gerberas with their hanging heads, and the sun-charred leaves of the alstroemerias fill me with sudden hopelessness. I think of the sunshine of the last few days and how I enjoyed the feeling of warmth on my skin, felt nourished and restored by it. And all the while it had been destroying the flowers I had lovingly put there for him.

It seems profoundly depressing that gain must always walk hand in hand with loss, that love and joy come only with the risk of pain, that though life gives, it also takes away. The world seems all of a sudden to be a place of bleakness. All day this bleakness stays with me. I can barely bring myself to look at photos of him. I cannot bear the waste, the unfairness and the pain.

Paddy is away. I let myself stay with the lowness of my mood. I do not try to lift myself out of it. I wait instead for it to pass.

It does. Out walking I see buttercups, their bright glazed petals like bursts of sunshine in the hedgerow; lacy heads of cow parsley, their white florets like tumbling snowflakes, captured and frozen mid-flight onto green fronds. In the lake, the oily black head of a cormorant protrudes above the water, rises up and dives. Around the point of entry ripples fan out in circles, ever reducing, until the water is calm again. I stop to watch and wait, and wait, until some metres away he re-surfaces beak first, like a missile breaking the water, shaking the water droplets from his glistening feathers.

And I realise that though life takes away it also continues to give, if only we can allow it to.

21 May 2015

THE LIGHT IS fading fast and blue is bleaching into grey as I pass Sugar Loaf towards the end of my drive to Wales. Above the summit, streaks of heather-grey are smeared across the sky – large smudges of cloud, thinning at the edges like the final brush-strokes of paint on canvas. There is beauty and quiet drama in the scene, but I shiver to think of Sam alone up there as dusk turns to dark. Only a sliver of moon will light the mountains tonight. I wish I could be there with him.

22 May 2015

I'M ON MY own for a couple of days in Wales. The cottage has been such a haven for me; more than somewhere to escape to, it's been a safe, containing space; a nest in which to hatch my grief.

Sometimes grief requires hatching. It's all too easy to ignore the pain of loss by filling one's life with activity and busy-ness, by pushing it away and pushing on through. Often those around us would like us to do just that: they want us to be okay. But I know that avoiding the pain – often without any conscious awareness that we are – doesn't work in the long term. So often it reappears at a later date and often in a different form, concealed behind unconscious defences that make it harder to reach and process.

I'm grateful for my nest.

25 May 2015

PADDY AND I are at the Hay Festival. Simon's here too. We go to hear Andrew Solomon talk about his book, *Far From the Tree,* which explores the challenges for parents when a child is different in some significant way from them. He is a riveting speaker and the audience is spellbound. I am aware of Simon, next to me, weeping silently as Solomon talks of the distinction between love and acceptance. It touches him and reaches the wound of Sam's loss.

For me, that moment comes when Solomon is describing a weekend spent with the parents of one of the perpetrators of the Columbine massacre. He describes their initial reluctance to engage with him at all, and then their inability to stop talking once they have begun. Within the twenty hours of recorded conversation he recalls a quiet moment when he asks them if there is anything they would want to say to their son if they could talk to him now. The father launches into a heartfelt, 'What the hell did you think you were doing?' The mother sits quietly for a moment before saying she would want to tell him she's sorry – sorry that, as his mother, she was unaware of all that was going on inside him.

For a moment, I share the pain of her quiet sense of having failed her son, the pain of opportunities missed, the loneliness of being a mother who has not been able to find a way to stay with her son on his journey. As mothers, we feel we should be able to. But some journeys are too far outside our own experience to allow us to be fellow travellers.

28 May 2015

IT'S A YEAR since Sam's service of thanksgiving. I walk on my own. At Sam's peg, I stand over the water amongst the reeds, look into the blinding glare of the early morning sun and think of him.

Back at home I read Simon's and Rosy's tributes to him; both so loving and respectful. Simon wrote:

Sam's time in and out of Prospect Park Hospital from July 2012 to August 2013 is a very hard thing to describe and I am not going to attempt it here. We should not forget Sam's position in all of this. Sam doesn't have a voice anymore and I think we owe it to him to give him a chance to tell us what he thought. This from a text to a dear friend: "I have never had any form of mental illness. The only thing that ever went wrong was the physical damage I suffered from the drugs I was forced to take. I was sent to Prospect Park by my family against my will having just returned from travelling with an open heart and mind and having enjoyed many new experiences. I want to put the record straight: there was nothing wrong with me when I got back and I had made so many wonderful new friends with whom I shared intimate stories and fantastic adventures. All of that has now been taken away from me by my family."

… I have to say that for me there was almost something heroic about Sam. He had to deal with some truly awful stuff in the last few years of his life and he bore his many challenges with great fortitude and dignity … There were so many things that made me very proud of him. In the shattering experience of being sectioned, Sam made what must have been one of the most difficult and painful decisions of his life: he decided to co-operate. We never had to experience the involvement of the police, of restraining techniques, of shouting matches, of forcible injections. Sam argued his case passionately and convincingly but ultimately he accepted his fate, always clear in his own mind that in his next life he would get a better deal.

Rosy wrote in language of such whimsical beauty that when she read out Sam's own writing from a notebook she'd found in his bedroom, it slipped in seamlessly within the whole:

'Sam was not to be grounded, least of all by me. His world was rich and textured, with the brightest colours, the most beautiful symphonies, the strongest vibrations and infinite possibility. In this world Sam was a prince, a scholar, a philosopher.

But he was always liable to float away from us.

His feet were only lightly secured to the ground; because Sam believed that the body that bound him to Earth was just a vessel for his spirit. And his spirit was destined for greatness. For Sam, death was not to be feared. It was the gateway to his next life. It would be the liberation of his spirit.

And Sam could never quite understand that we were attached to the body that his spirit inhabited. We were attached to the body that bound Sam to the Earth and to us.

And I can hear Sam saying, 'But it was only a body.'

And I want to say back, 'Yes, Sam, but it was the tiny body that I held when I was two and a half, the back that I drew tickly pictures on, the hair with the water-repelling properties of a duck's back, the hands that inflicted the deadliest Chinese burn, the feet grubby from bare-foot foraging, the arm that you would place around my shoulders, the body that had so much potential in this life on Earth.'

And so it is a tragedy for us, because Sam had so much love to give and so many lives to touch with his warmth and kindness. And I feel that it is a tragedy for Sam, because he had so much potential, and so much still to do and to discover. But it is also a liberation for Sam. Because his spirit is now free to soar and dance.

And Sam had big plans for his next incarnation. He wasn't destined to live his next life as a blade of grass or an ant. Oh no, he told me he'd probably be a planet. He told me that Ellie and I might end up as planets too, hopefully in the same solar system, so that we could still hang out together.

I now just want to read something that I found scribbled in Sam's barely legible spidery scrawl, in an old notebook of his:

Life is a beautiful orchestral symphony
Each moment in soul is perfection
Feeling is key
Breath is a paramount bliss
If you are ever feeling waves
It really comes down to enjoying
And welcoming each new moment
Remember life is a playfield
It's however you perceive it
You came in perfect
Remember your time
Be blissful and welcoming
It's all in your mind heart being

In Berlin, two months ago, Sam asked me, 'Would you rather be the Eiffel Tower or bratwurst or Pi?'

'Like apple pie?' I asked.

'No, like 3.142'

I said I'd like to be Pi, and Sam beamed his big smile, the one so big it almost made his eyes disappear, and said, 'Me too.'

> *So Sam might be a planet, or he might be Pi, or he might be flying above the clouds. But wherever he is, he's free.'*

29 June 2015

ELLIE'S FINISHED HER first year at university and is leaving for Indonesia in less than 24 hours. I'm terrified she is going to come to harm. I feel the terror most at night, a creeping anxiety that agitates my mind. My thoughts will not be stilled. Inside my head an LP is playing at 200 rotations a minute instead of 78. Fear comes in unbidden surges of adrenalin-fuelled discomfort. They shake me from my sleep and leave me prey to dreadful, negative thoughts that rove like assassins picking off anything good and positive in my life. I have failed as a mother. I couldn't make Sam feel my love. That's why he was reckless and took risks. I failed to keep him safe. I am to blame for his death. If I had done things differently perhaps he would be here now. I can't have loved him enough.

I pile misery on misery. I look for his text messages to me after his third admission to hospital.

7 April 2013: I'm not coming out today and I don't want to ever see anyone in the family ever again.

8 April 2013: Please don't come I wont see you.

8 April 2013: No more visiting I just spoke to Dr J.

14 April 2013: I really dislike you for your actions against me. I hardly have enough energy to get out of bed now due to the lead. Stop calling. I've said it all before.

I have nothing left inside me to fight the despair and self-recriminations. Everything good lies inert and broken, leaving negativity to roam, unchecked. I've failed as a mother. If Ellie doesn't return safely, that will by my fault too.

5 July 2015

I DON'T EVEN want to write.

8 July 2015

I'M SIMPLY TRYING to bear these feelings, rather than distract myself, or shake myself out of them. I know at some point they will pass, and I will start to see things differently.

10 July 2015

OVER SUPPER I read to Paddy a kind and thoughtful email from a friend. She writes of the strength I've shown over the last year and during Sam's illness. We talk about my ability to appear calm when under pressure – the moment he walked into our room covered in blood, the times he reappeared after going missing.

Suddenly I'm sobbing. Perhaps through being so strong I hid from Sam how devastated I would be if he were to die. I didn't cry when I sat with him waiting for the ambulance to arrive; nor as we sped, siren blaring and blue lights flashing to hospital; nor as I sat by his bedside in A & E as the medics debated whether or not to transfer him to the John Radcliffe in Oxford. And though the kindness of the nurse as she bathed his wounds and asked so gently, 'And how is Mum?' almost undid me, I managed to hold on still. I only *really* cried as I drove home at the end of that long, long day.

Then, in the safety of my car, I howled.

I howled and shouted until my throat was raw.

Suddenly it seems that in this strength, I might have failed Sam. I weep and weep for the thought that by finding a way to cope, I might inadvertently have made it easier for him to take risks with a life that was disappointing him.

12 July 2015

IN MY DREAM I'm on a journey. All around are rickety houses made of loosely garnered sticks, with glassless windows, tilting balconies and doorways without doors. Each balcony is hung with a swathe of fabric in a single, dazzling shade. I'm looking for vermillion. I find it and make my way inside. Next I must locate the house hung in byzantine blue. I glimpse it through the window, set at a right-angle to the one I'm in. When I go to step through the doorway, the hard-baked earth has disappeared and beneath me instead is a huge abyss, dropping away into nothing.

I steady myself, stop and look. The doorway to the second house is within jumping distance. I might be able to do it, but equally I might slip and fall. I know I have to continue my journey, I can't turn back, but I wonder if I can go a different way.

I see a staircase I hadn't noticed before. At the top is a tiny door. I bend myself double and squeeze through, emerging into the front room of a house. A swathe of byzantine blue hangs down from the balcony above me. I sigh with relief.

What might my dream might be telling me? Perhaps it's prompting me to find another way on this journey of grief; giving me permission to move on from torturing myself with doubts and fears. Perhaps I have stared into the depths of that abyss for long, and often, enough. I have needed to visit the possibility that I failed Sam – it's been a necessary part of coming to terms with his death – but perhaps I need do so no more.

I did my best.

Maybe that has to be enough.

***

I think of the dream on my morning walk. I stand on your fishing peg, look up at the sky, and ask you to forgive me for all the things I got wrong. I want the drizzle to stop and the skies to lighten: a sign from you that I'm forgiven. There is no change. I look across the lake, see the reeds trembling in the breeze, hear the throaty rasp and hoot of birdsong and think.

I'm looking for forgiveness from you, but it has to come from me, from within. I have a choice, to keep on staring into the abyss of self-reproach, or to forgive myself.

When I get home, I come across a newspaper article about something Julie Burchill has written about the death of her son. She lost him after she'd cut off contact with him in order to survive herself. I feel lucky never to have reached that point with you, Sam. I'm so glad that we managed to find a way through all the difficulties and keep our relationship intact.

I think of our trip to Berlin that so nearly didn't happen. I remind myself that even though you were angry with me, you did come. And though you remained wary of me – this mother who failed to see you as you saw yourself – we did, despite everything, have fun. I look again at the photos. There's a series of you and Rosy standing under the street sign, Frieda Glucksmann Strasse. In the first shots you're unsmiling and remote. It's me who's taking the photos and you're still punishing me. But in the last two you are grinning from ear to ear. Your eyes have disappeared. I'd made you laugh. I don't remember how, but I can recall it happening, and being grateful that I could still reach you.

There are two other photos, shot by Rosy, a few seconds apart. In the first you look towards me, wary and mistrustful. In one corner, I am in profile, smiling at you. In the next we're in the exact same place, but two things have changed. My hand now rests on top of your hand, on your leg. And your face has softened into a half-smile.

***

25 July 2015

ELLIE IS HOME safely. Thank God.

31 July 2015

THE EPITAPH FOR Sam's gravestone is preoccupying me. Getting it right feels every bit as important to me as my friends' worries about their children's futures. I send a suggestion to the rest of the family: the epitaph I saw on the tablet in Partrishow Church, *'He giveth his beloved sleep.'* It seems to contain a tacit acknowledgement that there is an escape for Sam in death from a life that wasn't the one he wanted. Ellie isn't happy with it. She says he didn't see death as a form of sleep. She's right. I keep on looking.

As soon as I see it, I know it's the right one. Everyone agrees. It's the words of Khalil Gibran in *The Prophet*,

> *'And when the earth shall claim your limbs,*
> *then shall you truly dance.'*

I August 2015

I WALK TO Sam's peg again. The sun is reflected on the water – a blinding glint of light. Around it flecks of flotsam float like a constellation of stars. The sharp line of a vapour trail cuts straight through the middle. With a sudden start a heron takes off with trailing feet, sending gentle ripples across the lake. The trail begins to dance, a gentle undulation like the slither of a snake across the surface of the water.

I think of Sam, but I do not feel him as I did before in the tumbling clouds above Ibiza, or the dancing sunlight and shadow leaves on the bed in the crenellated tower in Oxford. I feel that he is far away now, dancing his own dance of a new life, singing his own song.

And I can let him go.

2 August 2015

OUR FRIEND, BARRY is cycling in the Brighton to London bike race in memory of Sam. He raises £2500 for Rethink, the mental health charity. I see Sam's eleven-year-old face smiling out at me from Barry's top. He shows me the crossbar of his bike, where the same smiling face stared up at him during the race.

'I wanted to be able to see Sam while I cycled,' he says. 'I knew he would inspire me to keep going. And he did.'

6 September 2015

I MEET A man on the top of Sugar Loaf Mountain. I've been there a little while. It's 10am and I've just toasted Sam with a Bombay Sapphire and tonic. The man's shaved head appears before the rest of him. His arms are covered with tattoos and his eyebrows with piercings. He's perspiring heavily and doesn't look great. There's no one else around.

We exchange a few words before he asks, apologetically, 'Do you mind taking a photo of me next to the trig point?'

'No, that's fine,' I say. He hands me his mobile phone.

'I need to prove to my wife that I actually got here. She was fast asleep when I got up at four this morning. To be honest, I'm feeling terrible. Too many beers during the rugby yesterday. I'm trying to walk it off. I've already been up Pen y Fan.'

'Blimey,' I say, 'That's impressive. What time did you get to the top?'

'5.45. I was passing people already on their way down. Unbelievable. It was busy at the top, but then it always is. I run the burger van in the car park where most people set off from. I reckon there are sometimes 300 people on the mountain. It's mad.'

He looks around him and I look too.

'It's quieter over here,' he says.

'It is. I love the Black Mountains. Sometimes you can walk all day and barely see a soul. I love the silence and the space. It's such good thinking time.'

He takes a quick glance at me, to see perhaps whether he can gauge whether there's something I might *need* to think about, then takes his flask, pours himself a coffee and grimaces as he takes a mouthful.

'It looked alright when I made it at 4am.'

'You might need a swig of this,' I say, holding up my glass. I see him taking in the ice cubes and the slice of lemon as a small questioning frown appears between the piercings. 'It's gin and tonic.' The piercings shoot up. 'I know,' I say, shaking my head and smiling, 'It is a bit early, but I'm toasting my son. It was his favourite tipple.'

He hesitates a moment. 'Was?' he asks.

'Yes,' I say, and look down before I add, 'We scattered his ashes up here on 22nd February this year. It should have been his 23rd birthday.'

'Noooo,' he says. 'I'm sorry.' He sounds as though he means it, as though he'd stop it having happened if he could.

We stand on in companionable silence. The man sips his coffee as I move toward the trig point, scanning the ground for remnants of Sam. I find none. I didn't expect to. I stretch out my hand and trace the initials someone carved there long ago, 'SR.'

As if for Sam. As if they knew.

It's peaceful and I take my time, untroubled by the presence of the man from the burger van. It feels strangely comforting to know he's there.

'It was nice to talk,' he says as I prepare to leave. 'Now you take care.'

There's solace in the sorrow of strangers, people who know nothing of you, yet open their hearts for a moment to share your pain. It heals.

18 October 2015

SIMON TELLS ME about some new research into schizophrenia. It provides evidence of an already-suspected link between the illness, and the immune system and inflammation in the brain. The Head of Psychiatry at Edinburgh University describes schizophrenia as, 'one of the worst illnesses affecting mankind.'

Apparently, the brain has its own immune system in the form of cells called microglia. They prune weak synapses and neutralise bacterial infection. Brain scans of individuals suffering from schizophrenia reveal overactivity in this immune system. The report's author likens the effect to over-zealous gardeners pruning indiscriminately with shears, cutting healthy synapses as well as unhealthy ones, severing connections in the brain and leaving it wired incorrectly. 'You can see how that would lead to patients making unusual connections between what is happening around them,' he says, 'or mistaking thoughts as voices outside their head and causing the symptoms we see in the illness.'

***

I gaze at the photo of you by my bed, at the trust and innocence in your four-year-old smile. It's heart-breaking to think of this marauding, destructive force wreaking havoc within you. Gardeners sounds altogether too benign. I see instead a horde of undercover assassins clad in combat gear, stealthy, prowling, narrow-eyed and furrow-browed as they cut and snip at random and with dreadful effect.

Later, as I walk with Sig, I recall the moment you inexplica-

bly seized him — only six months old and tentatively dipping one paw at a time into the lake — raised him high above your head and flung him into the water. I hear the snip of those cruel shears.

I remember you proclaiming in awe and wonder at the beauty of a sky as dull and flat as a London pavement. I see you on the doorstep. You've been missing for days. You're cold and hungry and dishevelled, your eyes as large as marbles in the unnaturally stretched contours of your dehydrated face. You've drunk nothing for days, for fear of being contaminated by plastic bottles. I see synapses falling like scythed grass, like clusters of roses left to fade and wither on a severed shoot. I hear the steady snip of the shears which robbed you of the future you might have had.

One of the hardest things about losing you to schizophrenia was all the self-doubt and guilt I felt: wondering where Dad and I'd gone wrong as parents, whether we'd somehow caused it. Selfishly, there was some relief for me in reading the research and discovering evidence of a biological basis for it.

Of course, Dad and I both got things wrong. We knew you were sensitive and felt things keenly, despite trying to hide it. But there were some things we couldn't protect you from. When Dad told you all that he'd met someone else and planned to leave home I could see your bewilderment. You were only six. We all sat down in the green room before he left. He asked who hated him. Rosy hesitated for a moment then raised her arm. Ellie took her cue from her and raised hers too. When Dad asked if anyone hated me your arm shot *up in a flash and you looked at me defiantly. I understood. You were so wounded and afraid that you dared turn your anger only onto me, the person who wasn't leaving you.*

Two years later, when you were eight, you were assessed by an educational psychologist. Teachers were concerned about your rigidity and lack of focus. Your behaviour at home was nightmarish. Everything was a battle, even the simplest thing. I took you to drum lessons, at your request. Every time you refused to get out of the car when we arrived. I'd serve your favourite dinner and you'd refuse to eat it because one of the peas had touched the chicken. The psychologist said you exhibited several Aspergers-like traits, but you'd passed the 'theory of mind' test and seemed unusually connected in an emotional sense. She didn't feel you fulfilled the criteria for a diagnosis. She told me to praise you whenever I could and to choose my battles. I did both, but nothing improved. You became more contrary and angrier than ever.

We took you to see a child psychotherapist. Getting you there was torture, week after week. You'd refuse to get into the car at home and out of the car once we got there. But once inside she felt that you responded well. It was incredibly hard to leave you there, to trust my little boy to a complete stranger. I felt intensely vulnerable.

In one of the meetings Dad and I had with her, she told me you needed firmer boundaries, which seemed to be the opposite of what the psychologist had recommended. I felt she was blaming everything on me. Without warning she said she needed to leave the room for a moment. When she returned, I was crying. 'Aha,' she said, 'Something's happening.' It was.

I'd never felt so angry. Afterwards, outside, I insisted Dad drive you back, despite your protestations. I howled in the car all the way home: howls of frustration and anger. It all felt so unfair. I complained bitterly to Nic. She said the therapist was either a witch or a genius. It turned out to be the latter. My anger released something inside me. I became much more boundaried with you Sam. And with Dad. It wasn't before time. I'd been trying too hard to compensate for Dad not being there. Things improved a little.

You were diagnosed with dyslexia at thirteen and ADHD at seventeen. You took Ritalin and the difference was extraordinary. I'd never seen you sit still as you worked. You could stay in one place and focus. Academic work became easy. But not for long. Soon you'd decided you didn't like the side effects and you stopped taking it. By then you were at Henley College in your AS year. One of your subjects was Drama. You loved it. At the end of the year you played the part of Alan Strang in Peter Shaffer's 'Equus'. It was a challenging role – that of an emotionally disturbed young man receiving help in a psychiatric unit – but you embraced it with zeal. You adopted Stanislavsky's 'method acting' to help you deliver an authentic performance and immersed yourself in the role.

Your behaviour became quite strange. I felt worried and didn't know what to do but finally I spoke to your drama teacher. I didn't tell you. I knew you'd have been furious. Already I was learning to compromise on some of my fast-held beliefs about parenting, that honesty and openness were best.

'It's probably nothing,' I said to him. 'But I'm slightly concerned about Sam. I know he's meant to immerse himself

in the role, and he is, but I'm worried he might be slightly over-doing it. It's almost as though he can't pull himself out of character sometimes, which is probably what he's meant to be doing, but I'm worried he might go too far. He's always so extreme. I just wanted to let you know so that you can keep an eye on him and rein him in a bit if you think you need to.'

'Oh,' he replied, sounding bemused. 'Well, I haven't been aware of that but thanks for letting me know.'

I felt rather foolish for making the call. One of those neurotic mothers who's over-identified with her child.

You gave a sterling performance to much acclaim.

***

It's desperately hard, on many levels, to be the mother of a child or adolescent who is struggling with mental health issues. So often, when outside agencies become involved, we end up being made to feel we are part of the problem, that we are enmeshed with our children in some unhealthy way. I'm sure we are. It's hard *not* to become over-involved when you're worried, when you know your child so well and see things that others, even professionals, do not see.

22 October 2015

THE BOOMING TONES of John Humphries filter into my consciousness: 'and it is 7am on Thursday the twenty-second of October.' My mind stirs into action. Sam left for Thailand on the twenty-second. I count months in my half-sleep. It is exactly eighteen months since I last saw him. A half-anniversary. These dates that mark the passing of time have such power. I cannot shake off the sadness I feel now that this day has become connected to him.

I shower after my walk and use the shower gel I retrieved a few months ago from his room. There isn't much left. It was one of his stocking presents from his last Christmas. I can remember the small internal battle I went through when I walked past it in the shop. It was an organic brand Sam approved of. But it was expensive and I knew deep down that he would never use it. I picked it up and put it back down several times before I decided. I bought it in hope rather than expectation. He didn't show much interest in it when he opened it. And he never used it.

It's been hard to know what to do with it since. It sat on the windowsill in his room for a year after he died and it upset me every time I saw it, so I moved it to the bathroom, and eventually into the shower. Now I am fretting about finishing it and losing this link with him.

Sam gave everyone the same Christmas present that year. We each received a bottle of poppy seed tincture. He was in a fever of excitement as he presented his gifts to us, sitting on the bed on Christmas morning amongst five stockings-worth of discarded wrapping paper. He extolled its virtues to us in turn. I really wanted to share his enthusiasm, but instead I felt discomfort. It provoked so much anxiety in me, for tinctures were his then-current obsession. He bought them online and they arrived with alarming frequency. He would regularly consume an entire bottle at a go. Rosy, concerned, mentioned it to a homeopath. He said it was dangerous, that tinctures are the concentrated extracts from nature which form the basis for many modern medicines. That they are powerful. When she relayed this to Sam he shrugged his shoulders in irritation.

24 October 2015

I READ AN article saying that research spending on mental health is significantly lower than physical health – less than £10 per mental health patient per year compared to £1,500 per cancer patient receiving treatment. It is not well-supported by public donations either: a mere £0.003 per £1 of state funding, in contrast to £2.75 per £1 spent by the government on cancer research.

I am so angry.

Most people prescribed anti-psychotic medication stop taking it. They have every reason to: the side-effects are so devastating. In the summer of 2013 Simon and the children went for a holiday to Slovenia. Sam remembered his anti-psychotics but forgot the medication to counter their side-effects. He had so little energy that Rosy had to help him to dress and undress. His speech was slow and slurred. It made her weep. As Simon rowed them across Lake Bled, Sam said, 'I wish I could be a Dad and do what you do for us. I'd have liked to row my children across a lake.' It broke Simon's heart.

Why isn't there more research and development into new anti-psychotic medications? Why does schizophrenia seem to be a forgotten illness?

2 November 2015

SIMON POPS IN for coffee. He heard a professor of psychiatry talking about schizophrenia and suicide and saying that he describes a schizophrenic who takes his or her own life as having 'died of schizophrenia'. It feels suddenly less important to know exactly *how* Sam died. We know *why* he died. He died of schizophrenia.

And even more than this, it's a relief to know that someone in the media is talking about schizophrenia. Generally we only hear it mentioned in the context of a tragic news item about someone dying at the hands of 'a paranoid schizophrenic' – such a tiny part of the whole story. The vast majority of people with schizophrenia present no danger to anyone else. They are brave, good people struggling to live not only with the illness but with the often crushing side effects of medication. Too many of them, like Sam, die young.

17 December 2015

I MEET A woman in the park. We stop to talk about the weather and the mud and how hard it is to find some-where to walk after so much rain. She used to go to Crazies Hill with her daughter who knew the footpaths. 'But she's no longer with us,' she adds as a quiet aside, more almost to herself than to me. I ask about her daughter and tell her about Sam. We share with one another our children's names, their ages and illnesses. Most importantly we share, without the need for words, each other's sadness. And then we go our separate ways.

***

Your absence has hit me like a train this Christmas. There's been the space to feel it this year. I've managed to get through the lead up and Christmas Day itself and I don't think anyone has been aware of how much it's cost me. And now it's time for our Boxing Day walk with everyone. Amongst them all those lovely young men: Harry a year older, Tom a year younger, Ed two years younger …

… than you.

We're in the kitchen and it's all catching up with me. I can't seem to shake off the virus I've had for almost three weeks and the asthma it's triggered has worn me out. That and missing you. I tell the others that I'm not going to come on the walk, and maybe not lunch either. I'm going to go to bed instead. I start to cry as soon as they leave. I must have known somewhere that it's what I needed to do because in my hand I'm holding a strip of loo paper that I've torn off on my way upstairs. I sit on the bed, propped up on the pillows and I howl. There's no other word for it. I howl and I hammer the mattress with my tightly curled fists and I yell at the empty room and house.

'It isn't fair,' I shout, over and over again. I cry until I

can't catch my breath and my asthma makes me cough. I have to stop crying because I need to breathe.

But I haven't finished yet; I'm not done with feeling the pain and the anger about you. The unfairness of your life and death.

'I'm not going,' I yell. 'I'm not fucking going.'

I mean to the post-walk drinks at the pub and the Boxing Day lunch.

'I'm not,' I say conclusively, as though at the end of some intense and prolonged debate. 'I'm not going.' And I shake my head angrily as I stand up and pace round the room. 'I'm fucking not.'

'You fucking are,' another voice says, again out loud.

They're mine of course. The voices. And they are in debate. An internal battle actually, between two opposing pulls: Freud's life and death drives, the pulls towards light and darkness. You'll know them from when you did Psychology A level. I know them too, have been pulled by both. I've been clinically depressed and I know what it feels like when the death drive is stronger. I understand the lure of suicide.

I go into your room and pull out the white plastic bag twisted round and round to seal in the contents. Your jumper. I hold my arm out and watch the bag spin round in the air in an ungainly pirouette. It reminds me of you, at thirteen, performing on Dolphin Night in one of Rosy's dance leotards and tutus, mock-balletic, with a smile as wide as the Amazon. You'd stolen the idea from Harry but that didn't diminish your enjoyment one bit. I pull the jumper out, *unroll it, hold it so that the two joins of sleeve and body are close together, and bury my face into it. I breathe in deeply and wait. I wait for the smell of you to come.*

But it doesn't. There's nothing there.

I don't give up. I keep my nose and mouth buried deep into the wool; breathe in and out, hard, into the armpit. And with the warmth of my breath, it comes, barely perceptible, but still unmistakably you: that mix of acrid body odour and aftershave, sprayed liberally onto the outside of the jumper. 'It hides the smell Mum,' you'd say and, seeing my eyebrows rise in ironic disbelief, 'It does Mum, honestly.'

It didn't.

I roll the jumper tight again, underarms tucked in to preserve what's there. I always ration myself, saving the smell for future visits. I'm protective of the molecules which hold your scent. Each time I unroll it or breathe hard into it I see them breaking away, drifting into the atmosphere and dissipating into nothingness. Like ovarian eggs, a finite number, a little stash that's gone once spent.

I sit on my bed and I cry, quietly now. I cry for you, but also for me: for knowing that the day, inevitably, will come when no amount of warm, releasing breath will deliver your smell; for the pain of seeing other mothers' sons grow up and on, leaving you behind, overtaking you. I want to be able to rejoice in and for them. I do. But it's painful too. Sometimes I don't know what to do with the pain.

I sit on my bed and cry. And suddenly I realise how tired I am: tired of trying so hard. I've stayed involved, engaged with Christmas. I've carried on being a mother and a partner and a therapist. I've carried on living.

But I'm so tired.

And, as I write this, something dark and terrible dawns on me. Something about what I'm feeling. I'm not just talking about Christmas anymore. I'm talking about life. I'm sick of that pull towards it. It's simply too hard. I want to be with you. I actually want to join you.

There it is. I've said it and I'm truly shocked. But it's what I feel. Right now, in this moment, I want to die.

And now I don't know what to do with this terrible desolation that has engulfed me. Should I push it away and pretend it never existed, or stay with it and risk sinking into its depths?

I do neither, or perhaps I do both. I make myself think, and gradually things start to make sense. I've coped this Christmas, but underneath there's been so much pain. Perhaps that's why I've needed to be alone today and free to think about you: my attempt to recalibrate the balance between feeling the pain of losing you and remaining invested in life. And perhaps that's why I've been so angry.

When Paddy put on his new jumper yesterday, I told him I hated it, in front of everyone. A shocked hush fell but I didn't care. I ploughed on.

'If you don't mind looking eighty then that's fine,' I said. 'It's up to you, but just don't expect me to be seen with you when you're wearing it.' I could see he was hurt but a part of me didn't care. When he left the room Ellie and Rosy looked *at me in disbelief.*

'For God's sake, Mum,' Ellie said.

Rosy shook her head. 'You really need to apologise,' she said. 'That was so mean.'

Later she took me to task.

'But it's just a jumper,' she said.

'I know, but I hate it,' I replied, with quiet venom that took even me by surprise. 'He's welcome to wear it, but just not with me.'

'You make it sound as though it's a deal breaker.'

'It is,' I said defiantly.

'I'd no idea you were so superficial,' she said.

'Well, I am,' I replied. And then I repeated it to her retreating back as she stood up from the sofa and left the room. I felt rather pleased with myself for disappointing her.

It all starts to make sense now. I've tried so hard to allow myself to feel and process the difficult feelings: pain, guilt and anger. But more recently I've been ignoring the pain. And now it is beginning to make itself felt. Like a small child whose needs aren't being acknowledged or met, it's trying to be noticed. It's starting to kick off. It began with anger – a self-destructive sort, the sort that is unconsciously aimed at alienating the three people closest to me. And now it's moved up a gear. It's delivered a kick that I can't ignore, to shock me into acknowledging to myself how hard it all is – even now, a year and a half down the line – to be alive when you are not. It's hard enough to make me want to die.

I cry some more. And as I do, I think about my phone

call this morning with your uncle, Mike. He rang to thank me for his Christmas present. We talked about children. His three boys are all in the marines and they've all received top awards.

'They're doing so well,' he said, his voice a mix of pride and awe, as though he couldn't quite believe it.

And in my head I heard an inner voice ask, 'And how about Sam?'

'Oh yes,' I replied airily. 'He's still dead. He's doing really well at being dead.'

I'm tired. Exhausted by so much anger and grief. Outside the light is losing its potency, as though someone on high is rotating a giant dimmer switch very, very gradually. I switch my phone onto silent and lie down to sleep.

When I'm woken by the house phone I ignore it at first. But then I realise that I want to answer it. When I do I hear voices and laughter, then Rosy.

'You didn't come,' she says.

'No.'

'Have you been resting?'

'Yes.'

I feel I should say something more.

'Have you all had a nice time?'

'Yes, lovely,' she says, and I can tell she means it.

'I'm really glad,' I say.

And discover I mean it too.

'I didn't know you were feeling so crap. I wouldn't have guessed it from yesterday. I suppose you must just have *powered through and now you're paying for it.'*

'I think I've powered through the last few weeks.' I pause. 'In fact Ro, I think I've powered through the last few years.'

There's a moment of silence as she absorbs what I've said. And then we talk some more.

'I expect you want to sleep,' she says eventually. 'I'll let you sleep now because we'll be home soon.'

I do want to sleep, but I realise, more than that, I want to live. I get out of bed and pull on some clothes.

I'm downstairs when the crunch and swish of gravel signals their return. I smile as the door swings wide and they tumble inside.

I know it's what you'd want me to do.

***

1 January 2016

I DON'T STAY up to see the New Year in. I feel too angry with it for marking the passage of time. I don't want another year between a living Sam and me. I'm letting myself feel again.

7 January 2016

PADDY, THE GIRLS and I go away to Goa for a week. We're on a spit of land with the sea ahead of us and a creek behind. We walk over a long wooden footbridge to reach our destination. It reminds me of Pai.

Each morning I creep out of bed, make myself a cup

of tea and go to sit on the bamboo pontoon that juts out over the green and soupy waters of the creek. Fingers of sunlight reach me through the canopy of leaves. It is peaceful as I sit and think. I pick up my mug of tea from the jetty, cup my hands around it and, as I do so, realise that I'm feeling something close to contentment.

Perhaps time is both my enemy and my friend.

9 January 2016

WE WALK ALONG the beach to have supper at a nearby restaurant. When we emerge three hours later all the light has faded and the beach is in darkness. We arrive at the creek to find it much higher than when we waded across earlier. We haven't reckoned on the dark of a new moon or on the rising tide. As we're debating what to do, Ellie announces that she's going to give it a go anyway. With only the torch on her phone to guide her, she wades in. All we can see is a small pool of light where it catches the surface of the water.

'It's fine,' she shouts, then moments later, 'it's getting deeper.' Her voice becomes higher and higher in pitch as she exclaims in quick succession, 'It's deep, yes, it's really deep,' and then a final, 'oh my God it's deep.' Swinging the torch round she shines it onto herself. Spot-lit in the middle of the creek, she is fully clothed, with water up to her armpits. We laugh and laugh.

'It's okay,' she shouts as she takes another step, 'it's getting shallower again.'

I whip off my trousers and balance them on my head

with one hand. Rosy hoists her dress high as we follow
Ellie into the water and across to the spit of beach. Paddy
dithers on the bank.

'Come on,' we shout in unison. Ellie videos him as he
crosses. There is darkness and the sound of splashing and
cursing, and the three of us laughing, and then he emerges
from the wet and darkness, grinning despite himself.

'It's alright for you lot,' he says, 'I was carrying all of
these,' and he gestures down to the bundle he is clutching
in his arms: four pairs of shoes, his shorts, my handbag.
We laugh all the more.

We are able to laugh now. Sam would be glad.

***

*I miss your sense of humour. And your laugh. That more
than anything. It so often saved you.*

*Once I came to see you in hospital. You'd only just been
admitted. It was your third and last stay on Bluebell ward.
We were given permission to sit in a small room off the open
area of the ward. A man walked past the door. I saw you
clock him through the glazed panel. He was wearing a short,
frilly dress with little straps that strained over his bulky
frame. He had a bow in his hair, ankle socks and Mary Jane
shoes. You said he was called Lucy. He gave the finger to you
as he passed. You returned the gesture. He walked by again
and again, each time slowing his pace at the door just long
enough for you to engage in this exchange of provocations. He
didn't look like a man to mess with. I said as much. You*

brushed away my concerns.

When I came back the next day you and Lucy were standing together in the corridor, sharing a joke. You'd become best of friends.

I miss your off-the-wall cooking: the evening when you promised to make us all a meal. There didn't appear to be much activity in the kitchen, but you reassured us all was in-hand. Called to the table you presented each of us with a teaspoon of bee pollen. That was it. You'd never looked prouder.

Another time you were busy making flapjacks in the kitchen when I arrived home.

'Do you want a recipe?' I asked.

'Oh God no,' you replied loftily. 'I don't need that. I'm a master of cooking. You will never have tasted anything better.'

You melted some butter in a pan, theatrically poured oat flakes into it from a great height and pressed the mixture into a baking tin. I didn't bother to mention sugar and golden syrup.

'Now for my special touch,' you said, cracking an egg onto the top of it and shoving it into the oven.

'OH!' you exclaimed twenty minutes later as you took it out and started to hoot with laughter. Across the surface were several long trails of cooked egg white and a greyish lump where the yolk had congealed. You called us all to the kitchen and we guffawed.

'Might you use a recipe next time, Muelo?'

'Certainly not,' you replied indignantly as you tipped it all into the bin. 'A master I remain.'

I miss your excessiveness. You were beside yourself with excitement when the wheatgrass arrived. It took two men to carry it all in – tray after tray of young green shoots, organic capsules, fertiliser, water sprayer. For a week you walked around constantly chewing, moving the clump of stringy, mushed green from one side of your mouth to the other. A week after that the clump had disappeared and in the trays the shoots yellowed, wilted and died. You never mentioned wheatgrass again.

***

16 January 2016

PADDY AND I go to Shoreditch for the evening. Rosy is performing at the Zealous X Festival. We meet up with Harry and Tom and two of their friends for supper before the show. They were all at school with Sam. It's a treat to spend the evening with them.

But I'm not their mum.

Rosy plays to a full studio. Her piece – the Eg(g)o – is very funny; her main prop is a tray of fresh eggs. Whenever something goes wrong she has to give birth to a new ego – a process we watch on a huge screen above the stage – her face contorting in pain as an egg pops out of her mouth. Each time she catches it in her hands with a delighted, 'Oh.'

Towards the end she strips down to her underwear and rolls an egg yolk from the tips of her fingers, across the back of her hand, down her arm, shoulder, chest, stomach, thigh, calf, and finally her foot. The yolk drops from her toes onto the floor and breaks before she can catch it.

She bends down and scoops up the mess, cradles it in her hands, turns to the audience and says quietly, 'And I must live with my shame in my hands and hope that nobody turns away. This is me, this is real, messy me.' She smears it over her face to hoots of laughter, 'This is glorious ugly me. And I love it. I love mess. I love the glorious ugly mess, because ugly is the new beautiful,' and she smashes an egg into her hair, 'and broken is the new fixed,' as she hurls another at the floor, 'and maybe lost is the new found,' she shouts.

'And I am lost,' she bellows, as she bashes her forehead into the tray of eggs to uproarious laughter.

'I am broken.' Another bash. More laughter.

'I am a mess,' she yells as she smashes her head into the tray for a final time, to whistles and howls of laughter from the audience.

I want to stand up and tell them not to laugh, that she's still in pain from losing her brother. I don't of course, and needless to say she's grinning broadly as she takes her final bows.

22 February 2016

WE ALL GATHER in Wales and walk up Sugar Loaf again.

Sam would have been twenty-four. It isn't snowing this year.

22 March 2016

IT'S RAINING IN the woods. Great drops of leaf-trapped, overnight rain tumble noisily to the ground, dislodged by squirrels and the warmth of the sun. Around me the woodland hums with the constant slap slap slap of their landing. The sun streams through in places, illuminating the gloom with clusters of electric green leaves and shafts of misty light.

I'm out walking with Sigmund. These walks on our own have become a sort of therapy for me. They give me the time and space to think about Sam. And they give me nature. It reminds me of a wider world than that of my loss. A world that keeps on turning, the seasons changing, hedgerows now in the tangle of spring.

We leave the woods and emerge into the silence of a water and sun-drenched field. It's like a different world. Sig veers off, nose to the ground, zigzagging after some invisible trail. There's a roar of dragon's breath above me. I look up. Directly overhead hangs a hot air balloon. I glimpse green and flashes of vibrant pinky red. It resembles nothing more than a giant watermelon suspended against the milky blue sky of the spring morning.

I think of Sam in Sicily with his shopping trolley loaded high and I smile.

30 March 2016

I SOMETIMES WONDER if I'm coping too well and what that means. I recall again Sam telling me that I would 'get over it' if he were to die before me. Was the implication really that I didn't care enough, didn't love him enough? Is this what he meant? Have I got over it? I talk to a friend and voice my fear that I am doing too well, that perhaps it means I didn't love Sam enough – that same old worry coming back to haunt me. I see the answer in the kindness of her smile, in the knowing gaze she fixes on me, in the barely perceptible shake of her head. She doesn't need to say anything.

I'm in the shower the next morning when it comes to me, slowly but certainly, that it isn't lack of love that's at play, but the opposite. It's the *depth* of my love for him. And it isn't that I've 'got over it,' it's simply that I am learning to let him go. It is loving him so much that helps me now to start that process; and the fact that I loved him for himself, for his glorious, quirky self, rather than for what he was to me. I loved him for him and that makes it easier now.

In a quiet moment I pick up his Order of Service and gaze at the four photos on the back cover: Sam at four different stages of his life. On the top-left he's a baby, grinning his largely toothless, gummy smile, just two little pegs visible in his lower jaw. He's in a red baby-seat clipped on to the table and he's turning towards me. His right hand is splayed against the red canvas of the seat and his left is gripping the grey plastic bar which keeps it stable. His eyes are lively. He's a pickle. You can see it in his eyes.

On the top-right he's in monochrome, aged twelve. His nose is covered in freckles from the Corfu sun, his eyes are bright and he's smiling at me, his dark eyes flecked with light. It's a smile, not a grin and he looks knowing, thoughtful. It's hard to read his smile, hard to know what he's thinking. It is a few years after mine and Simon's separation.

On the bottom left he's grinning so broadly that his eyes have almost disappeared. He looks relaxed and happy, but there is something impish about his grin. He's sitting bare-chested on the balcony in Sicily holding a huge half watermelon, its flesh scooped out. He knows he's worrying me with his diet. I suspect that's the reason for the grin.

On the bottom right he's sitting on the bow of our boat on the Thames. It's the photo we put with his casket at his thanksgiving service. He's looking to his left, a dreamy smile on his face. He looks contented, at peace with himself and the world. It's a perfect summer evening and although it's often impossible to connect with him at this time, this is one of the exceptions, an evening when we seem to have the old Sam back. It's a happy evening and I take hundreds of photos.

I think somewhere I knew we were losing him, perhaps forever, and that I needed to capture the happy moments while I still could.

I'm always thinking about you: the person you were, the person you became. I've realised it isn't possible to separate the two, however much I'd like to. There was still so much of the old you in the new you. You'd always had such big ideas about yourself, about your place in the world. You didn't want to settle for mediocrity, and certainly not for illness and hospital admissions and a life controlled by others. You were brave, you were stoical and you were dignified in how you dealt with this new life but it wasn't unfolding as you'd expected. You'd felt your mind expanding, exploring new horizons, reaching dizzying heights of enlightenment. You knew what your spirit could do, its true potential. Only this life was holding you back. You'd never been one to stay with something difficult and see it through. You didn't recognise the benefits of delaying gratification. As a child when you'd return from some new hobby or club that had promised much, and announce triumphantly, 'I've quit,' it wasn't a cause for shame. It simply made sense if it wasn't delivering what you wanted, right then. I could talk to you about the merits of continuing until I was blue in the face – the satisfaction of something hard-won, the sense of achievement in seeing something through – but nothing changed.

I suppose I'm thinking about all of this because I'm still trying to make sense of how and why you died. I know schizophrenia changed the way your mind worked: how you saw the world, how you thought and felt, so I can rationalise your death and recognise that schizophrenia caused it. But I can also see so much of you in your death, and in a strange way that helps me to start to accept it. Because I loved you for being you, for seeing things differently, for having your own views, for rejecting the norm, for being so impossibly rigid, for making your own choices even though they were so often questionable ones. So even though I wish with all my heart that you'd seen things differently, more as Dad and I do, I recognise that you didn't. And I respect your right to see things your way, to do things your way, to take risks. I think it's this which allows me now to see that even though the outcome doesn't feel the right one for me, perhaps it might have felt right for you.

Perhaps it's you saying one last time, 'Mum, I've quit.'

***

18 April 2016

THERE ARE BLUEBELLS in the woods and the lingering call of the cuckoo in the air as I walk. It is early still and the light is golden as I cross Mill Green towards the churchyard. Ahead of me I see the vicar walking, head slightly bowed. It is a pensive walk; perhaps he's in quiet conversation with his God. He turns towards us as Hector, his black labrador, bounds up to greet Sigmund. The vicar greets me.

'How are you?' he asks.

'Fine,' I reply and then again, in confirmation to myself as much as to him, 'yes, fine.' It surprises me to realise that I am.

He knows I'm on my way to visit Sam's grave. We often meet as I'm coming in or out of the churchyard.

'And how are the rest of the family?' he continues.

It feels like a quiet acknowledgement that Sam is both already accounted for and still a part of the family. I like the feeling.

28 April 2016

I'M SITTING ON the sofa with my iPad, stealing a few early morning minutes of the day to spend with Sam. When the children were small and ever-present in my life I used to steal the early mornings for myself, creeping past their bedroom doors and hoping they would stay asleep as I tucked myself away on the sofa with a book or sat tapping at my computer, until I heard a plaintive cry of, 'Mu'um, where are you?' or the soft pad of feet on wooden floors and saw a tousled head come peering round the door. Sam was always the most vocal in his insistence that I should stop what I was doing and come to make their early morning drinks.

1 May 2016

MY MIND AND body know it's that time of year again. It's that same thing of the light, the colours, the scents, the sounds that link me without my even knowing it, to that moment of learning Sam was dead. It's part of my DNA now. I see the smokey mauves of the wisteria hanging outside my bedroom window, the droop of laden blooms pulling down the twisted branches, blossom falling like silent rain from the cherry tree, the oak tree yielding up its sticky clusters in neon green as the squirrels tear from branch to branch. I hear the insistent tap-tapping on the window as a long-tailed tit, confused, tries to gain entry. I smell the faint perfume of damp bluebells rising up as I walk through the woods. It's as though these things are all imprinted on a psychic retina that matches shapes and colours, sounds and scents and fits them into some sort of jigsaw of past experiences.

I feel the melancholy before I remember why.

6 May 2016

I ADD A slug of Bombay Sapphire gin to a half-full bottle of tonic water, slip a slice of lemon and ice cubes into a beaker and load them together with a packet of crisps into a small rucksack. I'm going with Sig for an early evening walk up Table Mountain. It's warm and sunny on the climb but gusty too and when I reach the summit the wind is wild.

In amongst a cluster of stone slabs, balanced like giant dice dropped carelessly onto the hillside, I find a sheltered spot. Sugar Loaf is directly ahead of me, only a sunlit valley and the village of Llanbedr in between. I pour my drink and raise my beaker to Sam then take a few photos on my phone. Only 28% battery left. I switch it off and put it on the stone beside me.

I am munching my way through my crisps when a young sheep appears round the slab of stone on my left. Sig is sitting at my feet, to my right. They look at one another. Neither moves. The sheep comes towards me. It has been shorn but its fleece is growing back thick and strong. I feel an urge to reach out and run my fingers through it, as I used to through Sam's thatch of hair.

The sheep directs its penetrating stare at me and Sig in turn, comes closer still and stops. It stands motionless for about thirty seconds before reaching out its head towards my left hand, wrapped around the beaker. Sig doesn't move a muscle. The sheep nudges my beaker with its nose, sticks out a strong pink tongue and licks my fingers. I do not move. It takes one finger in its mouth and presses it gently between its teeth. I feel their smooth flat surface against my finger. I do not withdraw my hand.

A moment later it releases me and turns its unblinking gaze on Sig. It walks towards him, stops a foot or two away. The sheep stretches out its neck until there are just a few inches between their noses. Sig stays perfectly still. I reach for my phone to capture these glistening noses – one pink, one black – with the silhouette of Sugar Loaf behind them. The screen goes blank. It does not revive. Still up to your old tricks then, Muelo, I think, thwarting your mother at every opportunity. You never would cooperate when I was trying to photograph you.

I pack my rucksack, zip up my coat. It's cold now in the wind, despite the sunshine.

But there is warmth inside me. I am smiling as I head back down the mountain.

***

You were so sure death wouldn't be the end. It's given me comfort since you died to know you had that certainty. Perhaps that's why it feels okay to say I sometimes feel you around me. Because I know you'd understand.

14 May 2016

WE'RE IN CORNWALL for my nephew's wedding. We rent a house for the weekend with my sister, Sue and family. We laugh a lot.

Saturday dawns bright and sunny. The wedding is lovely. I see my sister, Kate, beaming with maternal love and pride. A job well done. A mother's task fulfilled.

In the evening I sit by one of the fire-pits in the yard. My niece, Dorie comes out to join me for a moment.

'He's never forgotten, Gill,' she says. 'We loved Sam. We'll always remember him.' She hugs me.

I gaze into the glowing embers and remember this day exactly two years ago.

Then, 14 May 2014, I stood under the too-blue sky of a Bangkok morning and watched in numb disbelief as a coffin, apparently containing my son's remains, was manhandled into a crematorium. It isn't fair. Life isn't fair. But mine has been fairer than many. This week the Today programme has been dedicated to refugees with its 'World on the Move' theme. There have been interviews with those who have fled their homes for an uncertain future: past and present, young and old, tales of new lives built despite harsh beginnings. Life isn't fair. Sam's certainly wasn't. I feel the unfairness of it for him as I watch the spits and trails of fire fly out into the blackness of the night.

16 May 2016

I GO TO visit Sam at his grave. The grass is freshly cut and attaches itself in criss-cross swirls to the toes of my walking shoes: small spears of soft, vibrant green. It is young grass, cut down as it pushes its way up into the promise of spring.

At the grave I crouch low and trace Sam's name with my finger-tips. Tears fall onto the tablet, onto the epitaph, 'And when the earth shall claim your limbs, then shall you truly dance.' I think of the weekend in Cornwall.

I laughed. Properly laughed.

I rejoiced. Properly rejoiced.

I love my family. Only a few mentioned Sam by name. I understand why. Lives move on. Mine moves forward, but it doesn't move on. I cry now for my lovely lost son.

I properly cry.

Later I sit and read of journalist Sally Brampton's life and death. She fought depression all her life. She achieved great things, was loved by many. It was a brave and honest life. She walked into the sea and didn't turn back. In many ways it was a brave and honest death too.

I'd say the same of Sam's life. Perhaps of his death too, but we will never know. There are so many unanswered questions. Lying awake in my bed I find myself once again going over everything. The things we know of his final few days: his plans for travelling with the girl he had met in Bangkok, the buoyant text messages home, his Prospect Park friends' certainty that he left for Thailand intending to come home. And the things we would rather not know: his trip to the waterfalls – undoubtedly to buy drugs – the empty diazepam packets Simon found in his bin. I think too of all we can never know: how he was feeling on that day about his life, about all that he had lost, about his future. And as these thoughts are spinning round in my head a picture starts to form of Sam on that day. In my sleepy state I can see him and it is as if I am there with him, shadowing him on the last day of his life.

This has been my telling of Sam's story. Simon, Rosy, Ellie, Paddy, Kim and every person who knew him will each have their own version. Only he was privy to the real story of himself. Only he knew how it felt to be him. I know that his own telling of his story would have been very different from mine, but I hope that in this, my telling of his final day, I am somewhere near the truth.

***

I see you as you cross the rickety bridge and into town for something to eat. It's another hot and humid day and, walking back to your little hut on stilts you think of what you might do for the rest of the day. You haven't been to the hot springs yet but perhaps you will do that tomorrow. You've hired the moped so there's no hurry. You recall your earlier two trips to Pai – how you could meditate for hours on end, exploring the outward reaches of your consciousness. Those feelings have disappeared since you were forced to take medication. You miss them.

You find yourself back at your hut, with the day stretching out before you and you think about trying to recapture some of those feelings in the only way you can now. You get out the diazepam and the opium you bought at the waterfalls. Perhaps you will try them together to see if they might allow you to reach that world of pure bliss, once so familiar and now so frustratingly beyond your reach.

For the briefest of moments a thought flickers in the far depths of your consciousness as you wonder whether it might be too much to take them together, but that flicker is extinguished as quickly as it flares into being by another thought, a much more familiar and more compelling thought: let fate or God decide. If it is your time, then it is your time.

You close the door and window. You don't want to be disturbed. You turn on the fan. It's hot outside, 38 degrees, and airless in your small room. You take the diazepam and the opium and lie down on the bed, waiting for those first feelings of relaxation to come. You feel yourself slowing down, limbs becoming heavy, mind stretching out and easing itself into a place of total calm. You are as light and fluid as running water. Colours come too, swathes of luminosity swirling in hues and shapes and forms of breath-taking beauty: beauty you have known before. There is a comforting numbness within the beauty and the calm. You are in a place now where nothing can touch you, where nothing matters. All that has been falls away, tumbling like motes of dust on a breath of wind. Hurt, pain and disappointed dreams dissolve, fading like fireworks against a night sky. All that is and could be pulsates with promise, small orbs of energy and light, glowing green and blue in the distance.

It's hot in the room but in your barely conscious state you're unaware of the increasing heat. You're breathing more slowly now, shallow breaths that rise and fall on the gentle incoming tide of oblivion. The tide keeps rising, on and on, and with it your breaths grow ever fainter until the moment comes for it to turn, for it to begin its slow, silent retreat, and for life and consciousness and reality to reassert their unkind grip on you.

But instead there is a faltering and for the briefest fraction of time all is held, all is frozen and still, as God or fate decide what happens next.

And, in that moment of suspended time, while life hangs by only the finest of threads – mere gossamer holding you to this earth and to this life – a stillness falls. The you that we have known and loved lies still and silent. And in that final silence all is lost and all is gained.

It is both an ending and a beginning, a release.

That which was truly you – your soul – frees itself from your body, the vessel that's kept you tethered to a life that disappointed you. Your spirit soars, irrepressible and full of hope for the new life awaiting you. As planets spin and stars streak earthwards, small shafts of light catch threads of gossamer dancing in your wake.

Afterword

For a while the girls share a flat in London. Rosy is working for three months at the Coliseum and Ellie is starting with Teach First at a school in Penge. They love living together. I'm in awe of the honesty with which they each share their irritations with the other. Neither holds back. It's a real relationship; with love and anger, generosity and envy, delight and disappointment. It's entirely discrete from others within the family. They don't need Simon or me to mediate in any way. Their first port of call is now with the other if something between them needs to be talked about.

Sam is both the absent and the ever-present sibling. As their brother he shaped each of them. Losing him both to illness and in death has, perhaps more than anything else, made their relationship what it is now. Through this they discovered that even difficult things can be confronted and survived; that directness and honesty strengthen rather than diminish. They shared him as a brother. They continue to share the loss of him. It binds them now.

Ellie tells me about a recent yoga class they went to together. Towards the end of the session, as they lay on their backs relaxing, music came on. Although they'd never heard it before, it spoke unmistakably of Sam. Without a word each stretched out a hand and found the other. In the sharing of that silent moment he was back with them.

He's often back with me too.

He's been present for me in every moment of writing this. It hasn't been easy to write and it won't have been easy to read but I hope the joy comes across as well as the pain. Sam often struggled, and inevitably at times we struggled with him, but the joy of him lives on much more than the pain. I wrote because I needed to. I needed to spend time with him, to make sense of his life as much as his death. It was part of my grieving – the necessary but painful visiting and re-visiting of memories; part of allowing myself to face and feel difficult, uncomfortable feelings – guilt and anger, the pain of loss; part of feeling rather than pushing away, working through and pro-cessing rather than avoiding; part of my painful journey towards acceptance. Telling his story kept him alive for me. Putting it out into the world keeps him alive in a different way.

Sam's story is others' story too: one in a hundred young men and women the whole world over develop schizophrenia. Their lives change forever just as they're beginning to find themselves as adults. Many, like Sam, will not see the change. This is the story of their families too. I know there are no universal truths about feelings, that no two experiences are the same, but I hope for others there might be instances of recognition that ease the loneliness for a moment of being a parent who is worried for a child, or a brother or sister struggling with a sibling with mental illness, or a parent who's facing the loss all parents dread above all other.

I often ask myself what Sam might have felt about my telling his story. Ellie says he would have loved it, loved being immortalised and being able to brag, in his next life, about his mum being an author. I've often wished there were a way to know I have his blessing.

I go on an Arvon writing course and spend five days and nights with fifteen non-fiction writers and two tutors. I work on this.

On the first evening we're told about the Friday night showcase when we'll each read an extract from our writing. All week I think about what to read. Finally I decide. At lunchtime on Friday I go to the office to print it out. But later that afternoon, sitting in my attic room, I change my mind. I settle instead on something no one has seen: an extract from the summer of 2010, the watermelons and the rocket salads. I'm working on it, reading it through when I come to the sentence addressed to Sam, 'You ate only watermelons all week.' A picture comes to me of him standing in the street holding a whole tray of dusky black grapes – a wooden market tray with sharp upright corners, lettering in red and mauve and pictures of grapes and the island of Sicily. I hear him saying, what about the grapes, Mum? Okay I think, you didn't *only* eat watermelons. You ate grapes too. But the tutors have been telling us to be selective, to 'privilege the reader and the narrative,' that 'just because it happened, you don't have to include it.' So I'm sorry Sam but I'm leaving out the grapes.

After supper we all traipse up the wooden staircase in the barn with its three giant sofas and wooden settle at the front, where the reader sits. The tutors introduce us one by one. When it's Nettie's turn, I learn she's psychic. I didn't know, but it doesn't surprise me. She has the biggest heart. All week I've watched her feeling others' pleasure and their pain.

When it comes to me, my nerves simply evaporate. I don't know where the voice, the timbre, the poise come from. I'm living my writing as I share it with the group. At the end there's a hush before the applause. I see Nettie wiping away tears.

Afterwards I walk round the group to say my good-byes. Nettie sees me coming.

'I can't wait to see the fuckin' back of you,' she says, laughing. 'All you've done all week is make me fuckin' cry.' We hug.

Then suddenly she's serious. 'There's this word,' she says, 'I don't know what it means but I know I have to say it to you, so I'm going to. Grapes.'

'Oh my God,' I say again and again.

Nettie smiles. 'Think of Sam tonight,' she tells me. He won't be far away.'

I do.

And he isn't.

Acknowledgements

Sam's story has been unfolding for more than 28 years. I could not have found my way through it without the love and support of many people. My extended family and friends have been unfailingly generous with their love, time and patience, both during Sam's life and after his death; steadfast in their kindness and understanding and in helping me to keep Sam's memory alive. I am truly grateful to each of them. I hope they will forgive me for not naming them individually.

The writing of this story began in Pai, just 36 hours after Sam's cremation. At four o'clock in the morning I found myself sitting up in bed, reaching for my iPad and starting to write. For two years I sat and tapped away on it whenever and wherever I could. It became part of my grieving. It also became part of an entirely different journey: my writing journey.

My heartfelt thanks go to Mary McCallum of Makaro Press (and to Jane Meares for introducing her to me) for her sensitive feedback as my first reader/editor. Without her encouragement and gentle suggestions I might so easily have abandoned any idea of publishing and left my writing as a simple record for myself. She gave me the confidence and self-belief to embark on the monumental task of turning my journal into a book.

Along the way many others read my manuscript and helped me to hone it into a narrative I could send out into the publishing world. I cannot thank them enough: Wanda Whiteley of Manuscript Doctor, whose incisiveness and instinctive expertise helped me to reduce the word count to manageable proportions; author and beta-reader Adrienne Dines, whose insightful feedback and enthusiasm spurred me on. Who could not take confidence from words like 'glorious' and 'uplifting'? Also, huge thanks go to three of the 'Marks' in the publishing world (there seem to be many): most of all to Mark Ellen, who was unstintingly generous with his time, perceptive insights and expertise, and never failed to go the extra mile; Mark Ellingham for reading the manuscript and generously offering ongoing help with navigating the market; and Mark Lucas for his honest critique on the eve of a holiday when I'm sure he had many better things to do.

There are two people without whom I might never have got this far. Claire Dyer, writer and poet, facilitator of the wonderful writing group to which I belong and editor/critiquer supreme of Fresh Eyes. You could not have been more supportive, more generous with your time and expertise or more sensitive and encouraging at every stage. Thank you so much. And my publisher, Amanda Saint. Your steady belief in my book, your sensitivity in embracing Sam's story, and your willingness to listen to my views about its publication have meant so much to me. Thank you from the bottom of my heart.

I am extremely grateful too to the members of my writing group: Wendy Prové, Nicky Kaye, Alexis Wolfe, Emily Thornton, Heather Dyson, Simon Marshall and Monica Bothwell. I have learned so much from you all. Your careful, discerning critiquing helped me to develop a skin thick enough to risk putting my writing and Sam's story out into the world; and to the many friends and family who read some or all of earlier manuscripts and gave me thoughtful feedback and encouragement, often at times when I was full of doubt, not just about my writing but also about publishing.

Thank you to my lovely friends Teresa Johnstone, Hen Coleman, Pru Drysdale, Caroline Naish, Steph Seeley, Trish Steinhardt, Irial Eno and Alice Peck; to my cousin Nic Glucksmann, my siblings, Sue Jackson, Kate Manley and Mike Mann, and to David Cooke, Alice Martineau and Orlando von Einsiedel. This list is by no means exhaustive and I am as grateful to those I don't mention, as I am to those I do.

Thank you to the friends who made homes available to me when I needed an uncomplicated space in which to work on my writing: Karen Mann, Peta Sweet, Charles Irving and Hen Coleman. And thanks too to the Arvon Foundation for running such brilliant residential writing courses. Special thanks go to my tutors, Horatio Clare, Laura Barton, Marina Benjamin and Alexander Masters and also to all my fellow students for their generous feedback and encouragement and their lovely company.

I have been blessed to have two friends who walked beside me every step of the way when times were hard,

Sue Martin and Jo Roberts. Knowing that you were holding me in mind was a constant salve. It made me feel less alone and helped me to bear the unbearable. Thank you so much. I will be forever grateful for your friendship and love.

My most heartfelt thanks of all are reserved for the other people closest to Sam. The love of my two wonderful daughters, Rosy and Ellie, has sustained me at every turn and on even the darkest of days. They have been unwavering in their support of me, each contributing in their individual ways: Ellie, with her perceptive and thoughtful critiquing, and Rosy by putting her confidence and trust in me. I could not be more grateful to them for allowing me to put my version of their brother's life out into the world, even though they each have their own to tell. It is generous beyond belief.

Also, Simon, Sam's Dad, who gave me unstinting support in this endeavour and was always generous with his praise and encouragement. To Lily, Imogen and Kim who as part of our blended family have allowed me to tell parts of their stories too, thank you so much. And to Paddy, the steady rock in my life who has never once complained of the hours, days, weeks and months I have spent caught up in my writing – preoccupied and monosyllabic. You could not have been more generous or supportive. THANK YOU.

And, of course, to Sam, for giving me the story I'd rather not have had to tell, but which in its telling has given me so much. Thank you, Sam. I love you and miss you every day.

About the Author

Gill Mann has written for as long as she can remember but has only recently considered publishing her work. She has had a long and varied career, starting her working life as a solicitor and becoming a partner in a law firm.

In her early forties she re-trained as a professional photographer, becoming an Associate of the Royal Photographic Society, before deciding to return to university when she was in her late forties to study for a Post-graduate Diploma and Masters degree in Psychodynamic Counselling. She now works as a therapist.

It is her interest in and understanding of people that informs her writing. She writes mainly from life but has more recently turned to fiction, starting work on a collection of short stories based on the theme of therapy.

Credits

Many thanks to the following people and publications for allowing us to reproduce their work.

Reproduction of excerpts from *Lament* for a Son by Nicholas Wolterstorff, Eerdmans (1987)

"A Brief for the Defense" from *REFUSING HEAVEN* by Jack Gilbert, copyright © 2005 by Jack Gilbert. Used by permission of Alfred A Knopf, an imprint of the Knopf Doubleday Group Publishing Group, a division of Penguin Randomhouse LLC. All rights reserved

Twelve (12) lines from Selected Poems by Michael Rosen Copyright © Michael Rosen, 2007

Sally Williams, "*Paul Heiney's journey in memory of his sailor son*", The Telegraph, 04 April 2015.

Nicholas Heiney, *The Silence at the Song's End*, Songsend Books © 2007, E.M. Purves

The Economist 24 October 2015 p16 – article referred to in entry 24th October 2015

Printed by Amazon Italia Logistica S.r.l.
Torrazza Piemonte (TO), Italy